EARLY ENGLISH METRE

THOMAS A. BREDEHOFT

Early English Metre

UNIVERSITY OF TORONTO PRESS
Toronto   Buffalo   London

© University of Toronto Press Incorporated 2005
Toronto Buffalo London
Printed in Canada

ISBN 0-8020-3831-X

Printed on acid-free paper

Library and Archives Canada Cataloguing in Publication

Bredehoft, Thomas A.
  Early English metre / Thomas A. Bredehoft.

  (Toronto Old English series)
  Includes bibliographical references and index.
  ISBN 0-8020-3831-X

  1. English language – Old English, ca. 450–1100 – Versification.
  I. Title.   II. Series.

  PE257.B73 2005   829.1'009   C2005-901993-X

University of Toronto Press acknowledges the financial assistance to its
publishing program of the Canada Council for the Arts and the Ontario
Arts Council.

University of Toronto Press acknowledges the financial support for its
publishing activities of the Government of Canada through the Book
Publishing Industry Development Program (BPIDP).

Contents

Acknowledgments

This book would not have been possible without the support and guidance of a number of colleagues and friends, and I especially wish to thank the following folks. I owe a debt of gratitude to Dan Donoghue and Rick Russom (those self-alliterating metricists), for so usefully and supportively responding to some of my earliest attempts to write about Old English metre. I must also thank Nick Howe and Stacy Klein for their willingness to read this work in manuscript, despite their expressed reservations about their knowledge of metrical issues: their suggestions often materially helped me to improve the clarity of my argument. And little did Timothy C. Graham and Paul Szarmach know, when I worked with them during a 1997 NEH Summer Seminar on Anglo-Saxon manuscripts, that my promise (or was it a threat?) to turn my attention to metrical issues would ever have such a result. I owe a somewhat more diffuse (but no less seriously intended) thanks to all those scholars whose published works on Old English metre taught me everything I know about the subject. My occasional disagreements with their conclusions in no way diminish my respect for their works.

Portions of this book were previously published, a part of chapter 2.3 in *Notes and Queries*, and portions of chapters 3.1–3.3 in *Anglo-Saxon England*. I am grateful to the readers and editors of these publications for their helpful suggestions, and grateful as well to the editors and to Oxford University Press (*Notes and Querries*) and Cambridge University Press (*Anglo-Saxon England*) for the permission to reuse material from their pages.

I also wish to acknowledge the support of my colleagues at the University of Northern Colorado; the first draft of this book was completed during a sabbatical leave in 2001, and this work would not have been possible without their support and encouragement. Likewise, UNC's provost, Allen Huang; the Deans of Arts and Sciences, Curt Peterson and David Caldwell; and the Chair of English, Joonok Huh, all helped to bring this work to publication, and I gratefully acknowledge their support as well.

EARLY ENGLISH METRE

CHAPTER 1.1

Introduction

One should, perhaps, hesitate before offering up a new account of Old English metre. Dorothy Sayers's Miss Lydgate, English tutor at Oxford's fictional Shrewsbury College, exemplifies one reason for such hesitation:

> The English tutor's room was festooned with proofs of her forthcoming work on the Prosodic elements in English verse from Beowulf to Bridges. Since Miss Lydgate had perfected, or was in the process of perfecting (since no work of scholarship ever attains a static perfection), an entirely new prosodic theory, demanding a novel and complicated system of notation which involved the use of twelve different varieties of type ... there existed at that moment five successive revises in galley form, at different stages of completion. (*Gaudy Night* 39–40)

As this passage suggests, the work involved in revising established prosodical theories is complex and, as it seems, never-ending, with absolutely necessary adjustments and refinements always just around the corner; the work, it seems, is never done. And in the case of Old English prosody, one must wonder if the effort is even worthwhile: the 'five types' of traditional Sieversian scansion have such a powerful foothold in the minds and hearts of Anglo-Saxonists and others that one must have serious doubts that any new system can dislodge them. Yet the failures of the 'five-types' formalism have been significant, even if the consequences of those failures have not been fully appreciated by the community of Anglo-Saxonists.[1] How such a state of affairs could come about is worth exploring.

A useful place to begin is the appendix on Old English metre in

Bruce Mitchell and Fred C. Robinson's widely used introductory text-
book, *A Guide to Old English*, where we find Sievers's theory boiled
down to a scant half-dozen pages. Even as a graduate student concen-
trating on Old English (I am embarrassed to admit), I did not find
these pages very illuminating. They do serve to cover the ground
briefly, but it is worth noting that the very first half-line of Old English
verse encountered in the *Guide* (at the beginning of *Cædmon's Hymn*)
cannot be readily scanned either by the principles set out by Mitchell
and Robinson or by reference to the examples in their appendix: 'Nu
we sculon herigean.' Metricists will quickly identify this as a type A3
verse, but as common as such verses are, the *Guide* does not note either
their existence nor the details of their scansion, presumably because of
the difficulties these verses might cause for such categorical claims as
'each half-line has two syllables which are accented' (161).[2]

The metrical appendix in Mitchell and Robinson's *Guide*, then, can
only be intended as the most rudimentary survey of Old English metre;
students who truly wish to understand how Old English metre works
must turn elsewhere. One might begin with any of the numerous books
on the topic or (especially if one has a well-grounded instructor as a
guide) the introductory account found in John C. Pope's *Seven Old Eng-
lish Poems*, where the material on normal verses alone runs to over thirty
pages. But if a generation of Anglo-Saxonists is being trained from
Mitchell and Robinson (where a previous generation learned from
Pope), it is small wonder if few of them have much detailed understand-
ing of Old English metre, since most of the extensive treatments are
aimed at the specialist rather than the beginner and are thus relatively
inaccessible to even dedicated students.

Yet, at the same time as introductory textbooks have begun devoting
less space to discussions of Old English metre, critical studies of metre
(or of the interaction between metre and syntax) have proliferated, with
book length works by Hoover, Donoghue, Russom, Kendall, Cable,
Fulk, Whitman, Hutcheson, Momma, and Blockley appearing since
1985. But as an even cursory reading of such books will suggest, critical
studies of Old English metre have (in general) grown increasingly com-
plex and increasingly difficult, to the point that few, besides specialists
(and there are few enough of them), can even read such studies with
profit. When I have told other medievalists, for example, that I was
embarking on a project on Old English metre, more than one has asked
me, 'So have you actually *read* Fulk's *History of Old English Meter*?' as if
merely reading it, to say nothing of reading it critically, were itself a
monumental accomplishment.

On the one hand, the flurry of books on Old English metre published since the middle 1980s includes some (like R.D. Fulk's) which are replete with the sort of extensive and detailed philological argumentation which is becoming ever less familiar to Anglo-Saxon scholars trained in literary, rather than linguistic, analysis. Other recent books on metre, like B.R. Hutcheson's *Old English Poetic Metre*, employ equally dense and detailed statistical argumentation, which is perhaps even less accessible to most humanistically trained Anglo-Saxonists.[3] And both of these examples, in their separate complexities, might remind readers unpleasantly of Miss Lydgate's fictional prosodic notation, with its twelve varieties of type. Yet Anglo-Saxonist readers would undoubtedly make the effort to both read and grapple with these difficult books if they had a better sense of what is at stake. Or, more precisely, if they had a sense that what is at stake in the analysis of Old English metre made a difference to them.

Indeed, it seems that the contrast between the two trends I have been discussing (a decrease in attention to metre in introductory Old English textbooks and an increase in scholarly writing about metre) exposes a crucial problem in the current state of Old English metrical studies. To be blunt, modern critical analysis of Old English metre is usually carried out at a level of linguistic and technical complexity that, as all observers must agree, can have little to do with the intuitive, traditional (and hence transmissable, susceptible to being passed from poet to poet), and largely formulaic sytem which allowed actual Anglo-Saxon poets to compose.[4] The degree of mismatch between current descriptions of Old English metre and our own intuitive sense of how Anglo-Saxon poets operated is simply too great to bear. Introductory books, instead of investing the time and energy necessary to acquaint students with the complexities of modern metrical theorizing, have chosen the opposite strategy, backing off from that complexity and offering only a sketchy account of Sieversian metrics.

Ultimately, this very state of affairs is the greatest failure of Sieversian formalism: to the degree that modern metrical inquiry takes its primary task as correcting faults in Sieversian formalism as they come to the attention of metricists, the result has been a patchwork of bewildering (and increasing) complexity, and metrical study has become the province of specialists only. Another obvious failure of the Sievers-Bliss system is its inflexibility in dealing with metrical change, although it seems clear that linguistic change during the period ought to have occasioned metrical change as well. Finally, Sieversian metrics offers very little (if any) insight into Anglo-Saxon poetics. The metrical forms of Old English verse were tools that poets might use for effect, but the poetic effects of metrical options are still very poorly understood.[5]

A new metrical formalism, I believe, can help both to clear away a great deal of the confusing, troublesome, and complicated argumentation that has accumulated over the last century and to open up new areas of inquiry. After all, the very persuasiveness of Sievers's view of Old English metre has had important consequences for developments in Old English metrical studies: when cracks have appeared in the façade of Sieversian formalism, they have been patched (and repatched) to the point that now there must be serious questions about whether the underlying structure remains sound. Nevertheless, Sievers-Bliss formalism still seems to be virtually the only structure visible in the landscape of Old English metrical studies, to the point that metricists continue to employ it, sometimes despite their own reservations about its accuracy.[6] Those who have proposed alternative formalisms (e.g., Hoover, Russom, Hutcheson) have had little success in counteracting the inertia that a century's worth of teaching and research has given to Sievers's formalism.

Yet, as I have noted, Sievers-Bliss formalism has serious problems. One of the most troubling features of Sieversian scansion lies in the familiar claim that each verse of Old English poetry has 'two syllables which are accented' (*Guide* 161). In fact, this claim is one example of a Sievers-based dictum that can no longer stand. The general acceptance of such 'light' A3 verses as we see in line 1a of *Cædmon's Hymn* indicates that the general principle of the two-stress verse (and the four-stress line) must be inaccurate.[7] Bliss, who argued persuasively for one-stress verses, nevertheless claimed his results were nothing short of a 'triumphant vindication of Sievers' (v), although the two-stress verse has a foundational status in Sieversian formalism.[8] The under-cuttting of this foundation, however, has had little effect on the popularity of the Sievers (or Sievers-Bliss) system; although the existence of single-stress verses ought to have thrown Sievers's whole analysis in doubt, metricists have chosen to patch and save the system rather than revise it. Chapter 1.2 below addresses other pervasive problems with the descriptive aspects of Sieversian formalism.

Sieversian (or Sievers-Bliss) scansion is also problematic in terms of its rigidity, in that it cannot accommodate the ways in which Old English poetic practice was invented and reinvented by each generation of poets.[9] Certainly, we should expect the forms of Old English metre to have changed along with changes in the Old English language throughout the period, but other than a few remarkably brief (and often dismissive) comments, Sievers-Bliss formalism has little to say about poetic developments in the historical period. R.D. Fulk's massive *History of Old English Meter*, for example, devotes two lengthy chapters to the prehistoric processes of contraction and parasiting but has only one brief chapter on so-called Late Developments. Indeed, Fulk's *History* is more properly a history of phonological issues in Old English verse.[10] Since Fulk adopts Bliss's scansion system wholesale, he implicitly defines the *forms* of Old English verse as virtually unchanging: rather than discussing changes to the metrical system itself, Fulk's *History* is largely concerned with describing phonological changes in the words which fill out Sievers-Bliss verses. Fulk (and others who adopt a similar perspective) can make broad distributional claims (e.g., anacrusis is more frequent in later verse; C, D, and E types less frequent), but such observations explicitly insist upon the notion that the basic forms of metrical verses remained unchanged.[11]

When metricists do look at changes in metrical form during the Old English period, their comments almost invariably employ a 'rhetoric of decay,' describing the metrical tradition as 'breaking down' or losing its rigour.[12] All changes in metrical form are (according to this perspective) more or less explicitly identified in negative terms. The consequence of this viewpoint has been a more or less complete neglect of later Old English verse: when late verse maintains older forms, it merely manages to briefly succeed in a losing battle; when it exhibits new forms, it demonstrates a lack of adherence to 'the rules.' The very real possibility that later verse has rules of its own is too rarely addressed; later poems fail at classical verse, rather than succeeding at anything at all. The obvious privileging of the classical verse tradition which informs this perspective is rarely defended explicitly, but the convenience of the treatment of late verse as bad verse is clear: if late verse is defined as poor, sloppy, and out of control, it need not be addressed on its own terms.

Regardless, the assertion that the later poetry can be effectively compared to the earlier, or that later poets were, in fact, *trying* to compose verse under the same rules as earlier poets is deeply problematic. The reality is not that the poetic tradition was rigid, but rather that Sievers-Bliss formalism is rigid: it has limited the ways in which scholars and students have thought about poetry and poetic developments, to the point that any detailed understanding of late Old English verse still escapes us and a number of late poems have been explicitly excluded from the published canon of Old English verse, Krapp and Dobbie's *Anglo-Saxon Poetic Records (ASPR)*. Of course, these poems should merely be excluded from the canon of classical verse: our failings in understanding the metre of late poems should not necessarily be defined as the poems' failings.

The problems of this perspective become even clearer when one looks to early Middle English alliterative poetry, such as Layamon's *Brut*. Since it seemingly appears out of nowhere, scholars have frequently had a great deal of trouble accounting for the forms of Layamon's verse (and that of his less-well-known contemporaries). Recently, suggestions have been made that early Middle English poetry descends not from Old English verse, but rather from Ælfrician rhythmical prose (Blake, Brehe, Cable, Friedlander), while the traditional assertion that Layamon's use of rhyme is a borrowing from French practice is too rarely challenged (Friedlander is an exception here, however). An improved understanding of the history of late Old English verse also has the potential to clarify the origins of Middle English alliterative verse.

Finally, a new metrical formalism may offer the possibility of helping modern readers to an improved understanding of Anglo-Saxon poetics. Secondary poetic effects such as cross alliteration and rhyme have been very poorly accounted for from the Sieversian perspective, despite the likelihood that they were, in fact, used for effect. Likewise, hypermetric verses have not been particularly well understood by metricists, although the problem of the poetic value of shifting between normal verses and hypermetric ones clearly deserves our attention. Part of the difficulty, almost certainly, lies in the Sieversian conception of metrical verse-contours as abstract patterns of stress rhythms; recent work on the interactions of Old English metre and syntax (e.g., Kendall, Momma), however, offers powerful evidence that metrical verses are constructed far more subtly than by a mechanical analysis of stress and rhythm.

In this book, then, I attempt to rectify these troublesome aspects of the long-accepted Sieversian formalism. Borrowing more or less heavily from the recent books on Old English metre by such scholars as Geoffrey Russom, Calvin Kendall, Thomas Cable, and others, I present a new metrical formalism which is flexible enough to let us see the differences of poetic practice from one poet to another, including the systematic differences which separate classical Old English verse from later works.[13] In addition, I try to put forth a metrical system with an inherent simplicity, yet one which accounts for the enormous variety of individual verse 'types.' Along the way, I offer new interpretations of many of the features of Old English versification which have been only poorly explained by previous theories: restrictions on anacrusis, double alliteration patterns, cross alliteration and rhyme, and hypermetric verses.

At its centre, my formalism attempts to allow a diachronic perspective on Old English verse. Rather than imagining the formulaic system of composition as essentially static and unchanging, I begin with the expectation that poets and poems differ in their metrical practices, and that these differences might arise from differences in authorship, time of composition, or even subject matter and tone. In presenting a new descriptive metrical system, I attempt to account for both how Old English poems are like one another and how they differ from one another. At times, the differences are quite radical, and a brief summary of what I see as the chronological development of Old English verse is worth presenting here as a kind of road map to the chapters which follow.

At the heart of what are usually considered as the earlier and more technically competent Old English poems lies a versification system which is deeply and thoroughly formulaic. In this system (which is used in 'classical' Old English verse, and described in detail in chapters 2.1–2.4) verse types are generally structured as pairs of what have been termed 'feet,' and each foot is patterned (as Geoffrey Russom has compellingly argued) on a commonly occurring word stress-contour. A small number of simple rules define how these feet can be combined into metrical verses and how verses combine into lines. Because many feet are patterned on compound stress-contours, lexical compounds (and formulaic compounding) play a large role in this classical verse, as does the rule of resolution, which metrically equates long stressed syllables with disyllabic sequences consisting of short stressed syllables and their immediate successors.

Classical verse is notable for several features. It includes two main foot-combination modes: normal verses (combinations of two feet) and hypermetric verses (combinations of three feet). Generally making use of alliteration as a primary linking feature to connect verses into lines, the classical tradition occasionally allowed the secondary devices of rhyme and cross alliteration to substitute for some of the effects of primary alliteration. The conservative and formulaic nature of the classical tradition includes some notable archaisms, especially in the metrical preservation of linguistically archaic forms which predate the phonological processes of 'contraction' and 'parasiting.'[14] During the classical period, however, it seems that these processes resulted in the reanalysis of certain forms and the authorization of new verse types which had previously been excluded. A poem like *Beowulf*, in which contracted and uncontracted forms are both sometimes metrically required, should be expected to exhibit at least some of these innovative forms, and (as I argue below) it does, as do virtually all of the longer classical poems.

Just as the persistence of some metrical forms (justified by the prehistoric linguistic processes of parasiting and contraction) led to a reanalysis of acceptable metrical forms, the difficult and confusing process of resolution eventually led to even more extensive formal revisions, as I discuss in chapters 3.1–3.3. The changes brought about by the elimination of resolution as a part of the poetic system were accompanied by changes which served to dissociate the forms of metrical feet from word stress-contours. These changes appear to have occurred during the tenth century, and they mark the beginning of a second major period in the history of Old English verse forms.

Among the most prominent formal changes seen in this 'post-classical' or 'late' Old English poetry (discussed in chapters 3.1–3.3) was the loss of metrical compounding (late feet have only two stress levels, not three, so secondary stress is no longer metrically significant and compounds are no longer metrically required). But further, new metrical forms were authorized. Many of the new verse types were superficially similar to Sieversian A-type verses with anacrusis; others appeared to overlap classical hypermetric forms (indeed, the tenth-century changes seem to have eliminated true hypermetric verses altogether). Alliteration no longer needed to link the first full stresses in the two half-lines, but could, in principle, link any two stresses. In the work of some poets (especially in the eleventh century), rhymes at the end of half-lines (an ornamental, secondary poetic feature in the classical period) were used as the only linking device to join half-lines.

The postclassical verse forms that arose as a result of the tenth-century changes characterize a surprising amount of Old English verse, including the *Metrical Psalms*, much of the poetry of the *Anglo-Saxon Chronicle*, *The Judgment Day II* (and other poems from CCCC 201 and Junius 121), many of the *Metrical Charms*, and other assorted odds and ends. This corpus of postclassical tenth- and eleventh-century poetry works on metrical principles markedly different from those of classical verse but clearly descended from them. Further, however, I argue that another large group of texts can be described by precisely the same metrical forms: the so-called rhythmical prose works of Ælfric. Long misunderstood simply because it failed to fit the norms of classical verse, Ælfric's rhythmical prose is actually a clear and straightforward example of late Old English verse. The long-needed identification of the principles behind Ælfric's characteristic alliterative form serves to identify him as one of the Anglo-Saxon period's most prolific versifiers.

Unfortunately, the complexity of its foot forms meant that late Old English verse lacked some of the simplicity and straightforwardness of the classical verse system, and its redundancies and ambiguities also made it ripe for reanalysis by later poets. At a point very late in the period (perhaps in the twelfth century) postclassical verse seems to have been further reinterpreted by poets, and the resulting verse form can be conveniently characterized as 'early Middle English alliterative verse' (discussed with specific reference to Layamon in chapters 4.1–4.2).

This early Middle English verse form retains the alternative forms of linking seen in late Old English verse: half-lines may be joined by either alliteration or verse rhyme (and sometimes by both). Individual verses generally have two, three, or four 'feet,' each stressed foot held by a single word (as late Old English verses had up to four stresses), and extrametrical syllables are allowed before each foot. Where the feet of classical and postclassical Old English metres were often filled by groups of words, the simplifying principle which led to early Middle English alliterative metre involved the reidentification of stressed feet and individual words. The metre of Layamon thus returns, to some degree, to the simplicity of the classical Old English system, although the metrical forms themselves have been radically altered.

As the preceding summary should indicate, the metrical study contained in this book attempts nothing less than a thorough-going revision of much of early English literary history. On the one hand, this fact indicates just how valuable metrical study and analysis can be to students of literary works: an analysis purely formal in its origins has major consequences for our understanding of the literature of the period. On the other hand, however, the very scope of the project demands that I sometimes move quickly through complicated and detailed arguments. And since this book hopes to find an audience among Anglo-Saxonists and medievalists in general, I leave a great deal of the detailed argumentation so common in books on metre to the footnotes, where interested parties and metrical specialists can find it. Nevertheless, I make no claim that my own prosodic theory has 'attain[ed] a static perfection' (Sayers 39), aiming for clarity and usability instead of exhaustive and (one fears) stultifying detail. Most readers, I hope, will examine the formalism I propose here at its own face value, as an attempt to codify the inherent simplicity of Anglo-Saxon verse, despite the ways in which that simplicity could (and did) generate an extraordinary variety of metrical forms.

Sieversian Formalism

In the previous chapter, I briefly explored some of the problems of a Sieversian metrical perspective. Nevertheless, it seems worthwhile here to provide a somewhat more extensive survey of Sieversian formalism – and what it can and cannot do – before embarking upon the task of offering a replacement.

At its heart, Sieversian metrics should be understood as a descriptive formalism that provides a taxonomy for metrical Old English verses according to abstract patterns of linguistic and metrical stress. To put it another way, Sieversian formalism identifies certain stress sequences as metrically acceptable while identifying others as unmetrical; the identification of metrical and unmetrical stress contours is descriptive and inductively derived, based upon observation, categorization, and analysis. The power of Sievers's formalism is that it allows the bewildering variety of observed specific types to be gathered together into five 'basic' types, each of which, in turn, has certain allowed (and sometimes disallowed) subtypes. Thus, any account of Sieversian formalism must include two things: an account of stress in Old English verse and a description of metrical types. It seems appropriate to begin with stress.

Stress in Old English

Sieversian formalism (like many other descriptive metrical systems) operates on the assumption that there was a general poetic tendency to match linguistic stress and metrical stress. That is, Sieversian analysis works by comparing the linguistic stress of an individual phrase (e.g., 'gomban gyldan,' *Beowulf* 11a) to an abstract stress contour (such as stress, unstress, stress, unstress: type A).[1] The process of analysis is simplest when (as here) the linguistic stress of the individual words in a verse matches their metrical stress assignment most closely: the similarity allows us to easily conclude that *Beowulf* 11a is a type A verse. In a verse like the following

Beo 197a: on þam dæge[2]

however, we know from alliteration that 'þam' must be metrically stressed (since it is the alliterative element), and thus we must analyse the verse as type C (unstress, stress, stress, unstress), although the identification of this verse's type is made difficult by the mismatch between the low linguistic stress of the definite article and the high metrical stress it takes in this particular verse. To a large degree, the extent to which scanning Old English verse is difficult in the Sieversian system is due to the difficulty of correctly identifying the link between the linguistic stress on individual elements and the metrical stress of those elements.

In linguistic terms, we can identify stress of two sorts: word-level stress and sentence-level stress. Every word pronounced in isolation, of course, receives (or may receive) full stress, but in connected discourse (such as a poem) sentence-level stress also plays a significant role. In terms of word-level stress, the general Germanic rule is clear and familiar: words receive primary stress on their first root syllable (excluding prefixes), with declining stress on succeeding syllables, and with secondary elements of compounds generally receiving secondary stress. Within sentences, however, it appears that words of high semantic import generally continue to receive prominent, primary stress, while those of less semantic import are unstressed. Thus, nouns, adjectives, and nonfinite verbs receive prominent stress, while pronouns, articles, prepositions, indefinites, and conjunctions are generally unstressed. Some words occupy a kind of middle ground, being stressed sometimes, unstressed other times (finite verbs, some adverbs).[3]

With such a stress hierarchy in place, the Sieversian scansion system offers some additional insight into metrical trends. Most often, there is a close match in verses between the 'sentence level' stress-pattern of the words involved and the metrical contour. To return to the verse 'gomban gyldan' cited above, since it consists of a noun and an infinitive verb, its words perfectly match the alternating stress pattern of a Sieversian A-type verse. Occasionally, however (as in *Beowulf* 19b, 'Scedelandum in'), there is a mismatch between metrical stress and linguistic stress: in this verse, the metrical contour suggests that a normally unstressed element (the preposition 'in') has been promoted to full metrical stress. Sieversian formalism generally accounts for many such mismatches by a rule of displacement: unstressed free (that is, 'mobile') sentence elements remain unstressed if occurring before the final stress of the first verse of the clause, but they are 'promoted' to positions of metrical stress if displaced from that unmarked position (displaced proclitics are similarly promoted, as in *Beowulf* 19b).[4] In principle, the complexity and ambiguity of such mismatches between linguistic stress and metrical stress are minimized by the fairly regular effects of this displacement rule.

Finally, one other feature of metrical stress is an essential component of Sieversian scansion: resolution, which is a principle of syllabic equivalence that equates a long stressed syllable with a two-syllable sequence consisting of a short stressed syllable plus an unstressed syllable.[5] Stressed syllables in Old English verse are generally long (either by virtue of having a long vowel or by falling in a syllable which is 'closed' by a final consonant), but short syllables are occasionally stressed, and for the majority of such stressed short syllables, resolution applies.[6] In practice, resolution is a purely metrical phenomenon: although its origins may lie in Old English linguistic history, its only function in surviving texts seems to be in making syllable counts of metrical verses come out right, and in terms of syllable counting, a resolved sequence (which is, linguistically, two syllables) counts as a single syllable. The complexity of resolution (even more than the difficulty of assessing stress levels in words) is the chief hurdle that beginning students of Old English metre must master to effectively scan verses.[7]

Metrical Types

Given the definitions of stress and resolution described above, we can wrap up this summary of Sieversian scansion with a brief account of just what metrical contours are allowed and how they are grouped into basic 'types.' The following table identifies the major Sieversian types (including allowable variations).

As the table indicates, in Sieversian formalism, most metrical verses consist of two 'feet,' each of which includes an element with primary stress. Anacrusis (the optional presence of unstressed material before the first stress of a verse) is allowed before types A and D. Secondary

TABLE 1
Sieversian Basic Types

Type	Anacrusis	First foot	Second foot	Examples (from *Beowulf*)	Scansion
A	[xx]	/x(xxx)	/x	gomban gyldan (11a) Aras þa se rica (399a)	/x /x [x]/xx /x
A3		xx(xxx)	/x	ac me geuðe (1661a) Hæbbe ic eac geahsod (433a)	xxx /x xxxxx /x[8]
B		x(xxx)/	x(x)/	ne hie huru heofena Helm (182a) Ðonne sægdon þæt (377a)	xxxx/ x/ xx/ x/
C		x(xxx)/	/x	þæs þe him yplade (228a) geseon moston (1875b)	xxx/ \x x/ /x
D	[xx]	/(x)	/ \x	atol angengea (165a) gesette sigehreþig (94a)	/ / \x [x]/x / \x
D4[9]	[xx]	/(x)	/x(x)\	swefan sibbegedriht (729a) yðe eotena cyn (421a)	/ /xx\ /x /x\[10]
E		/ \x(x)	/	Licsar gebad (815b) Nihtweorce gefeh (827b)	/ \x / / \xx /

Notes: / = a stressed syllable or resolved sequence
  \ = a syllable with secondary stress (occasionally a resolved sequence)
  x = an unstressed syllable
  (x) = one optional syllable of expansion allowed
  [xx] = one or two optional syllables allowed in anacrusis in a-line; anacrusis
  limited to one syllable in the b-line
  (xxx) = one or more optional syllables allowed, with no clear theoretical
  maximum
For readers' convenience, syllable stress (according to Sieversian formalism) is here
marked with a double underline for primary stress and a single underline for secondary
stress; resolved sequences, of course, are counted as single syllables.

(or tertiary) stress is mandatory in types D and E, and it also may
appear in other positions (specifically, / \ is often an optional replace-
ment for a foot of the form /x).[11] In addition, secondary stress can
sometimes be used to replace primary stress, in that compound words
can be counted in scansion as if their components were independent
elements (as in the first of the two C verses listed on the table).

Expressed in such a fashion, Sieversian scansion has an admirable simplicity, and it can be readily used to scan passages of Old English verse as follows (where I again indicate full stress with a double underline and secondary stress with a single underline):

Geseah ða on searwum   sigeeadig bil,
eald sweord eotenisc,   ecgum þyhtig,
wigena weorðmynd;   þæt [wæs] wæpna cyst,
buton hit was mare   ðonne ænig mon oðer
to beadulace   ætberan meahte,
god ond geatolic,   giganta geweorc.   (*Beowulf* 1557–62)

With the stress of each syllable (or resolved sequence) marked like this, it is easy to simply write down the individual scansions of each verse, as follows:

Scansions		Types (a-line)	(b-line)
(x)/xx /x	/ \x /	A (with anacrusis)	E
/ \ /x	/x /x	A (with / \ foot)	A
/x / \	xx/ x/	A (w/ resolution and / \ foot)	B
xxxx /x	xxxx/ /x	A3	C
x/ \x	x/ /x	C (w/ resolution and secondary stress)	C (w/ resolution)
/x /x	/ \xx /	A (w/ resolution)	E

Of course, each of these subtypes can be given a more specific name, but doing so is not actually necessary once we have identified the metrical contour appropriate to each verse. Regardless, as even such a brief passage indicates, the chief difficulty in scanning most verses of Old English poetry lies simply in correctly identifying the stress-bearing syllables and sequences, although the frequency of alliteration does much to make even that task easier. The brilliance of the Sieversian scansion system lies in its essential simplicity and its descriptive validity. It is simple in that the basic principles can be expressed (as I have expressed them here) in a remarkably short space, although the details certainly grow in complexity the more closely one tracks them down. Its descriptive validity is shown by the simple fact that the system works: the great majority of Old English verses can, in fact, be scanned according to such a system.

But neither of these facts, of course, indicates that Old English verses *ought to be* scanned in this system. The Sieversian system can taxono-mize verses according to abstract stress contours, but it seems clear that Old English poets did not, in fact, conceptualize their metrical sys-tem this way.[12] Further, Sieversian taxonomy (as I have suggested above) may group subtypes together incorrectly: in many ways, type A3 is more like types B and C than like type A; likewise, type D4 may be mistakenly associated with other type D verses. A taxonomy that groups items together incorrectly is obviously problematic and subject to replacement by a more useful taxonomy. Finally, the Sievers system gives little insight into the logic behind the metricality of verses: if a compound disyllable (/ \) can replace a /x foot in an A verse, for example, why not in a C-verse? In the following paragraphs, I briefly discuss several other issues of scansion or verse-form that reveal weak-nesses or insufficiencies in Sieversian scansion

1. Tertiary Stress. Tertiary stress, as its name seems to indicate, is a stress level somewhat less prominent than secondary stress and some-what more prominent than no stress at all.[13] Unfortunately, it is not at all clear that tertiary stress has any phonological reality or consequences.[14] As it turns out, tertiary stress seems to be a phenomenon strictly limited to Old English verse, and Bliss's comment that it is a kind of 'secondary stress which can be ignored' (*Metre* 25) is telling. In fact, tertiary stress appears, on closer examination, to be merely an artifact of Sieversian scansion. In the most revealing kinds of example, tertiary stress is invoked in Old English verse merely to account for the conventional scansion of certain types of lines. Consider a verse like the following, for example:

Beo 96a: ond gefrætwade

In Sieversian formalism, such a verse is scanned with 'tertiary stress' on '-wad-': the reason for doing so appears to be none other than to preserve the principle that a verse must have two stressed syllables.[15] When verbs similar to 'gefrætwade' appear at the beginning of a verse, the 'tertiary stress' is, in fact, ignored in the scansion, as leading to unmetrical types. Tertiary stress, then, seems to be little more than a mechanism to grant ad hoc scansions the appearance of consistency.[16]

The case of tertiary stress is a fascinating example of the power and pervasiveness of Sieversian formalism and its consequences. Although Bliss is more than willing to discard the necessity for two-stress verses in the case of A3 verses (and in his type 'e' verses) his treatment of verses like *Beowulf* 96a relies more or less directly on precisely that principle. Bliss backs away from the extensive renovation of Sievers which his foundational revisions would seem to demand, and Sievers-Bliss formalism ends up appearing to grant linguistic reality (seemingly buttressed by statistical calculations) to something which is, in fact, produced by the scansion system itself, rather than being present in the poetry. In another scansion system, tertiary stress need make no appearance at all, and it makes none in the analysis presented here.

2. Anacrusis is limited to two syllables. The limitation of anacrusis to two syllables is frequently remarked for Old English verse, and while Thomas Cable's important 'Constraints on Anacrusis' article associates anacrusis with verbal prefixes and the negator, the association is not complete. We can observe this apparent constraint, but Sieversian formalism offers no explanation for it.

3. Anacrusis is excluded before E verses. In Old English, anacrusis is limited to occurring before verses that begin with a stressed syllable, but it is not allowed before E-type verses, which also begin with a stressed syllable. This commonly observed limitation also cannot be accounted for in the Sievers system.

4. Except for the simplest di-trochaic (/x /x) A verses, A, D, and E verses regularly take double alliteration in the a-line, while B and C verses generally have double alliteration only optionally. If we except full-verse compounds and A verses made up of two '/x' feet[17], where each foot is filled by a single word, the remaining A, D, and E verses in the a-line have double alliteration (in *Beowulf*) 89 per cent of the time by my count, while B and C verses (again excluding the relevant compound forms) have double alliteration only 37.4 per cent of the time.[18] While I am not aware that this observation has been made before, there is nothing in Sieversian formalism (where each foot of a B or C verse has a full stress), to explain the difference. Geoffrey Russom's word-foot formalism (discussed in more detail below) would offer a clear and compelling account of the difference.

5. Second elements of compound personal names have secondary stress only when inflected. That is, the name 'Beowulf' is conventionally scanned as '/x' but the inflected form 'Beowulfes' is scanned

'/ \x.' This rule has clear exceptions, and I have argued elsewhere that there is clear alliterative and manuscript evidence to suggest that this conventional interpretation of nominal stress patterns is incorrect (Bredehoft, 'Secondary Stress'). Yet these scansions are required according to all traditional accounts of Sieversian metrics, and this conclusion about stress has even made its way into grammars of Old English.[19]

6. Formally similar verses are often scanned differently solely on the basis of alliteration. For example:

Beo 614a: grette goldhroden	/ x / \x	type D
Beo 640b: eode goldhroden	xx/ \x	type C

The variable treatment of finite verbs in such cases seems ad hoc; Kendall's analysis, in fact, suggests that such verses are essentially the same in their scansions, despite the conventional association of alliteration with full stress.[20]

As a descriptive formalism, Sieversian scansion is not essentially *wrong*; it may in fact continue to serve a useful purpose as a simple and clear way of talking about Old English verse, much as traditional grammatical terms continue to be used by modern linguists and taught in grammar classes. Yet, like all descriptive systems, Sieversian scansion should give way if a better descriptive system can be found. What the next section of this present book offers is such an improved descriptive system, one which can describe metrical Old English verses with all the precision of Sieversian formalism, making no reference to tertiary stress and offering a clearer and explanatory account of constraints on anacrusis, patterns of linguistic stress, double alliteration patterns, and finite verbs.

A New Formalism for Classical Old English Metre

The schemes and designs to be explored here include: the structures of lines of verse; patterns of rhyme, alliteration, and assonance; schemes of syntax and word order ... and larger arrangements of these.

John Hollander, *Rhyme's Reason* 3

It may seem somewhat incongruous to begin an account of Old English alliterative metre by quoting from a book called *Rhyme's Reason*, but Hollander's list of the formal characteristics of verse can stand as a salutary reminder of what sorts of formal features we might need to pay attention to. Indeed, in the chapters that follow, I will suggest that the underestimation of the role of rhyme in Old English verse has been endemic on the part of metricists, who have too readily limited the metrical tools of Old English poets to stress and alliteration. Likewise, alliteration itself has been misunderstood, with a focus on primary alliteration obscuring the effects and functions of secondary alliterative patterns. Hollander's catalogue of poetic 'schemes and designs' lists the very building blocks of poetry itself: our understanding of Old English verse must take more into account than patterns of stress and alliteration. Ultimately, any detailed understanding of Anglo-Saxon poetics must attend to all of the formal tools available to Old English poets, and the formalism I present here is, I believe, sensitive enough to give us valuable insights into the issues of poetics.

The metrical system described here (and discussed in chapters 2.1–2.4 of this book) is that which can be called 'classical' Old English metre. Distinguished from later verse by certain formal characteristics, classical metre appears to be a relatively consistent metrical form in use before the middle of the tenth century and perhaps even later. Chrono-

logical estimates, of course, are difficult here: as Old English verse com-
position was notoriously formulaic and traditional, the continuing
existence and employment of traditional forms is only to be expected,
even in the context of the more or less sweeping changes that overtook
the poetic tradition itself. I take my examples in these chapters primarily
from a variety of the longer poems which can be assigned to the classical
metrical period with some confidence. These include *Genesis A, Beowulf,
Andreas, Exodus, Elene, Guthlac A, Guthlac B*, and *Judith*. My procedure
thus explicitly avoids problems caused by a too-exclusive focus on any
one poem, and the system I describe is not perfectly reflected in any one
poem. But in its flexibility, the formalism I propose here is able both to
account for the metre of these various poems and to allow us to describe
the metrical differences between them.

The work of previous metricists is, of course, enormously valuable,
and much of what I include in my account of Old English verse is
included or anticipated in their work. What a new system can offer is a
new way of putting old ideas together, hopefully allowing both new
answers to old question and new questions. Much of what is brought
forth in the following description, then, should seem familiar to any-
one who has studied even a little Old English verse. Some of the basic
principles which have been articulated by previous scholars go com-
pletely unchallenged here, as I find the logic behind them compelling: I
agree, for example, with previous scholars on the importance of tradi-
tional definitions of long and short syllables,[1] on what sounds alliterate
with one another, and (at least in general terms) in the assignment of
linguistic stress to words.[2] But before going any further, it seems
important to begin with what is best known about Old English verse,
and I will take three general principles as fundamental (although there
are notable exceptions to each).

*P1. Alliteration (the repetition of initial sounds of stressed syllables) generally
links Old English verses (sometimes called half-lines) into full lines. All initial
vowels are considered to alliterate with one another and the clusters 'sc-', 'st-',
and 'sp-' count as separate alliterators and thus do not alliterate with one
another.*

P2. Each normal metrical verse is formed by the combination of two 'feet.'

*P3. Classical Old English verse feet are generally patterned on the stress pat-
terns of Old English words.*

Note that Principle 1 (P1) suggests that alliteration only links verses into full lines as a general principle, not an exclusive one. Single, unpaired verses are occasionally used, sometimes for what appears to be deliberate poetic effect, as in the final lines of *Wulf and Eadwacer*:

> Þæt mon eaþe tosliteþ   þætte næfre gesomnad wæs,
> uncer giedd geador.   (ll. 18–19)

Here, where the poem itself discusses the separation of things never truly joined, we find an unpaired half-line: the formal use of the lone verse here seems to provide a perfectly appropriate parallel to the sense.[3]

In other cases, however, it is worth noting that alliteration does not seem to provide a link, even where there are two half-lines. Consider this line from *Genesis A*:

> *GenA* 1956: mon for metode,   þe him æfter a

Here we see what is sometimes labelled 'AABB-alliteration.' Such lines are, of course, comparatively rare in classical verse, but lines without alliterative linking are numerous enough to suggest that while P1 is a general rule, some exceptions are, in fact, allowed.[4]

Some version or another of P2 has appeared in virtually all of the major metrical theories of Old English verse. The two-part structure of Old English verses gives rise (in different ways) to Sievers's feet, Pope's measures, Bliss's breath groups, and Russom's feet. P3 corresponds closely to Russom's analysis of metrical feet as being patterned on word forms, although (as we shall see) my system nevertheless includes a broader range of allowable feet.

P1–P3 are the basic principles of Old English verse. As should be clear, they are simple and plausible. In fact, nothing in P1–P3 is new; rather, these three principles capture much of the basic structure of Old English verse which all metricists must describe. What remains in a useful description of Old English verse are rules of three separate sorts: detailed rules of foot structure, rules for combining feet into verses, and rules for combining verses into lines. I will take each sort of rule in order.

1. Foot structure rules

FS1. Resolution. Resolution is a principle of syllabic equivalence in which a short, stressed syllable plus a following unstressed syllable in the same word is metrically equivalent to a long stressed syllable. As such, resolved positions can also be designated as 'syllables,' especially for the purposes of syllable-counting rules. Restrictions on resolution are noted in the foot combination rules (FC1).[5]

The existence of resolution in classical Old English verse strongly suggests that Old English metre is not primarily rhythmic, in the sense that what is 'measured' by the metre is not time, but rather syllables (or syllable equivalents). Classical Old English metre is perhaps best described as 'stress-syllabic.'[6]

FS2. x-feet, s-feet, S-feet. Metrical feet are based upon the stress contours of typical Old English words, and they can be conveniently grouped into three basic varieties, each of which has several specific forms.

FS2a. x-feet are completely unstressed feet, patterned on and generally exemplified by function words, particles, or prefixes. Examples:

> x: ac, for, þa, to, and, ge-
> xx: oððe, under, sona, hwilum
> xxx: nænigne, hwæþere, uncerne

It seems likely that scansion occasionally demands an xxxx foot, but it is not clear that such a foot would be patterned on an actual word. Consider, however, the following verse:

GenA 1456b: Nohweðere reste fand

Here the primary alliteration is on 'r,' and if Krapp's word division is correct, an xxxx foot is indeed necessary.[7]

Note that in scansion, multisyllabic x-feet can generally be filled by either single words or groups of words. Syntactically, it may be useful to distinguish two sorts of x-feet: those which contain so-called sentence particles (e.g., pronouns, conjunctions, adverbs) and those which contain only proclitic elements (e.g., prefixes, prepositions, articles). Since x-feet are always initial in verses (see Foot-Combination rules, below), x-feet which include sentence particles must be clause-initial.[8]

FS2b. A second group of feet can be labelled as 's-feet' in this formalism; these feet are patterned on finite nonauxiliary verbs, and they are generally filled by such verbs and associated particles, prefixes, and pronouns. Examples:

s: sceal,[9] eteð, hiold, bat
sx: setton, hwearf þa, grette, ferdon
xs: gesægd, onband, ða com, nu sceal
xsx: gesette, wiðhæfde, ne sohte, ne mæg ic, gewat him
xxs: forðon sceall, þonne cwið, ac he hafað
xxsx: ne gefeah he, oferwearp þa, ne gefrægen ic

Paradigmatically, s-feet are filled by single-word finite verbs and their prefixes; the initial unstressed portions of s-feet are limited to two syllables because 'ofer-' is the longest available verbal prefix.[10] The inclusion of enclitic particles (especially pronouns and 'þa') after the s-element is rhythmically authorized by disyllabic forms like 'setton' as well as justified by the close linguistic link between verbs and these following elements. In *Andreas* 220a, we see an s-foot of the form 'Scealtu' with the enclitic subject pronoun phonologically assimilated to the verb; such forms are very familiar from Middle English, and the appearance of this form in *Andreas* confirms that such pronouns, at least, should often be considered as enclitic to the associated verbs.[11]

Note also that the scansions imply that resolution applies in s-feet. It is somewhat difficult to find conclusive evidence for this claim, although the following verses from *Beowulf* are significant here:

Beo 1701a: fremeð on folce
Beo 3101a: Uton nu efstan

In both cases, initial finite verbs with short root syllables appear, followed by single additional syllables (each functioning here, I believe, as the x-position in an sx foot). If resolution did not apply in these s-feet, we would expect to see four-syllable verses with these types of finite verbs, but we do not see them. The case of *Beowulf* 3101a is especially clear here, as the adverb 'nu' may well be included for the sole purpose of bringing the verse up to the minimum number of positions.[12]

FS2c. S-feet are feet patterned on (and frequently filled by) fully stressed words of high semantic value: nouns, adjectives, adverbs, nonfinite verbs. Examples:

S: god, beorht, eorl, atol, gryre
Sx: sweorde, beagas, lices, byrgean, wrætlic[13]
Sxx: fultuma, ealgian, maðelode[14]
Ss: Beowulf,[15] fyrheard, wisfæst, seleweard
Ssx: Hroðgares, lagustreamas, Scyldingas, murnende[16]
Sxs: wundenhals, Hrefnesholt, hildedeor
Sxxs: sibbegedryht

Note that, while S-feet are paradigmatically filled by single words, they may also be filled by groups of words. S-feet can also be filled by words of less semantic import through the assignment of 'metrical stress.' That is, while words of high semantic content are generally scanned on S-feet, S-positions are not limited to such words in practice.

Note that only in s-feet are prefixes scanned as part of the foot; in words with S-feet, unstressed prefixes are scanned as separate x-type particles in a preceding foot, or as extrametrical syllables.[17] Two additional feet are needed to scan a small number of 'inverted' verses; see the rules for inverted verses in the foot-combination rules below. It is worth mentioning, though, that all of the feet listed here would have been intuitively familiar to all Anglo-Saxon speakers. These foot patterns, then, are part and parcel of both Old English linguistic knowledge and Old English poetic knowledge.

It is important to realize that there are frequent 'mismatches' between the paradigmatic form and content of a foot and its actual representation in particular verses. For example, s-feet are sometimes filled by nonfinite verbs by a process of analogy, and certain verse patterns which have conventionally been labelled as featuring 'anacrusis' seem to be patterned on verses with s-feet, even though they may contain no verbs at all. Likewise, pronouns and articles can sometimes be mapped onto S-feet, and even bear the weight of the alliterative link, as in the following line:

Beo 197: on þæm dæge   þysses lifes

Note that the alliterating (and thus metrically stressed) articles here are not 'displaced' as is often required in metrical theories;[18] instead, both are in their proper syntactic location. A more detailed analysis of this line is offered in the next chapter. Regardless, such 'mismatches' are an unavoidable part of Old English versification, although it probably remains true that such mismatches must remain relatively few in comparison to properly matched words and feet, or the basis of the metre would be lost.[19]

2. Foot combination rules

FC1. All metrical, nonhypermetric verses must have at least four metrical syllables.[20] *Resolution is 'blocked' or 'suspended' if resolution would drop the number of metrical syllables to less than four, or if it would change the class of the verse (see below).*[21]

FC1 offers what is perhaps the most straightforward account of when resolution does and does not apply, as well as eliminating three-syllable (or three-position) verses.[22]

FC2. Up to four unstressed extrametrical syllables can appear between metrical feet, although there appear to be additional constraints operative in certain specific types.[23]

FC2 accounts for much of the great diversity of specific verse-types in Old English. While extrametrical elements are generally only one or two syllables, up to four are sometimes necessary for scansion. It is possible that extrametrical elements and x-feet are patterned identically, giving some support for the existence of an xxxx foot.[24]

Occasionally extra syllables may appear to be present, as in the following verse from *Beowulf*:

Beo 2172a: Hyrde ic þæt he ðone healsbeah   ?sx/(xxxxx)Ss

It seems probable, however, that elision links the first two words, leaving only four extrametrical syllables, and that the limit of four such syllables is a firm one in classical verse.[25]

FC3a. Normal Verses: Normal verses must end with an S-foot of at least two syllables; Ssx, Sxs, and Sxxs are excluded from the first foot.

The vast majority of verses in Old English (about 93 per cent of the verses in *Beowulf*, for example) can be considered 'normal' verses, in that they are all generated by a simple set of combining rules. There are three basic types of normal verses, and the form of the final foot identifies the basic type of verse, according to the following definitions:

A-type verses end with	Sx, Ss
B-type verses end with	Sxs, Sxxs
C-type verses end with	Ssx, Sxx

Initial feet can be x-feet, s-feet, or S-feet, and thus there are nine types of normal verse, as seen here:

Initial Foot Type	Second Foot Type	Verse Types
x	A	xA, xB, xC
s	B	sA, sB, sC
S	C	SA, SB, SC

Note, again, that Ssx, Sxs, and Sxxs are excluded from the initial position in normal verses while Ss is always allowed (although comparatively rare) as an initial foot. Thus, a trisyllabic compound having a short root-syllable in the second element must be scanned as Ss (i.e., with resolution) in the first foot of a normal verse, while being scanned as Ssx in the second foot of a verse. These nine types of normal verse correspond to Sieversian A, B, C, and D verses, and I maintain the use of the letters A, B, and C in order to make this system seem as familiar as possible.

FC3b. Inverted Verses

Inverted verses are those which have either an inverted foot, or an inverted foot order. The latter include those verses labelled as E verses in Sieversian scansion. I maintain that designation for the overall class identification of E-type verses, but offer more precise designations for individual types. E-type verses can simply be listed:

CsS: Ssx/S and Ssx/(x)S
CxS: Sxx/S and Sxx/(x)S
BS: Sxs/S and Sxxs/S

The appositeness of the term 'inverted verses' for E-type verses can be seen by comparing the following pair of verses from *Andreas*:

And 617b: agef ondsware	xs/Ssx	sC
And 628b: ondsware agef	Ssx/(x)S	CsS

Both verses have their primary alliteration on vowels, and the poet seems to use the variation between the two here to avoid the troublingly close repetition of identical verses (especially since 'agef ondsware' is used again at 643b). As both this example and the abbreviated type-descriptors I use indicate, E-type verses can be conceptualized as inverted SB and SC verses. Almost all inverted verses are of the E type, and the great majority of these are of the specific type CsS. A few additional rare inverted verses, however, have inverted feet ('b-feet'), of the form sxS or sxxS: these feet are not based upon extant Old English words, and may have developed through comparisons or analogies between E-type verses (Ssx/S) and SB verses (S/Sxs).[26] Regardless of their origins, however, xb verses constitute the final metrical type to be described in my system:

xb: x-foot plus b-foot (x/sxS or xx/sxxS, etc.)[27]

The foot combination rules thus allow for a great variety of basic verse-types, including a small number that have not generally been included in previous theories, primarily because they are rare or nonexistent in *Beowulf*.[28] Further, the rules given explain the extraordinary numbers of specific types seen in Old English verse.[29] Nevertheless, the foot combination rules are themselves quite simple: except for the rare xb types with the inverted sxS and sxxS feet, all other types result from simple combinations of x-feet, s-feet, and S-feet. Where knowledge of feet would have been available to all Old English speakers, it is the foot combination rules which allowed composition of metrical verses. The verse combination rules described below allowed composition of lines. A few additional comments about the implications of the foot combination rules are in order, however.

Note, for example, that the constraint on resolution which disallows resolution from changing the class of a verse prevents xC-type verses with a final Ssx foot from becoming xA verses, even when the s-position of the C verse is short. Thus we see resolution operating in quite straightforward (and hopefully familiar) ways:

Beo 2779b: mundbora wæs	Ssx/S (without resolution)
Beo 1480a: Wes þu mundbora	xx/Ssx (without resolution)

Beo 2438a: his freawine	x/Ssx (without resolution)
Beo 2357a: freawine folca	Ss/Sx (with resolution)

Resolution in 2779b and 2438a would lead to three-syllable verses (in keeping with the notion that resolved sequences count as single syllables in syllable-counting rules); in 1480a, it would change the class of the verse.[30] In 2357a, resolution is required because Ssx is not allowed as the first foot of a normal (noninverted) verse. Consider also the following verses:

GenA 2697a: mines fæder	xx/Sx
Beo 2048a: þone þin fæder	xx/(x)Sx
Ex 149a: mihtmod wera	Ss/Sx

In these sorts of verses, resolution in the second foot would conflict with FC3a, which requires that the second foot be an S-foot with at least two metrical syllables; resolution in the second foot is accordingly blocked in these verses.[31] In classical verse, it is clear that resolution is suspended far more often in Ss/Sx verses (such as *Exodus* 149a) than in Sx/Sx verses. The simplest account of this difference would seem to revolve around the 'weight' of the verses, the 'light' unresolved second foot being more acceptable after the heavy Ss foot than after the normative Sx foot.

Occasionally, the use of resolution can lead to ambiguities of scansion, as in the case of the following verse:

ChrC 1011b: æþelduguð betast	Ss/Sx	or	Ssx/S

The resolution of 'æþel-' is certain, as is resolution of either '-duguð' or 'betast.' Since (as in *Exodus* 149a above) short unresolved syllables are not uncommon on the second S-position of Ss/Sx verses, either scansion is plausible, although the frequent contraction of 'betast' to 'betst' might argue in favour of scanning this verse as an E verse. Either way, however, the verse is clearly metrical; fortunately, examples of such ambiguity are relatively uncommon.

3. Verse combination rules

VC1: Alliteration links the first S-positions of the two verses in a line.

VC2: Double alliteration is generally mandatory (occurring on more than 90 per cent of examples) or quasi-mandatory (in more than 75 per cent of exam-

ples) in a-lines with two S positions (SS verses), with the exception of the specific type Sx/Sx.[32] *Where it is not mandatory, double alliteration is optional in a-line verses with additional S or s positions.*[33]

The requirement for mandatory or quasi-mandatory double alliteration is suspended for full-verse compounds and for verses where one S-position is filled by a proper name.[34] In addition, double alliteration is occasionally replaced by three other (relatively uncommon) linking devices: in cases where rhyme replaces alliteration, where secondary alliteration is employed, and where traditional semantic doublets are used.[35] Finally, double alliteration is generally excluded in the b-line.

VC3. In classical verse, xA and sA verses are excluded from the b-line.

VC3 is the familiar constraint disallowing Sieversian A3 verses from the second half-line. There are occasional exceptions to VC3, even in classical poems.

Note that VC2 accounts for the rarely observed fact that double alliteration is often mandatory for specific types of Sieversian A, D, and E verses, but never mandatory for Sieversian B or C verses, since only A, D, and E verses have two S-positions. This observation is easily explained in my account by the fact that double alliteration cannot be mandatory in verses with only one S-position (since the S- and s-positions in the relevant feet are paradigmatically filled by the elements of a compound, which cannot be expected to co-alliterate).[36] Since alliteration patterns are always acknowledged to be a central feature of Old English metre, the fact that previous metrical theories have neither identified nor explained the restrictions on where double alliteration can be required should be seen as a sign of their incompleteness.

Further observations can be made. For example, compounds (i.e., single words with the patterns Ss, Sxs, Sxxs, and Ssx words with secondary stress), as Calvin Kendall has argued, are always marked for alliteration.[37] As a consequence, many SA, SB, and SC verses are especially clearly marked for double alliteration in the a-line and are rare in the b-line. Consider the following basic verse-forms:

Sx/Ss   SA
S/Sxs   SB
S/Ssx   SC

In each case, if the second foot is filled by a compound (which, as I have noted, is marked for alliteration), then the pattern ought to have problematic double alliteration if it occurs in the b-line. As it turns out, all such verses are, in fact, rare in the b-line. In fact, examples of S/Ssx in the b-line are plentiful where the second foot is a single word only if that word is a name (such verses being excluded from the normal alliterative requirements) or if the Ssx foot has a long second syllable without secondary stress.[38] There are, of course, exceptions such as *Beowulf* 164b ('feond mancynnes') or 495b ('hroden ealowæge'), but the general trend is nevertheless quite clear.[39] Likewise, in *Beowulf*, SA-type b-lines with Ss second feet are virtually nonexistent unless the second foot consists of a compound name.

One of the unexpected consequences of these findings is the confirmation of my earlier claim about Ssx feet, where I suggested that the s-position of an Ssx-foot must either have secondary stress or be long. These two varieties of Ssx feet (which are clearly distinct from Sxx feet, which can appear in the first foot of normal verses) are distributed differently in this example, according to whether or not they have secondary stress. Presumably, poets were paying attention to the alliterative requirements of compounds, and this attention results in the distribution noted, but regardless, it is crucial to see that the ways in which we define elements of scansion and analysis can have an impact on the observations we make.[40] In the case of S/Ssx verses in the b-line, we see a complex interaction between alliterative expectations, foot-form identity, and foot combination rules.[41] Nevertheless, the complex distribution observed can be accounted for by a remarkably simple set of rules and guidelines (compounds are generally marked for alliteration; names are excluded from some alliterative requirements). Once again, a complex metrical distribution can be seen to develop straightforwardly from poetic rules that are simple enough that we can believe poets might actually have employed them.

A few additional observations about double alliteration are worth making at this point. Geoffrey Russom's remarkable insight that much of Old English alliteration can be understood as deriving from a system of metrical subordination is extremely useful here. Russom's analysis, adapted to s-foot scansion, lies behind the suggestion that primary alliteration occurs on the first S-position of each half-line. In the a-line, additional S or s positions may also optionally alliterate, although Russom suggests that doubly-subordinated elements cannot alliterate. The following interesting patterns of alliteration are thus allowed in classical verse:

Beo 264a: Gebad wintra worn	xs/Sxs	sB	(Ss-alliteration)
Beo 1616a: forbarn brodenmæl	xs/Sxs	sB	(sS-alliteration)
And 107a: Geþola þeoda þrea	xs/Sxs	sB	(sSs-alliteration)
Wand 66a: ne sceal no to hatheort	xs/(xx)Ss	sA	(Ss-alliteration)
Beo 743a: synsnædum swealh	Ssx/S	CsS	(SsS-alliteration)
ChrC 1006a: woruldwidles wom	Ssx/S	CsS	(SsS-alliteration)

In the first example, there is additional alliteration on an s-position following the first S-position; in the second example, we see alliteration on an intial s-foot plus the intial S-position. In the verse from *Andreas*, both kinds of additional alliteration appear, and we have a case of triple alliteration; such examples are infrequent, as we would expect.[42] In the verse from *The Wanderer*, we have an alliteration pattern similar to that in the first example, although the S-foot here is Ss, rather than Sxs. Because self-alliterating compounds are few, such alliteration is relatively rare. The triple alliteration seen in E-type verses involves only singly subordinated elements. Further examples of triple alliteration are worth noting, however:

Sat 644a: Georne þurh godes gife	Sx/(x)Ssx	SC
Hell 19a: Open wæs þæt eorðærn	Sx/(x)Ss	SA
Ruin 20a: weallwalan wirum	Ss/Sx	SA
Dan 539a: heahheort ond hæðen	Ss/(x)Sx	SA
ChrC 1630a: beorht boca bibod	S/Sxxs	SB

In the first two examples, doubly subordinated s-positions do, in fact, participate in the alliteration. Thus, while Russom's account offers a nice explanation for why subordinated S- and s-positions are generally blocked from alliterating in the b-line, it seems likely that the actual form of the constraint must refer to the b-line itself, rather than simply relying on degree of subordination.[43]

Note also that double alliteration occasionally takes unexpected forms, as in the following verses:

Whale 45a: heoloþhelme biþeaht	Ssx/(x)S	Ss-alliteration
Ex 149a: mihtmod wera	Ss/Sx	Ss-alliteration

Such examples are rarer than verses with SS-alliteration, but these kinds of example do seem to fulfil the requirement for double alliteration demanded by SS-verses (notably, the *Andreas* poet uses Ss-alliteration no fewer than five times;[44] the *Meters* poet seems especially fond of Ss alliteration in E verses).[45] The examples of triple alliteration in SS-verses given above, of course, also fulfill the double alliteration requirement.

In the end, the metrical system outlined here is useful precisely because of its flexibility and descriptive power. As I will discuss below, many conventionally troublesome features of Old English metre are easily accounted for in this system: 'anacrusis,' alliteration of finite verbs, and so forth. Further, variations between Old English poems can often be described as resulting from alterations or changes in the basic rules as given here (e.g., double alliteration is often only optional, rather than quasi-mandatory, in E-type verses). In order to address some of these specific issues, however, it is worthwhile to demonstrate how my metrical system works in practice.

Scanning Old English Verse

The outline of classical Old English metre presented in the preceding chapter was brief, and some account of how to use that outline as the basis for a system of scansion is in order. In the present chapter, I will use a number of examples to demonstrate the basics of my scansion system and to discuss how it deals with some of the verses which have traditionally been identified as problematic or unmetrical. It is conven- ient to begin with the following familiar passage from *The Wanderer*:

	Swa cwæð eardstapa, earfeþa gemyndig,	xs/Ssx	Sxx/(x)Sx[1]
	wraþra wælsleahta, winemæga hryre:	Sx/Ssx	Ssx/S
	'Oft ic sceolde ana uhtna gehwylce	xxsx/Sx	Sx/(x)Sx
	mine ceare cwiþan. Nis nu cwicra nan	xx/Ssx	xx/Sxs
10	þe ic him modsefan minne durre	xx/(x)Ssx	Sx/Sx
	sweotule asecgan. Ic to soþe wat	Sx/(x)Sx	xx/Sxs
	þæt bið in eorle indryhten þeaw,	xx/(x)Sx	Ssx/S
	þæt he his ferðlocan fæste binde,	xx/(x)Ssx	Sx/Sx
	healde his hordcofan, hycge swa he wille.	sx/(x)Ssx	Sx/(xx)Sx
15	Ne mæg werig mod wyrde wiðstondan,	xs/Sxs	Sx/(x)Sx
	ne se hreo hyge helpe gefremman.	xx/Ssx	Sx/(x)Sx
			(ll. 6–15)[2]

As the scansions to the right of the passage show, most of the basic verse-types are represented here; the only major type missing is type SB, and we can find an example in *The Wanderer* at verse 23a: 'hrusan heolstre biwrah' (Sx/Sxxs).[3] With that inclusion, this brief passage from *The Wanderer* includes nearly all of the major verse categories, and can serve well for a brief examination of the important issues of

Table 2.1
Representative Types from *The Wanderer*

Type	Scansion	Example Verses
xA	xx/(x)Sx	12a: þæt bið in eorle
sA	xxsx/Sx	8a: Oft ic sceolde ana
SA	Sx/Sx	13b: fæste binde
	Sx/(x)Sx	11a: sweotule asecgan
	Sx/(xx)Sx	14b: hycge swa he wille
	Sxx/(x)Sx	6b: earfeþa gemyndig
xB	xx/Sxs	9b: Nis nu cwicra nan
sB	xs/Sxs	15a: Ne mæg werig mod
SB	Sx/Sxxs	23a: hrusan heolstre biwrah
xC	xx/Ssx	16a: ne se hreo hyge
	xx/(x)Ssx	13a: þæt he his ferðlocan
sC	xs/Ssx	6a: Swa cwæð eardstapa
	sx/(x)Ssx	14a: healde his hordcofan
SC	Sx/Ssx	7a: wraþra wælsleahta
E (CsS)	Ssx/S	7b: winemæga hryre

Old English scansion in my system.[4] Table 2.1 presents these scansions according to types, as a basis for the discussion that follows.

In the following section, I will address the key issues raised by the scansion of these verses, specifically focusing on just how one arrives at these scansions. Along the way, I will also discuss a number of verses that prove troublesome for many metrical thoeries and describe how they are dealt with in this formalism.

The first, and probably most important, step in scanning verses is to identify those semantically important nouns, adjectives, adverbs, and nonfinite verbs that are generally mapped onto S-positions. In this passage from *The Wanderer*, the following verses are made up entirely of such words:

6b: earfeþa gemyndig
7a: wraþra wælsleahta
7b: winemæga hryre
11a: sweotule asecgan
12b: indryhten þeaw

15b: wyrde wiðstondan
16b: helpe gefremman

In each case, correct scansions may be arrived at by simply marking the root of each word as S, secondary elements of compounds as s, and all the remaining syllables as x. Resolution must apply in 7b ('hryre') to prevent an unmetrical type (*Ssx/Sx; Ssx is allowed as the first foot only in class E), and it also occurs in 11a ('sweotule'), since such resolution would not change verse-class. Such marking results in the following notation:

6b: earfeþa gemyndig	Sxx xSx
7a: wraþra wælsleahta	Sx Ssx
7b: winemæga hryre	Ssx S
11a: sweotule asecgan	Sx xSx
12b: indryhten þeaw	Ssx S
15b: wyrde wiðstondan	Sx xSx
16b: helpe gefremman	Sx xSx

In these mark-ups, I have simply preserved word boundaries for clarity, but to finish these scansions, we need only identify the proper foot boundaries: for verses such as these, nothing could be simpler, as the foot boundaries correspond to the word boundaries, and the elements proclitic to the second foot of each verse are considered to be extrametrical, leading to the following scansions:

6b: earfeþa gemyndig	Sxx/(x)Sx
7a: wraþra wælsleahta	Sx/Ssx
7b: winemæga hryre	Ssx/S
11a: sweotule asecgan	Sx/(x)Sx
12b: indryhten þeaw	Ssx/S
15b: wyrde wiðstondan	Sx/(x)Sx
16b: helpe gefremman	Sx/(x)Sx

In some cases, foot boundaries will not correspond with word boundaries so directly, as the following examples show (although in two cases, I include examples with unstressed words):

Beo 48a: heah ofer heafod	Sxx/Sx
GuthB 881a: meaht ond mundbyrd	Sx/Ss

And 984a: maga mode rof   S/Sxs

In *Beowulf* 48a, we must scan the unstressed syllables of 'ofer' as part of the first foot (even though this preposition is syntactically attached to 'heafod'), in order to avoid an unmetrical type with only three metrical syllables: *S/(xx)Sx. In the verse from *Guthlac B*, 'ond' must be scanned as part of the first foot for a similar reason. In *Andreas* 948a, we have two possible competing scansions: S/Sxs and Ssx/S, since there are two word-boundaries present. The first scansion is preferable here because the syntax associates 'mode' and 'rof' more closely together; that such a scansion is substantially correct is confirmed by the double alliteration in this verse.[5] Either way, however, one of the three S-words must be scanned as subordinated, and actually placed on an s-position. Such verses are not especially common, but inspection is usually sufficient to determine the subordinated element and scansion follows straightforwardly.

Further, verses which feature both naturally stressed words and unstressed elements (prefixes, conjunctions, pronouns, prepositions, light sentence adverbs, and finite forms of 'wesan' and 'weorþan') can generally be scanned straightforwardly:

9a: mine ceare cwiþan	xx/Ssx
10a: þe ic him modsefan	xx/(x)Ssx
12a: þæt bið in eorle	xx/(x)Sx
13a: þæt he his ferðlocan	xx/(x)Ssx
16a: ne se hreo hyge	xx/Ssx

In both 9a and 16a, we have xC verses. In 9a, resolution must occur in 'ceare' to prevent the unmetrical type *xx/Sxsx, while in 16a, resolution is blocked in 'hyge' to prevent a change of verse class (treating 'hyge' as resolved would make the verse into type xA).[6] In 12a and 13a, foot boundaries and extrametrical syllables are determined as above: the preposition 'in' and the pronoun 'his' are both proclitic to the following nouns, and are scanned as extrametrical. In 10a, I also scan 'him' as extrametrical, simply because xx is the normative x-foot, and scansions with xx are clearly less metrically complex than those with x or xxx (in *Beowulf*, I count 89 verses with the specific scansion x/Sxs, 510 with the scansion xx/Sxs, and only 36 with the scansion xxx/Sxs).[7] The first two words in 16a are also scanned as xx on the same basis.

As the preceding examples suggest, many verses formed by ele-

ments in the 'naturally' stressed and unstressed classes are relatively
easy to scan. In some cases, however, we must use additional strate-
gies, the most important of which involves scanning the final word of
any verse as stressed.[8] Using this rule allows us to scan the following
verse correctly:

13b: fæste binde   Sx/Sx

Here, the finite verb ('binde') is scanned upon an S-position by the 'last
word stressed' rule, and the scansion is clear. Consider also:

10b: minne durre   Sx/Sx
14b: hycge swa he wille   Sx/(xx)Sx

In these examples, the 'last word stressed' rule allows us to (again)
scan the finite verbs ('durre' and 'wille') as Sx; but the rule which
excludes xA and sA verses in the b-line (VC3) comes into play to sug-
gest that some preceding syllable must also be scanned with full ('S')
stress: the only candidate in 10b is the first syllable of 'minne' and thus
we scan it also as Sx, and in 14b, 'hycge' is clearly the strongest preced-
ing element and is likewise scanned with Sx.[9]
    The 'last word stressed' rule also allows straightforward scansion of
the following verses in the passage from *The Wanderer*:

8b: uhtna gehwylce   Sx/(x)Sx
9b: Nu is cwicra nan   xx/Sxs
11b: Ic to soðe wat   xx/Sxs

In the first of these verses, the pronoun 'gehwylce' is stressed by the
'last word stressed' rule; the proclitic prefix 'ge-' is scanned as extra-
metrical, because the complexity of an Sxx foot appears to be greater
than the complexity of extrametrical syllables in type A verses.[10] In 9b,
a final word that also belongs to the 'naturally' unstressed class
receives stress as the last word in its verse, while the finite verb 'wat' in
11b must also be stressed. Since these verses end in monosyllables and
begin with unstressed elements, both must be xB verses (since E
verses, the only other types to end in stressed monosyllables, never
begin with unstressed syllables). The use of an Sxs foot in each verse,
then, becomes easy to identify.
    The remaining four verses from the passage in question feature finite

verbs to be scanned on s-feet, the most innovative component of my system. They are:

6a: Swa cwæð eardstapa	xs/Ssx
8a: Oft ic sceolde ana	xxsx/Sx
14a: healde his hordcofan	sx/(x)Ssx
15a: Ne mæg werig mod	xs/Sxs

In three cases, the finite verb fails to coalliterate with the following S-position; only in the case of 14a, 'healde his hordcofan' would we even be tempted to scan the verb as Sx. Calvin Kendall has very usefully discussed such alliteration as 'extra-metrical alliteration,' meaning alliteration that is supplementary to the alliteration of the later S-element, rather than primary.[11] In the case of 15a, on the other hand, we have a situation in which the finite verb alliterates with an s-position in the same verse; such alliteration occurs in many Old English poems and it generally seems to be allowed, but not used for any clear effect (for fuller discussion, see chapter 2.3).

As I hope the extended example and analysis of this passage from *The Wanderer* has made clear; there is surprisingly little difficulty in scanning verses with this system, especially once the importance of the 'last word stressed' rule has been recognized. In the remainder of this chapter, I will discuss some additional complications and issues surrounding s-feet, the most innovative feature of my system, and work through two further brief examples of scanning.

Scanning Verses with s-feet: Auxiliaries, Alliteration, and 'Anacrusis'

As I have suggested above, I first devised 's-feet' in order to scan Old English verse in an attempt to integrate Calvin Kendall's observations about the alliteration of finite verbs into Geofrrey Russom's metrical formalism. In this section, I discuss three issues relevant to this new tool of scansion. First, I consider what might be called 'metrical auxiliaries': cases where finite verbs are actually scanned on x-positions. Second, I look at ways in which s-feet can clear up certain ambiguities of scansion that Sieversian metrics have never dealt with well. Finally, I discuss how s-feet account for so-called anacrusis (which actually turns out to be a much more restricted phenomenon than previous metricists seem to have realized).

Some of the verbs I have scanned with s-feet above might, at least at first glance, appear to be auxiliary in function (especially 'sceolde' and 'mæg'), and my earlier claim that finite forms of 'wesan' and 'weorþan' should be scanned on x-positions deserves further comment in the context of s-feet. The distinction drawn between most finite verbs, on the one hand, and forms of 'wesan' and 'weorþan' on the other amounts to a distinction (as far as classical poetry is concerned) between auxiliary verbs and main verbs, or perhaps between auxiliary usage and main-verb usage. Forms of 'wesan' and (less frequently) 'weorþan' are often used by poets in positions where they can only be scanned on x-positions, as the following examples suggest:

Beo 1302a: Hream wearð in Heorote	Sx/(x)Sx
Wand 50b: Sorg bið geniwad	Sx/(x)Sx
Ex 19a: Heah wæs þæt handlean	Sx/(x)Ss
And 320b: Selre bið æghwam	Sx/(x)Sx
Soul I 157a: forðan wyt bioð gegæderode	xx/(xxx)Sxx
Ruin 21a: Beorht wæron burgræced	S/(xx)Ssx

Many more examples can be found, especially with forms of 'wesan.' In all of these cases, the scansions seem relatively unambiguous, with the verbs falling on x-positions. In most cases, these positions are in the 'dip' between two S words, but in the verse from *Soul and Body I*, the possibility that 'bioð' might be scanned on an s-foot is definitively ruled out by the three syllables which precede the verb (likewise, in the example from *The Ruin*, 'wæron' must correspond to xx, since *Ssx/Ssx is unmetrical). Such scansions appear in a wide variety of classical poems, and it seems that we must treat these verbs, at least, as being normally scanned on x-positions. The conclusion that virtually all other verbs, including finite forms of 'sculan,' 'magan,' and 'willan,' should generally be scanned on s-positions is supported by the fact that they rarely appear in such positions, and, while often present at the beginning of clause-initial verses, they are rarely preceded by more than two syllables. That is, they scan readily as s-feet, and rarely need to be scanned otherwise, while forms of 'wesan' frequently are scanned as x.

When, as sometimes happens, forms of 'sculan' or 'magan' are scanned on x-positions, I believe we should properly identify them as 'metrical auxiliaries': finite verbs being scanned as unstressed elements. Gnomic statements in particular use 'sculan' in this way, as the following examples confirm:

Max I 71a: Forst sceal freosan	Sx/Sx
Wand 70a: Beorn sceal gebidan	Sx/(x)Sx
Vain 82a: Forþon we sculon a hycgende	xxx/(xxx)Ssx

The reason behind the authorization of such 'metrical auxiliary' usages in gnomic statements remains obscure, and some poems seem to allow such usages while others reject them. The presence or absence of metrical auxiliaries seems to be a stylistic feature, perhaps at least sometimes related to considerations of genre (cf. the frequent use of metrical auxiliaries in *Maxims I* and *Maxims II*).

One of the primary advantages of scanning most finite verbs on s-feet, however, is that doing so eliminates the need for a great deal of ad hoc argumentation and scansion. Because of their variable alliterative characteristics, scholars have long debated the stress-levels to be assigned to finite verbs, and many scansion systems treat them variably, depending on whether they alliterate or not.[12] In s-foot formalism, finite, non-auxiliary verbs are to be treated as stressed (i.e., they seem to be subject to resolution, as I suggested in chapter 2.1), but since they are assigned to s-positions, we can easily account for their alliterative characteristics without resorting to variable stress. Instead, it is best to interpret s-feet (and hence finite verbs in the first foot) as simply being marked as secondary in terms of alliteration, with the alliteration of the verse generally being determined by the following S-foot.[13]

Indeed, s-foot scansions greatly help to clarify certain seeming inconsistencies in the alliteration of finite verbs. Compare the following verses from *Beowulf*:

Verse	Alliterator	Scansion	Type
Beo 391a: Eow het secgan	s	xs/Sx	sA
Beo 424a: forgrand gramum	g	x/Ssx	xC
Beo 740a: ac he gefeng hraðe	f	xx/(x)Ssx	xC
Beo 1265b: Þanon woc fela	w	xx/Ssx	xC

Similar examples can of course be found in other poems. In 391a the finite verb does not alliterate, while in 424a it coalliterates with 'gramum,' and the verbs in 740a and 1265b carry the primary alliteration.[14] Such inconsistency has been troublesome for many metrical theories; s-feet, however, make the seeming inconsistency understandable.

In the case of *Beowulf* 1265b, the scansion is clear: as the final word, 'fela' must be stressed (by the 'last word stressed' rule), but it cannot be the primary stress of the verse (because xA and sA verses are excluded from the b-line), and the strongest earlier syllable must be scanned as S.[15] The same logic, of course cannot apply in *Beowulf* 740a, since xA and sA verses are allowed in the a-line; here, the three syllables which precede the finite verb prevent it from being scanned with an s-foot. The sequence of three unstressed syllables demands that we have an initial x-foot, and the root of the verb is scanned on an S-position in the second foot. The succeeding syllables ('hraðe') indicate type xC.

In the case of *Beowulf* 391a, scansion as an sA verse is both possible and correct (as the alliteration of this verse indicates), but verses like 391a are somewhat rarer than those like 424a. In 424a, two possible scansions present themselves: xs/Sx or x/Ssx. I believe the latter scansion is correct, because unresolved short lifts would be rare in type sA, but they are common in the '-sx' portion of the Ssx foot of an xC verse.[16]

As my discussion of all four of these verses indicates, the use of s-feet in scansion allows us to correctly scan these verses (and to understand their alliteration) without resorting to notions such as 'reduced stress.' Finite verbs are simply marked as secondary in terms of alliteration. They may (under certain circumstances) be scanned on S-positions, to take on the role of the primary alliteration of verses, but they generally do so only when there is a clear metrical reason.

The use of s-feet, of course, also explains one of the most puzzling features of Old English verse: so-called anacrusis. Anacrusis is, technically, the use of unstressed syllables before the first foot of a verse actually begins. The following verses, however, which have usually been identified as featuring anacrusis, are scanned with s-feet in my system:

Exo 21a: ofercom mid þy campe	xxs/(xx)Sx
Dan 700a: Gesæt þa to symble	xsx/(x)Sx
Dream 122a: Gebead ic me þa to þam beame	xsx/(xxxx)Sx
El 1147a: Ongan þa geornlice	xsx/Ssx
Beo 2367a: Oferswam ða sioleða bigong	xxsx/Sxxs

When verses like these are scanned with s-feet, the association between verbal prefixes and syllables in so-called anacrusis is obvious: the vast majority of verses conventionally identified as having anacrusis have finite verbs in the first foot, often accompanied by prefixes. The limitation on anacrusis to two syllables must derive from the fact that no verbal prefix is longer than 'ofer-'; it might be more precise to say that anacrusis is limited to two syllables because no s-foot has three x syllables before the s.[17] By using s-feet to scan verses such as these, however, we see that these examples can no longer be accurately labelled as anacrusis, since the first foot of each of these verses does include the syllables in question; only a small number of Old English verses truly feature anacrusis; these shall be discussed below as scanning mismatches.

Mismatches and Scansion

The scansion of finite verbs on S-positions, as in a verse like *Beowulf* 740a, 'ac he gefeng hraðe,' exemplifies a certain sort of scanning 'mismatch,' where the metrical value of an element fails to exactly match its 'natural' value. Scanning mismatches of various sorts are not uncommon in classical Old English verse, and the most frequent sorts involve alliterative mismatches, word-class mismatches, and what Russom has called 'bracketing mismatches.' Each sort deserves at least a brief discussion.

In alliterative mismatches, we generally see finite verbs which serve as the primary alliterators of verses, even when scanned on s-positions. Consider the following examples:

GenA 1175a: Lifde siððan	sx/Sx
Sat 683a: Loca nu ful wide	sx/(xx)Sx
And 1163a: Fregn þa gelome	sx/(x)Sx
Ruin 2b: brosnað enta geweorc	sx/Sxxs
Beo 758a: Gemunde þa se goda	xsx/(xx)Sx
Beo 2717b: seah on enta geweorc	sx/Sxxs

Of course, these verses might be 'regularized' by scanning each finite verb on an S-position (leaving *Beowulf* 758a with anacrusis; see below), but the small number of verses in classical Old English poetry which feature this sort of mismatch strongly suggests that finite verbs did not regularly take on the role of primary alliteration in such verses.[18] The two 'enta geweorc' verses suggest that some mismatches of this sort may have had some currency in the b-line, but they nevertheless remain quite unusual.[19]

A second category of mismatches ('word-class mismatches') involves the placement of nonfinite verbs on s-positions, as in the following cases:

Beo 756a: secan deofla gedreag	sx/Sxxs
Soul I 104a: secan hellegrund	sx/Sxs

Ex 207a: geseon tosomne	xs/(x)Sx
Sea 17a: bihongen hrimgicelum	xsx/Ssx
GenA 1520a: besmiten mid synne	xsx/(x)Sx

In the first two cases, the mismatch (as the alliteration of these verses suggests) involves the placement of infinitive verbs on (nonalliterating) s-positions. These two might be scanned with the nonfinite verbs on x-positions, but the number of alliterative mismatches of this sort is so small that a clear choice is probably not possible.[20] The final three examples (and there are many other similar cases), have infinitives and particples scanned as s-feet, and these suggest that cases of anacrusis involving nonfinite verbs should still probably be scanned with s-feet. Such verses involve a scanning mismatch (since nonfinite verbs are scanned on s-feet), and the resulting complexity of these verses is presumably compensated for by a requirement for double alliteration, even though no such requirement applies to s-feet filled by finite verbs. Further, these verses suggest that the relatively small number of verses which truly feature anacrusis not involving verbal prefixes may arise by analogy to such mismatched s-feet, where nonfinite verbs are mapped onto s-positions. Examples of such analogically authorized verses include:

GenA 892a: on treowes telgum		xsx/Sx	sA (mismatch)
	or	(x)Sx/Sx	SA (anacrusis)
GenA 1182a: Se eorl wæs æðele		xs/(x)Sx	sA (mismatch)
	or	(x)Sx/Sx	SA (anacrusis)
Beo 1248a: ge æt ham ge on herge		xxs/(xx)Sx	sA (mismatch)
	or	(xx)Sx/(x)Sx	SA (anacrusis)
Beo 93b: swa wæter bebugeð		(x)Sx/Sx	SA (anacrusis)

Alternative scansions are given for the a-line verses because it is difficult to determine whether these are sA verses with a mismatch on the s-position, or SA verses with true anacrusis, although patterned on the rhythmically similar sA verses.[21] Either way, of course, the verses are metrically acceptable (as long as they remain relatively few in number). The occurrence of such verses in the b-line (slightly less common than in the a-line, in both *Beowulf* and *Genesis A*) demands the SA scansion, because of the general prohibition against sA verses in the b-line.[22] What is important here is the fact that the limit of two initial syllables in s-feet becomes the practical limit on true (analogical) anacrusis. Trisyllabic anacrusis in classical verse is disallowed precisely because verses with so-called anacrusis are either scanned with s-feet or formed by analogy to such verses.[23] Previous metrical theories have frequently noted this restriction on anacrusis, but no previous theory has offered a clear justification for the constraint, and these verses thus provide useful support for the scansions I propose here.

An additional category of word-class mismatch involves the scansion of B-type verses, especially xB and sB verses. In the second foot of such verses, secondary stress is sometimes suppressed, and 'natural' s-positions are scanned as x. This suppression happens relatively frequently with proper names, but examples with other compounds do occur often enough to be considered metrical. Consider:

Brun 1a: Her Æþelstan cyning	x/Sxs
Beo 1162b: Þa cwom Wealhþeo forð	xs/Sxs
And 889a: Þam bið wræcsið witod	xx/Sxs
Phoen 433a: þæt he feorhgeong eft	xx/Sxs
Beo 1236a: ond him Hroþgar gewat	xx/Sxxs
And 770b: Þær orcnawe wearð	x/Sxxs

Such formations may have originally been authorized by triple compounds, such as 'inwitgæst' and the other 'inwit-' compounds, since these compounds frequently fill Sxs-feet. We might note a handful of verses as potential support for this possibility:

Beo 2891b: þonne edwitlif	xx/Sxs
Dan 183a: efndon unrihtdom	sx/Sxs (vocalic alliteration)
Rid 14 2a: geong hagostealdmon	S/Sxs[24]

Of course it might also be possible to scan the second feet of these verses as Ssx, but the compounds are suggestive, at the least. Why names seem to be especially attracted to this particular scansion mismatch is not clear, although it may simply be the case that once the mismatch became authorized, poets found it especially useful for fitting compound names into B-type feet.

Finally, it is important to examine the nature and functioning of bracketing mismatches, where the foot boundaries of a verse fail to correspond to the most powerful linguistic boundaries. Bracketing mismatches characterize the following types of verse:

Beo 48a: heah ofer heafod	Sxx/Sx
GuthB 881a: meaht ond mundbyrd	Sx/Ss
El 236a: werum ond wifum	Sx/Sx

These types of examples (the first two were discussed above) involve cases where unstressed elements that are linguistically proclitic to the second foot are, in fact, scanned as part of the first foot. The mismatch certainly introduces a significant degree of metrical complexity; as indicated in chapter 2.1 (n. 32), the specific type Sx/Sx does not require double alliteration as a general rule, but in *Beowulf*, at least, 90 per cent of Sx/Sx verses with such a bracketing mismatch do, in fact, have double alliteration.[25]

Final Scansion Examples

At this point, it is worthwhile to offer scansions and commentaries upon a couple of other passages, in order to indicate the possibilities and difficulties of scanning Old English verse, even in this system. First, we can take a look at a particularly interesting passage from *Elene*:

Nu ge geare cunnon		xx/Ssx
hwæt eow þæs on sefan selest þince	xx/sxS	Sx/Sx
to gecyðanne, gif ðeos cwen usic	xx/Ssx	xx/Ssx
frigneð ymb ðæt treo, nu ge fyrhðsefan	Sxx/(x)S	xx/Ssx
ond modgeþanc minne cunnon.	x/Sxs	Sx/Sx
		(ll. 531b–5)[26]

In many of these verses, there is absolutely no difficulty, but 532a and 534a both involve quite difficult choices in the scansion. In 532a, 'sefan,' of course, has a short root syllable, and thus is susceptible to resolution: the scansion given above treats the verse as an 'inverted' xb verse; this possibility seems to be supported by the resulting cross alliteration, which would help in the identification of the unusual verse form.[27] Yet it might also be possible to simply scan 532a as xx/(xx)Sx, with an unresolved sequence filling the Sx foot. Choosing between these alternatives is difficult, because both forms are quite rare, but I feel the xb scansion is most likely. In the case of 534a, we have two apparent anomalies involved. On the one hand, the finite verb alliterates, and on the other, 'treo' seems unambiguously monosyllabic.[28] The scansion given above appears to make sense of the line, however: the monosyllabic final foot demands an E-type verse with a trisyllabic initial foot.[29] The placement of the finite verb, therefore, is on an Sxx foot (in this case) and as a result the fact that it alliterates is not anomalous at all. The Sxx/(x)S verse, on the other hand, is somewhat unusual. Such verses do appear occasionally (and are thus included in my system in the previous chapter), and they seem to be a rare variant of the typical inverted E verse, Ssx/S. Consider also the following verses:

GenA 2278b: hunger oððe wulf	Sxx/S	CxS[30]
El 394a: witgena word	Sxx/S	CxS
Rid 15 1a: Hals is min hwit	Sxx/S	CxS
GenA 2359a: Bletsian me	Sxx/S	CxS
Ex 108a: æfena gehwæm	Sxx/(x)S	CxS

In 2278b, I take 'hunger' as featuring a parasite vowel (Fulk identifies this line as ambiguous: 77, n. 29), and thus I scan it as a monosyllable. In these verses, where the possibility of resolution is not a source of ambiguity because all the relevant syllables are long, the use of Sxx/S style E verses seems to be clear. The existence of such verses appears to support scansions of familiar Beowulfian verses in similar ways:

Beo 183b: Wa bið þæm ðe sceal	Sxx/(x)S	CxS (cf. *Beo* 186b)
Beo 603b: Gæþ eft se þe mot	Sxx/(x)S	CxS
Beo 658a: Hafa nu ond geheald	Sxx/(x)S	CxS

Verses of these types have previously been scanned in ways analogous to CsS [Ssx/(x)S] or SB [S/Sxxs], but it seems just as likely that if CxS verses are metrical that these scansions should here apply, especially since the CxS scansion does not demand that we stress 'bið' in 183b, which is generally an unstressed particle.[31] We might note that the *Beowulf* poet's use of these forms is, in these verses, almost certainly formulaic[32]; these formulaic uses may well justify other verses which may be best scanned as CxS:

Beo 2150a: lissa gelong	Sxx/S[33]
Beo 881a: eam his nefan	Sxx/S

The second of these verses, with contraction in the first word, is otherwise a fairly anomalous case where resolution is not employed and so this verse may be best considered as an uncertain example. Russom usefully gathers together the verses from *Beowulf* which might seem to demand similar scansions (*Linguistic Theory* 116–17), but offers alternative explanations for most of them, as do most metricists who would like to exclude the Sxx/S pattern. If the Sxx/S verse is rare but allowed in *Beowulf*, the alternative explanations are unnecessary.

As a final example of scansion, the following passage from *Beowulf* is also worth examining:

Wundor is to secganne		Sx/(xx)Ssx	
hu mihtig God	manna cynne	x/Sxs	Sx/Sx
þurh sidne sefan	snyttru bryttað,	x/Sxs	Sx/Sx
eard on eorlscipe;	he ah ealra geweald.	Sx/Ssx	xs/Sxxs
Hwilum he on lufan	læteð hworfan	xx/sxS	Sx/Sx
monnes modgeþonc	mæran cynnes	Sx/Sxs	Sx/Sx

(ll. 1724–9)[34]

Again, most of the verses here are quite straightforward. But 1724b is notable for demanding scansion with extrametrical syllables in type SC; even if 'wundor' is scanned as a monosyllable due to parasiting, there is still at least one extrametrical syllable. In 1728a, we again see an inverted xb verse, again supported by cross alliteration (the only such example out of five xb verses in this poem). Certainly, not all xb verses receive such support, but as noted above, they do so with surprising freqency. In the case of 1727b, we have an interesting example of double alliteration in the b-line, involving the s-foot as well as the S-foot. As noted elsewhere, such alliteration is relatively infrequent (and, indeed, is generally excluded), but cases like this do occasionally appear.

The examples and discussion in this chapter should be sufficient for scanning virtually any passage of classical Old English poetry (barring those containing hypermetric lines, to be discussed in the next chapter). The key element of my formalism, the introduction of s-feet into scansion, allows for a somewhat larger range of basic types than Sieversian formalism, but it covers the ground of the specific types far more precisely, and the symmetry of the foot combination rules discussed in the previous chapter allows the wide variety of specific types to be generated from an easily mastered basic system. Further, this formalism allows straightforward explanations for anacrusis, patterns of double alliteration, and for limits on unstressed syllables. In the following chapter, I will describe rules for classical hypermetric lines, the use of rhyme in classical verse, and discuss supplementary alliteration patterns such as cross alliteration. Each of these topics, usually treated only briefly or dismissed entirely by previous metrical theories, is in fact an important component of classical Anglo-Saxon poetics.

Additional Rules: Hypermetric Verses, Rhyme, and Alliteration

In the preceding two chapters, I have discussed the basics of the classical Old English verse system, but it is worthwhile to identify a few more rules used by Old English poets involving hypermetric verses, the use of rhyme, and the use of secondary alliteration patterns such as cross alliteration. As I will suggest, the hypermetric verse system stands as an alternative set of foot-combination rules. The poetic use of rhyme and secondary alliteration, on the other hand, involves alternative verse-combination rules (VC2, in particular). As I will show, rhyme and secondary alliteration patterns are not merely random or purely ornamental features of classical Old English verse; they are secondary – but nonetheless effective and functional – features of the classical verse system, and as such they need to be described in a metrical account of classical verse.

Hypermetric Verses[1]

A significant number of verses in classical poems do not fit the scheme described above for normal verses by being too large. Conventionally labelled 'hypermetric verses,' these enlarged verses have not been particularly well understood by modern readers. Nevertheless, the classical form of the Old English hypermetric verse can be accounted for by simple foot-combination rules and verse-combination rules, just as normal verses can.

There are, as I will show, three basic varieties of hypermetric versification, two of which appear to use modifications of what we can therefore label as basic (or Type 1) hypermetric rules, as described below:

Type 1 Hypermetric Rules

HFC1: Hypermetric verses have three feet, rather than two. The final two feet must be S-feet, and generally, the final two feet must combine according to the rules for normal SS-verses.[2] The initial foot can be an S-foot, s-foot, or x-foot, but it must always contain at least two syllables.

HFC2: Extrametrical syllables may appear between either the first and second or the second and third feet. Between the second and third feet, rules limiting extrametrical syllables are analogous to the rules for similarly patterned normal verses (e.g., if the final feet of a hypermetric verse are Ssx and S, then only one extrametrical syllable is allowed).

HVC1: Type 1 hypermetric a-lines can usually be schematized as SSS verses or sSS verses; Type 1 hypermetric b-lines must generally be xSS or sSS verses. (Alternatively, *the first foot of a Type 1 hypermetric a-line may be an S-foot or an s-foot; Type 1 hypermetric b-lines begin with x-feet or s-feet.*)

HVC2: Alliteration. Alliteration links together the initial S-positions of the two half-lines. Double alliteration in the a-line is generally mandatory and must occur in the first two feet.[3]

HVC3: Hypermetric verses must generally be paired with one another, but hypermetric verses may be paired with normal verses.

It is crucial to understand that the rules for hypermetric verses and lines do not merely serve to define a separate variety of Old English verse; instead, the hypermetric rules function in concert with the rules for normal verses, as I will discuss in more detail below. Geoffrey Russom, following the conventional wisdom, has suggested that hypermetric lines must occur in clumps or clusters in order to allow readers or listeners to understand their alternative structure.[4] While it is true that hypermetric lines are clustered in *Beowulf* (which is Russom's primary data base) and often in other poems as well, a fair number of isolated hypermetric lines do occur, which suggests that the claim of hypermetric clustering cannot be supported as a general rule in the larger corpus of Old English verse.[5]

For the most part, potential areas of confusion are limited by the hypermetric rules, as we can see by considering the general requirement for double alliteration in hypermetric a-lines (HVC2). Since hypermetric verses stand as a rarer (and more complex) alternative to normal verses,

double alliteration seems to function to minimize complexity and max-
imize audience recognition of structure. Metrical confusion between
normal and Type 1 hypermetric forms is minimized in other ways as
well. Specifically, Type 1 hypermetric lines have the following structural
possibilities:

a-line	b-line
SSS or sSS	xSS or sSS

Since Type 1 excludes the possibility of alliteration on the last S-posi-
tion of the a-line, any line that features alliteration on three consecuive
feet can generally be immediately identified as a normal (rather than
hypermetric) line.[6]

Further, the requirement that the initial foot of a hypermetric verse
must contain at least two metrical syllables has a nonobvious conse-
quence where normal verses are concerned. This consequence is the
frequently noted limitation of anacrusis to one syllable in the b-line of
normal verses. Consider, for example, the following two b-lines:

GenA 1907b: ymb mearce sittað   (x)Sx/Sx
GenA 2859b: and me lac bebeodan   xx/Sx/Sx

The first of these verses occurs in a stretch of normal verses, and must
be scanned as one of the rare verses with anacrusis, modelled on an sA
verse, although here appearing in the b-line. The latter verse occurs in
a cluster of hypermetric verses, and is to be scanned accordingly.[7] The
limit of one syllable of anacrusis in the b-line can be explained as an
effort to eliminate metrical ambiguity by preventing formal overlap
with hypermetric verses. Since Type 1 hypermetric a-lines cannot have
initial x-feet, no such limit applies to a-lines with analogous anacrusis,
and two syllables of anacrusis are allowed in normal a-lines.

As these observations confirm, the hypermetric system and the nor-
mal verse system operate complementarily, and the metrical formalism
I offer here can account for both systems. Indeed, certain features of
both normal and hypermetric verses can only be understood by con-
sidering both types of verse as products of a larger system.

Now that the basics of Type 1 hypermetric verses have been covered it
is worthwhile to consider a specific passage in detail. The following
passage from Beowulf offers a familiar starting point:

Þa cwom Wealhþeo forð		xs/Sxs
gan under gyldnum beage,   þær þa godan t
wegen	Sxx/Sx/Sx	xx/Sx/Sx
sæton suhtergefæderan; þa gyt wæs hiera sib ætgædere,	sx/Sx/(x)Sx	xx/(xxx)Sx/Sx
æghwylc oðrum trywe. Swylce þær Unferþ þyle	Sx/Sx/Sx	xx/(x)Ss/Sx
æt fotum sæt frean Scyldinga; gehwylc hiora his ferhþe treowde,	(x)Sx/(x)S/Ssx	xx/(xxx)Sx/Sx
þæt he hæfde mod micel, þeah þe he his magum nære	xxsx/Ssx	xx/(xx)Sx/Sx
arfæst æt ecga gelacum. Spræc ða ides Scyldinga:	Ss/(x)Sx/(x)Sx	sx/S/Ssx
'Onfoh þissum fulle, freodrihten min,	xs/(xx)Sx	Ssx/S
		(ll. 1162b–9b)[8]

The first verse and the final line here are normal verses, and the rest
constitute a hypermetric 'cluster.' Most of these hypermetric verses
have straightforward scansions, but a handful of them demand special
comment. In 1165b, for example, we have an ambiguous verse:

Beo 1165b: Swylce þær Unferþ þyle

I have scanned this verse as hypermetric, but the short root syllable in
'þyle' might suggest that this word should be resolved, yielding a nor-
mal xB verse similar (in the second foot) to the sB verse in 1162b. While
the pairing of a hypermetric a-line with a normal b-line is not particu-
larly unusual, I choose instead to treat the word 'þyle' as unresolved, as
is relatively common in normal verses after initial Ss-feet. In 1166a, we
see that unstressed syllables may occasionally precede the initial S-foot
of a hypermetric verse; the rules permitting this are identical to those
permitting anacrusis by analogy to s-feet in normal verses. Note also,
however, that 1166a includes a finite verb that must be scanned on an x-
position; such usage is notably rare in *Beowulf*, and its appearance in a
hypermetric verse here may result from the fact that hypermetric pas-
sages may be less formulaic and less traditional than passages of normal
verses. In 1167a, we have a normal verse in the a-line being paired with
a hypermetric verse in the b-line. As noted above, such pairings occur
relatively infrequently, but often enough to be deemed acceptable. The
relative lack of ambiguity in the form of individual verses (whether nor-
mal or hypermetric) allows readers and listeners to scan even mis-
matched verses correctly.

Passages of Type 1 hypermetric lines can be found in many poems,
and the following poems should probably be understood as using Type
1 rules exclusively (or nearly so): *Beowulf, Judith, Genesis A, The Dream of
the Rood, Elene, Guthlac B, The Pheonix, The Wanderer,* and *The Riming
Poem.*

While Type 1 rules seem to be used most often and to keep hypermetric and normal verses distinct most clearly, it is important to note that two additional hypermetric systems were indeed used by Old English poets. As discussed below, each is characterized by modified forms of HVC1 and HVC2. I will label these modified varieties of hypermetric verse Type 2 and Type 3; each will be discussed separately below.

Type 2 Hypermetric Rules

HCV1 (Type 2): Type 2 hypermetric lines allow xSS in the a-line.
HCV2 (Type 2): Type 2 hypermetric lines allow alliteration to fall on the final two feet of xSS a-lines and allow triple alliteration in SSS a-lines.

The poet of *Guthlac A*, for example, uses Type 2 hypermetric rules, allowing x-feet in the first foot of the a-line and (as a result, one suspects) also allowing double alliteration on the second and third feet of the a-line. Thus:

næfre ge me of þissum wordum onwendað þendan mec min gewit gelæsteð.	xxx/(xxxx)Sx/(x)Sx[9]
Þeah þe ge hine sarum forsæcen, ne motan ge mine sawle gretan,	xx/(xxx)Sx/(x)Sx
ac ge on betran gebringað. Forðan ic gebidan wille	xx/(x)Sx/(x)Sx
þæs þe me min dryhten demeð. Nis me þæs deaþes sorg.	xx/(xx)Sx/Sx
	(ll. 376–9)[10]

Here I have scanned only the a-lines; the b-lines offer no real difficulties (although 379b, of course, is a normal verse).[11] The general requirement for double alliteration still applies to even these a-lines, and in fact we see double alliteration on the two S-positions in each of the quoted a-lines. But because the third foot of each of these a-lines participates in the alliteration, these lines would have been correspondingly difficult for a contemporary audience to interpret correctly.

Because Type 2 hypermetric passages allow alliteration to fall on the final S-foot in the a-line, it makes sense to suggest that examples of triple alliteration in a-line SSS hypermetric verses also belong to Type 2. Three clear examples from *Daniel* (lines 204a, 266a, and 270a), a poem that clearly uses Type 2 rules in other lines, confirms the connection.[12] Including such examples, we can conclude that the following poems use Type 2 hypermetric rules with some consistency: *Daniel, Guthlac A, Riddle 16, The Meters of Boethius,* and *Against a Dwarf.* [13]

Type 3 Hypermetric Rules

HVC1 (Type 3): Type 3 hypermetric lines allow xSS in the a-line and allow SSS in the b-line.

HVC2 (Type 3): Type 3 hypermetric lines allow alliteration to fall on the final two feet of xSS a-lines and allow triple alliteration in SSS a-lines.

The chief modification that marks Type 3 hypermetric rules is that which now allows SSS in the b-line. As an example, consider the following passage from *Maxims II* (preceding the C-version of *the Anglo-Saxon Chronicle*):

Cyning sceal rice healdan. Ceastra beoð feorran gesyne,	Sx/Sx/Sx	Sx/(x)Sx/(x)Sx
orðanc entageweorc, þa þe on þysse eorðan syndon,	Ss/Sxxs	xx/(xxx)Sx/Sx
wrætlic weallstana geweorc. Wind byð on lyfte swiftust,	Sx/Ssx/(x)S	Sx/(x)Sx/Sx
þunar byð þragum hludast. Þrymmas syndan Cristes myccle,	Sx/Sx/Sx	Sx/(xx)Sx/Sx
wyrd byð swiðost.	Sx/Sx	(ll. 1–5a)[14]

In line 2, we have a very heavy normal verse in the a-line, followed by a standard hypermetric verse, but in all of the hypermetric b-lines, we see S-feet in the initial position. In addition, verse 3a has triple alliteration. Although there is only one example (l. 45a), it is clear that this poet also allows x-feet in the first foot of hypermetric a-lines (with double alliteration on the second and third feet). For the poet of *Maxims II*, the restrictions on initial feet that apply in Type 1 do not seem to apply to either the a-line or the b-line. This practice, then, is distinguishable both from Type 1 hypermetric practice (as exemplified in *Beowulf* and *Judith*) and from the Type 2 practice as seen in *Guthlac A, Daniel*, and *The Meters of Boethius*. Type 3 hypermetric rules are used less frequently than either Type 1 or Type 2; besides fairly numerous examples in *Maxims I* and *Maxims II*, a handful of other lines suggest that Type 3 rules are also used in *Christ III* and *Solomon and Saturn II*.

What is important about hypermetric verses from the perspective of classical verse is the realization that hypermetric verses (and the rules which generate them) function in concert with the rules for normal verses. Rather than standing as a completely separate metrical system, hypermetric lines are structured merely as different combinations of the same metrical feet as make up normal lines. Although different classical poets apparently disagreed about what the precise rules for hypermetric lines were, the basics, as I hope to have shown, are simple, clear, and sensible. Once again, the metrical rules for this variety of classical Old English verse can also be seen as simple enough to learn and transmit.

Even so, the diversity of hypermetric systems found in classical poems remains remarkable. Much rarer than normal verses, hypermetric verses exhibit far less consistency of form from one poem to another. Without the same weight of traditional and formulaic expression to promote formal consistency, rules for hypermetric verse composition seem to have varied (perhaps even evolved) at a different rate and frequency from rules for normal verses. In the ways in which even the 'modified' Type 2 and Type 3 hypermetric rules resulted in increased metrical ambiguity and difficulties of scansion (by allowing alliteration on the third foot of the a-line and S-feet in the first foot of the b-line), we can see an important crack in the formal structure of classical Old English versification. The accumulation of precisely such cracks brought about the radical changes to be discussed in the late Old English and early Middle English sections of this book.

Rhyme and Secondary Alliteration

In order to finish my description of the rules for classical Old English verse, it is necessary to describe a small number of supplementary rules for the use of secondary patterns of alliteration and the use of rhyme. Both sorts of secondary poetic feature could function as poetic adornment (both within the half-line and across the caesura) and as integral and functional parts of verses and lines. There is clear evidence that, at least in some cases, the use of rhyme and secondary alliteration patterns was structural and governed by rules; this section will provide a brief account of those rules. Because rhyme and secondary alliteration patterns are not understood as well as many of the issues discussed previously, however, I will provide a bit more of the supporting evidence for the claims made here.[15]

S1. Rhyme and supplementary alliteration may poetically link syllables which have either primary or secondary stress.[16]

S2. Rhyme, cross alliteration, or secondary alliteration may occasionally substitute for expected alliterative links. Cross alliteration is defined as the alliterative linking of syllables across the caesura (in addition to primary alliteration); secondary alliteration is the alliterative linking of two syllables within the half-line beyond the links demanded by primary alliteration.

Rule S1 is essentially definitional and simply ensures that any secondary effects involve only those verse elements that poets and audiences are already paying attention to for purposes of stress and alliteration.

Thus, in a verse like the following:

Beo 656a: siþþan ic hond ond rond   xx/(x)Sxs

rhyme should be understood as linking 'hond' and 'rond,' although neither is meaningfully linked to 'ond' through rhyme.[17] Note that, according to S1, Ssx feet without secondary stress will not employ rhyme or supplementary alliteration on the s-position.[18]

While S1 defines what sorts of syllables might be affected by rhyme or supplemental alliteration, S2 identifies rules for the poetic usage of such secondary poetic effects. Crucially, S2 allows us to distinguish between examples of rhyme and supplementary alliteration that are random, accidental, or even purely ornamental and those which are poetically functional.

That some sorts of rhyme and supplementary alliteration can be accidental, unintentional, or perhaps strictly ornamental (rather than functional) seems clear. Consider the following types of examples:

GuthB 1156b: Ongon þa hygegeomor   xsx/Ssx[19]
El 792b: Forlæt nu, lifes weard   xsx/Sxs[20]
Rid4 7a: Winterceald oncweþe   Ssx/S[21]
Beo 1726b: snyttru bryttað   Sx/Sx[22]
GuthA 24: lærað ond læstað   ond his lof rærað   sx/(x)Sx   xx/Ssx[23]

In the first two examples, finite verbs scanned on s-positions coalliterate with syllables within the same verse. In a-lines, of course, traditional scansion has seen coalliteration of finite verbs with the primary alliterator as especially significant (leading to the common conclusion that alliterating finite verbs receive full stress). But examples like Elene 792b: 'Forlæt nu, lifes weard,' where the finite verb in the b-line coalliterates with the primary alliterator strongly suggest that this sort of alliteration (at least in the b-line) is accidental and nonfunctional, since functional alliteration in such cases would be problematic double alliteration in the b-line.[24]

In cases like Riddle 4 7a: 'Winterceald oncweþe,' we see coalliteration of two stressed positions after the first S-position in the verse; it is not clear that most such examples are used for any particular reason or effect. Likewise, the sorts of rhyme seen in the final two examples above do not seem to have any clear poetic function: they stand as examples of more or less random sorts of rhyme, where stressed syllables within the same verse or line simply happen to be phonologically similar.

In at least three sorts of cases, however, it is clear that rhyme and supplementary alliteration are, at least sometimes, nonrandom and poetically functional. Examples of functional secondary alliteration, cross alliteration, and functional rhyme each demand separate discussion.

Secondary alliteration within the half-line

In the poems *Genesis A*, *Exodus*, and *The Pheonix*, the following verses are the only examples of Ss/Ss types:

GenA 9a: soðfæst and swiðfeorm	Ss/(x)Ss
GenA 899a: fah wyrm þurh fægir word	Ss/(x)Ss
Ex 61a: mearchofu morheald	Ss/Ss
Phoen 299a: nioþoweard ond ufeweard	Ss/(x)Ss[25]

Ss/Ss types are notably heavy and correspondingly complex, and this undoubtedly accounts for their relative rarity. But it seems to be especially noteworthy that, in these three poems, these extremely complex verse-types show, without exception, both double alliteration and secondary alliteration.[26] Although I should probably hesitate to draw a conclusion based on four verses, it nevertheless seems likely that these poets felt that the complexity of this superheavy type could be minimized by employing secondary alliteration, just as double alliteration seems to be required consistently in all poetically complex types with two S-feet.

The likelihood of such an interpretation, however, is supported by four verses from *Beowulf*:

Beo 367b: glædman Hroðgar	Ss/Ss
Beo 457b: wine min Beowulf	Ss/Ss
Beo 1148b: Guðlaf ond Oslaf	Ss(x)Ss
Beo 1704b: wine min Beowulf	Ss/Ss

As I have discussed elsewhere ('Secondary Stress'), scanning proper names as Ss compounds marks these verses as unusual, in that the alliterative requirements of Ss compounds (generally marked for alliteration as 'Class 1' compounds) ought to exclude Ss/Ss verses from the b-line. There are exactly five Ss/Ss b-lines in *Beowulf* (the fifth, 530b,

participates in cross alliteration, to be discussed below); the pattern sim-
ply cannot be accidental, and it is clear that the *Beowulf* poet feels these
heavy verses can be used in the b-line only if they feature supplemen-
tary alliteration.[27] Of course, in the b-line Ss/Ss verses from *Beowulf*, the
secondary alliteration does not truly replace primary alliteration, but it
seems clear, nevertheless, that it provides an alliterative link that the
poet feels is necessary in these verses.

It is important, of course, to recognize that some poets used Ss/Ss
verses without secondary alliteration. In *Beowulf*, for example, Ss/Ss
verses in the a-line must have double alliteration, but they need not
have secondary alliteration as well. Regardless, the evidence presented
here certainly indicates that these patterns of secondary alliteration
were sometimes deemed necessary by certain poets in certain circum-
stances; such differences in usage offer the possibility of distinguishing
among various 'metrical styles' used in different works.

Cross alliteration substituting for double alliteration

In the poem *Christ II*, the following specific verse types are among
those which have mandatory double alliteration in the a-line: Ss/Sx,
S/Ssx, and Ssx/S.[28] All of the lines from this poem that feature a-lines
of these types without double alliteration are listed below:

ChristB 465: efenece bearn, agnum fæder	Ssx/S	Sx/Sx
ChristB 528: heahengla cyning, ofer hrofas upp	Ssx/S	xx/Sxs
ChristB 536: up stigende eagum segun	S/Ssx	Sx/Sx
ChristB 618: cyning anboren. Cwide eft onhwearf	S/Ssx	S/Sxs
ChristB 636: freonoman cende, ond hine fugel nemde	Ss/Sx	xxx/Ssx
ChristB 687: cyning alwihta, cræftum weorðaþ	S/Ssx	Sx/Sx

Four of these six lines clearly feature cross alliteration (528, 618, 636,
and 687), while a fifth (465) has unusual Ss-type double alliteration in
the a-line. The sixth (536) appears to feature neither Ss alliteration nor
cross alliteration, but the near-alliteration of 's-' and 'st-' might make
us at least wonder whether cross alliteration was intended. Regardless
of the status of line 536, however, it is clear that, for the poet of *Christ II*,
cross alliteration (or, less frequently, Ss alliteration) is used as a regular
substitute for double (SS) alliteration in the a-line.[29] Once again, the
numbers are too consistent to be ascribed to random chance.

Other poets also seem to use cross alliteration (and Ss alliteration) as a substitute in a-lines for which double alliteration ought to be mandatory. Consider the following examples:

Phoen 637: forð butan ende.	Næs his frymð æfre	Sxx/Sx	xx/Ssx
GuthB 1014: þeoden leofesta,	þyslicne ær	Sx/Ssx	Ssx/S
GuthB 1078; Upeard niman	edleana georn	Ss/Sx	Ssx/S
GuthB 1378: siðfæt minne.	Ic sceal sarigferð	Ss/Sx	xs/Sxs
Beo 653 Hroðgar Beowulf,	ond him hæl abead	Ss/Ss	xx/Sxs

For each of these poems, these stand as the only examples of these specific types in the a-line that fail to feature double alliteration; four of these lines have cross alliteration, and one (*Guthlac B* 1078a) has Ss alliteration in the a-line.[30]

As the examples gathered here indicate, it is clear that cross alliteration (and Ss alliteration, which might be best understood as a variety of secondary alliteration within the half-line) could operate functionally in a-lines where double alliteration is expected. The examples given come from poems where these patterns are especially clear, but it seems probable that similar usages occur in other poems, and that this sort of substitution was a functional part of classical Old English practice.

Rhyme subsitituing for double alliteration

The following verses belong to types that demand double alliteration in their respective poems:

And 176a: eard weardigað	S/Sxx
Beo 2440a: broðor oðerne	Sx/Ssx
Beo 1422a: flod blode weol	S/Sxs[31]

In each case, it is clear that rhyme substitutes for double alliteration; in a number of other examples, rhyme pairs also appear to substitute for alliterating word pairs, although often in types that generally occur at least occasionally with single alliteration. Although the number of examples that are unambiguous is relatively small, the *Beowulf* and *Andreas* poets certainly use rhyme within the half-line as an acceptable substitute for double alliteration, and when we see such rhymes operating in other poems (or in other specific types within these poems) we should probably interpret those rhymes, too, as substituting for double alliteration. The fact that rhyme did at least occasionally substitute for double alliteration confirms that it was a functional aspect of Old English poetics, although the infrequency of the substitution indicates that, like cross alliteration or secondary alliteration, rhyme was a secondary poetic effect at best in classical Old English verse.

As the examples of rhyme, cross alliteration, and secondary alliteration given here indicate, all three of these secondary poetic effects could occasionally substitute for the primary linkages generally accomplished through primary alliteration. In that sense, these secondary effects must be accounted for in descriptions of Old English verse. But further, it seems important to point out that these secondary poetic linkages might well have been used by poets for artistic ends (perhaps especially when they were *not* substituting for primary alliteration), and that modern readers might do well to attune themselves to these linkages as well as to the links afforded by primary alliteration. The following chapter discusses the implications of the secondary rules identified in this chapter in terms of Old English poetics.

Classical Old English Poetics

In previous chapters, I have attempted to describe the basic forms of metrical Old English verses, including the rules for their use. These basic forms, of course, constituted the very tools used by Old English poets. In this chapter, I hope to at least begin considering the poetic value of various formal features of the classical system of Old English verse. At the heart of my analysis here is the supposition that any and all of the formal features recognizable by Anglo-Saxon poets and audiences (alliterative patterns, normal-hypermetric verse distinctions, rhyme, cross alliteration, and so on) could be used to contribute to the poetic effects of Anglo-Saxon poems. In the examples I discuss from *Judith* and *The Ruin*, I hope to show how much modern readers of Old English poetry can sometimes benefit from a greater attention to these formal, metrical features.

Judith

Judith has frequently been identified as exceptional within the corpus of classical Old English verse for its usage of hypermetric lines and rhyme, and it is appropriate to begin an examination of Old English poetics by asking just how the poet of *Judith* uses these formal devices (and others) in the poem.[1] As a careful examination will show, I believe, the *Judith* poet uses a remarkable variety of poetic effects to vary the pacing of the narrative and, at some moments, uses the sound-patterning possibilities offered by rhyme and cross alliteration for remarkably powerful poetic effects.[2]

Although the fragmentary nature of the poem which survives makes categorical statements difficult, most would agree that at the beginning of *Judith* as we have it, the action is quick. By line 121 of the surviving 349 lines, Holofernes lies dead in his own chamber, and the rest of the poem serves primarily as a more-or-less anticlimactic denouement describing the consequences of the death scene: the important action of the poem takes place at the beginning. Notably, the poet's use of secondary effects also seems to be concentrated at the beginning. Forty-nine of the poem's sixty-nine hypermetric lines occur before line 100;[3] thirteen lines with cross alliteration occur before line 121 (there are only fourteen such lines in the remainder of the poem).[4] The first 121 lines also contain three verses with supplemental alliteration (vs. three more verses in the rest of the poem)[5] and eight lines with linking rhyme or off-rhyme (vs. five such lines in the rest of the poem).[6] Almost two-thirds of these secondary metrical effects, then, are concentrated in the first one-third of the poem.

Two passages in particular deserve close examination. One describes the actual death of Holofernes and the departure of his soul for the torments of hell:

> Næs ða dead þa gyt
> ealles orsawle;   sloh ða eornoste
> ides ellenrof   oðre siðe
> 110 þone hæðenan hund,   þæt him þæt heafod wand
> forð on ða flore.   Læg se fula leap
> gesne beæftan,   gæst ellor hwearf
> under neowelne næs   ond ðær genyðerad wæs
> susle gesæled   syððan æfre,
> 115 wyrmum bewunden,   witum gebunden,
> hearde gehæfted   in hellebryne
> æfter hinsiðe.   (ll. 107b–17a)[7]

The secondary poetic effects employed in this passage are subtle, and modern readers might easily miss them. But cross alliteration appears in lines 108 and 112, and 'verse rhyme' appears in 113 and 115.[8] An example of secondary alliteration can be seen in 111b. Further, however, we might note that the primary alliterators continue in consecutive lines in 108–9 and 116–17; such continuation is not particularly unusual in *Judith*, but it may well contribute a bracketing effect to this passage.[9] Finally, we see a case of off-rhyme in line 110. In fact, this particular off-rhyme is probably the most effective off-rhyme in all of Old English verse, as the 'hund'/'wand' off-rhyme pair implicitly evokes, for readers or listeners, each of the corresponding true rhymes, calling to mind both the 'hand' of Judith, and the 'wund' of Holofernes. As the passage insists, this crucial moment of separation (Judith from Holofernes; head – and soul – from body) is simultaneously a moment of binding (Holofernes's soul is bound in hell), and the use of rhyme and secondary alliteration serves to emphasize the binding aspects of the passage through a kind of linguistic or poetic interlacing.[10] The effect is strengthened by the repeated use of the same specific verse type, Sx/(x)Sx, in three consecutive half-lines: 115a–16a (and see 114a, as well); one can almost feel the bonds tightening.

In a somewhat earlier passage, we can see the use of cross alliteration for a different effect. Here, Judith stands over Holofernes's unconscious body and begins her prayer for strength:

> Ic ðe, frymða god,   ond frofre gæst,
> bearn alwaldan,   biddan wylle,
> 85 miltse þinre,   me þearfendre,
> ðrynesse ðrym.   Þearle ys me nu ða   (ll. 83–6)[11]

As I have noted elsewhere ('Estimating Probabilities'), these four lines are remarkable for each featuring cross alliteration.[12] There can be little doubt that the poet uses this strategy at this particular narrative moment for a powerful poetic effect: Judith's words here are rhetorically heightened by the additional alliterators.[13] The interlacing effect of this passage of cross alliteration serves to ornament Judith's speech, and the prayer takes on the feeling of almost supernatural eloquence.

And yet there are even further examples of the *Judith* poet's use of ornamental alliteration, in lines featuring what Mark Griffith has labelled 'cluster alliteration' such as the following:

> *Jud* 23: hloh ond hlydde   hlynede ond dynede
> *Jud* 37: hringum gehrodene.   Hie hraðe fremedon
> *Jud* 164: ðreatum ond ðrymmum   þrungon ond urnon
> *Jud* 240: þæt him swyrdgeswing   swiðlic eowdon

In *Judith*, I count over twenty examples of lines where at least two alliterating elements in a line share not just initial consonants, but initial consonant clusters.[14] Since I count over forty-five lines with vocalic alliteration in *Judith*, we see this cluster alliteration in about one in every fifteen possible lines. Cluster alliteration can be seen occasionally throughout the corpus, but rarely with the frequency or insistency we see in *Judith*; the sound-play we see in the example from line 23, 'hloh ond hlydde, hlynede ond dynede,' supplemented as it is by rhyme in the b-line, is an especially effective counterpoint to the semantic content of the line itself, with its description of the (presumably repetitive) carryings-on of Holofernes at the feast. It is clear that such cluster alliteration was not mandatory for the *Judith* poet or for any Anglo-Saxon poet, but it seems equally clear that it could be used, as here, to increase the poetic quality of a work.

As all of these passages suggest, the intensified sound patterning accomplished by the *Judith* poet's use of rhyme, secondary alliteration, cross alliteration, and cluster alliteration allows, at the very least, for a kind of emphatic effect, calling attention to these passages and lines even in the context of continuing poetic expression. The accumulation of such effects in the first third of *Judith* serves to focus our attention especially strongly in this portion of the poem. At the same time, the dense clustering of hypermetric verses in *Judith*'s first hundred lines very probably accomplishes much the same thing. In Type 1 hypermetric lines (such as are used in *Judith*), we still have (at most) three primary alliterators per line; the difference between normal and hypermetric verses involves the number of non alliterating stresses, with their numbers roughly doubled in hypermetric passages. In one important sense, then, the 'pace' of a hypermetric passage is slower, in comparison to normal verses, and in *Judith* the slowed pace of the first hundred lines also forces us to pay special attention to the beginning passages.[15] The final 250 lines of the poem, where normal lines predominate, really do seem to hurry along, drawing to a logical conclusion what has already been determined by the action in Holofernes's bedchamber.

In *Judith*, as I have suggested, we find a remarkable testimonial to the power of at least one Anglo-Saxon poet to put the possibilities of the traditional verse form to good use. In this poet's hands, we can see secondary poetic effects like rhyme and cross alliteration working in understandable ways, as well as see at least one possible way in which the distinction between hypermetric and normal verses was used for effect. A more careful examination of similar strategies in other poems might likewise be productive. In the case of *The Ruin*, the exercise is clearly worth the effort, as I suggest below.

The Ruin

In *The Ruin*'s forty-nine fragmented lines, there remain thirty-five whole lines, and an additional five verses also survive which are apparently complete, for a total of only seventy-five surviving complete verses. Surely, this poem accomplishes more in these few lines than virtually any passage of similar length in Anglo-Saxon poetry. Part of the *Ruin* poet's efficiency lies in his use of compounds (e.g., nine compounds in the first ten lines), but part of the power of the poem also lies in *The Ruin*'s use of secondary poetic effects. Consider the following passage:

> Beorht wæron burgræced,   burnsele monige,
> heah horngestreon,   heresweg micel,
> meodoheall monig,   [mon]dreama full
> oþþæt þæt onwende   wyrd seo swiþe.
> Crungon walo wide,   cwoman woldagas,
> swylt eall fornom   secgrofra wera;
> wurdon hyra wigsteal   westen staþolas
> brosnade burgsteall   (ll. 21–8a)[16]

Here we see ten compounds in fifteen verses (six in the first six verses). But notice the cross alliteration seen in line 27, and the even more remarkable case of line 25, where the two finite verbs (on s-feet) coalliterate with one another. Twice, the final stress of one line coalliterates with the primary alliterator of the following line (22b–3, 26b–7), and twice secondary elements in the a-line coalliterate with stressed elements in the preceding line (23a, 28a).[17] Such coalliteration occurs frequently and accidentally, but in *The Ruin* it seems likely to be used for effect.[18] The poem's first two lines exhibit a more impressive sort of linkage:

> Wrætlic is þes wealstan,   wyrde gebræcon;
> burgstede burston,   brosnað enta geweorc.   (ll. 1–2)[19]

Line two picks up alliteration on 'b' from the last stressed element of the preceding verse, while the final stress on 'w' in line two echoes the primary alliteration in line one.[20] Together, these elements form an alliterative bracketing pattern, and these two lines function as a remarkable introductory synopsis of the poem as a whole: the formal features imply wholeness through their circular linking effects, while the explicit content of the lines invokes the notions of breakdown and decay.

But even more notably, perhaps, the specific alliterators used in *Ruin* 1-2 deserve our attention. Three of the four b-words ('gebræcon,' 'burston,' and 'brosnað') refer directly to destruction and decay, while three of the w-words ('Wrætlic,' 'wealstan,' and 'geweorc') seem to invoke the the marvellous beauty and wonder of human (or giantish) creation. Alliterative associations thus link 'wyrde' ('fates' or 'events' in Mitchell and Robinson's glossary) with ideas of marvellous creative skill, in marked contrast to the role of the 'wyrde' as agents of destruction or decay. Likewise, the alliteration ironically associates the marvellous 'burgstede' (a citadel, a place of protection) with the very act of destruction itself. Pairs of lines with similarly dense alliterative patterning do occur elsewhere in Old English verse, but rarely with such powerful or apposite poetic effect.

Elsewhere, *The Ruin* uses a great deal of rhyme, specifically in the b-line (4b, 5b, 7b, 11b, 31b, 39b). Indeed, the *Ruin* poet's fondness for b-line rhyme is one of his hallmarks. But perhaps the most fascinating passage in *The Ruin* immediately precedes the longer passage quoted above:

mod mo[. . . . .]yne swiftne gebrægd
hwætred in hringas,   hygerof gebond
weallwalan wirum   wundrum togædre.   (ll. 18–20)[21]

The combination of cross alliteration in line 19 and triple alliteration in 20a powerfully supports the image of the braided thoughts and encircling wires which together gave the structure its strength.[22] Throughout *The Ruin*, in fact, the use of both rhyme and secondary alliteration patterns serves to present the poem itself as a marvel of careful construction and functional beauty. Although the accident of the *Exeter Book*'s fire damage has prompted many a facile observation about the degree to which *The Ruin* is itself a ruin, a far better comparison should be drawn between the marvellous construction of the baths and the equally ingenious and intricate formal construction of the poem.

As I hope to have suggested with these brief examinations of formal features in *Judith* and *The Ruin*, Anglo-Saxon poets had ways of making the most of the metrical system in which they worked. While the structures of primary alliteration and metrical form certainly imposed some constraints on Anglo-Saxon poets, enough freedom remained that poets could still use formal structures for ornamental and poetic effects. Modern readers, I think, have had too little understanding of the form and its possibilities to effectively address the poetics of Old

English verse, and one of my main purposes in this work is to at least attempt to provide a vocabulary for talking about Anglo-Saxon poetics. In my examination of these passages from *Judith* and *The Ruin*, then, I hope to have suggested just how illuminating a consideration of poetics can be, even in some of the best known and most frequently read Old English poems.

Late Old English Verse

Studies of Old English metre have generally focused on classical metre, with the metre of a single poem, *Beowulf*, dominating even that field. Yet it is undeniable that a great deal of Old English verse has always resisted Sieversian analysis, and commentators' suggestions that these works stand as 'poems of irregular metre' (Sedgfield) or 'debased verse' (McIntosh) have too rarely been challenged. The appeal of these pejorative terms, it appears, derives from the fact that, by employing them, scholars have been able to simply dismiss the evidence of poems that do not fit the Sievers-Bliss formalism. The possibility that classical Old English verse simply evolved into a different sort of verse is too rarely considered with any degree of seriousness.[1]

In this and the following chapters, I will suggest that the details of late Old English verse can, in fact, be readily understood as developing from the formal features of the classical system. Metrical changes, which (on the evidence of the *Chronicle* poems, the charm *For the Water-Elf Disease*, and inscriptions such as the Sutton Brooch) must have taken place in the mid- to late tenth century, defined a new variety of Old English verse, operating by new rules.[2] But, of course, these rules were simply different from those of classical verse, and the later poems are (in principle, at least) no less poetic for using them.

The metrical changes in question involved three areas, although they were almost certainly interrelated. These areas (loss of resolution, loss of metrical subordination, and reanalysis of anacrusis) all demand some discussion before we turn to the specific rules of late Old English verse.

Loss of Resolution

To put it briefly, resolution played no role at all in late Old English verse; in other words, late verse made no meaningful distinctions between stressed syllables based on their length. Two types of evidence can immediately be brought forth to test the accuracy of the claim that resolution was nonfunctional in late verse: cases where short stressed syllables appear in positions where classical metre allowed only long syllables and (conversely) cases where long stressed syllables occur in positions previously open only to short syllables.

Examples of the first sort occur (although rarely) even in *Beowulf* (e.g., line 262a: 'Wæs min fæder'), but with somewhat more frequency in late poems:

PPs 54.16 3a: and bodie
PPs 55.5 3a: and wiðer me
PPs 73.11 3b: efenmidre

Other, similar examples can also be found, but such verses might be explained (in classical terms) on the basis that resolution is blocked in them by a four-position rule. Such an explanation, however, cannot account for the following verses, in which long stressed syllables appear in positions where resolved sequences would be required in classical verse:

PPs 72.5 1b: ungemete swyþe   Sxxx/Sx
Dur 17b: and he his lara wel genom   xx/(x)Sxxxs
JDay II 102b: ungerydre sæ   Sxsx/S

I have placed tentative 'late Old English verse' scansions to the right of each verse here for clarity's sake.[3] All three of these verses, of course, would be unmetrical in classical Old English poetry. In each verse it is the long (four- or five-position) foot which would cause difficulty in the classical system; each of the long feet in these verses corresponds to an acceptable classical foot (Sxx, Sxxs, and Ssx) where the initial S-position (in classical verse, optionally filled by a resolved sequence) has been replaced by Sx. In other words, such verses are, in fact, precisely what we should expect to see in a system in which resolution does not apply. Further examples will be given below, but these verses should be sufficient to suggest the plausiblity of the succeeding analysis.

Metrical Stress and Subordination

Late Old English verse seems to have made use of only two levels of metrically significant stress, not three, as were employed in classical verse. That is, where classical verse had feet with two stressed positions with differing stress-levels (the same forms in Russom's account and above: Ss, Ssx, Sxs and Sxxs), late Old English verse made distinctions only between stressed and unstressed metrical positions. In practice, this change in metrical stress-assignment rules amounted to a virtually complete dissociation of acceptable verse feet from the stress patterns of existing words and compounds. Such a dissociation, of course, represents a radical change, since (as I have argued above, following Russom), a link between word-stress patterns and metrical patterns was the very basis of classical metre. But the evidence for the use of only two metrically significant stress levels in late verse is two-fold. First, there is a clear tenth-century decline in the use of verse types with three stress levels. But further, it seems clear that the late verse system allowed alliteration to fall in positions where it was excluded in classical verse, including on the second elements of compounds. Each type of evidence, and its relation to the issue of stress levels in late verse, demands at least a brief discussion.

The dissociation of word-level stress patterns and patterns of metrical stress appears to be directly related to the frequently observed decline in the numbers of Sieversian C, D, and E types found in datably late poems.[4] C, D, and E verses are precisely those that have feet with both primary and secondary stresses; such feet are paradigmatically filled by compound words. The use of compounds in classical verse, then, both authorized and (in a sense) generated these types, but compounds no longer played any definitive role in metrical verse structures once the conceptual equation between two-stress feet and compound words failed to hold. To put it another way, there was no longer any metrical impetus for poetic compounding in late Old English verse, since the principles of the verse form made no reference to compound like stress structures.[5]

While the decline in types C, D, and E can be understood as the result of a dissociation of word stress and metrical stress patterns, the most direct evidence for the claim that late verse made use of only two stress levels rests on changes in alliteration patterns, which had formerly relied upon subordination of all rightward elements within the verse.[6] Such subordination, in Russom's account, explains why leftmost elements of verses and compounds take alliteration. In late verse, however, the 'subordinated' elements of compounds may alliterate, if only occasionally:

Mald 242a: scyldburh tobrocen	alliteration on 'b'
DAlf 18a: to Eligbyrig	alliteration on 'b'
PPs 88.29 1a: Gif hi mine rihtwisnessa	alliteration on 'w'

Such examples certainly suggest a shift in the rules for where primary alliteration can occur, but the simplest account of such verses seems to be to interpret these compounds as having two stressed positions of equal metrical weight. We should, perhaps, scan such verses as follows:

Mald 242a: scyldburh tobrocen	SS/(x)Sx
DAlf 18a: to Eligbyrig	x/SxSx
PPs 88.29 1a: Gif hi mine rihtwisnessa	xx/(xx)SSxx

With such scansions, we can see that alliteration must still fall on a stressed syllable, but the position of that syllable is not determined by the rules of wordlike or compoundlike subordination, which (in each case) would demand that the alliterating syllable should be the leftmost S-position.

It is worth noting, of course, that alliteration is even more frequently delayed in verses without compounds; in the following examples the alliteration also fails to fall on the first stressed position:

PPs 118.71 3a: þin soðfæst weorc[7]	alliteration on 'w'
PPs 88.29b: fracoðe gewemmað	alliteration on 'w'
Mald 298a: Þurstanes sunu	alliteration on 's'
MCharm2 31a: Wyrm com snican	alliteration on 's'

Russom's argument that the alliteration rules in classical verse were derived from the rules of stress assignment (where alliteration, like word stress, was attracted to the left-most element of a structure, while rightward elements were subordinated) cannot be used to explain these sorts of alliteration. Rather, it seems likely that simply the presence or absence of stress was the key criterion for whether an element could alliterate; once all the stresses in a verse became conceptually equal, alliteration was allowed to fall on any stress, even the last stressed element in a line.[8] What both types of evidence suggest, I believe, is that metrical subordination no longer worked in late verse as it had in classical verse; rather than having metrical verses patterned on the juxtaposition of two word-stress patterns, late verses were defined by patterns of stressed and unstressed syllables. In short, secondary elements of compounds (which, linguistically, had secondary stress) were treated in the metre as either stressed or unstressed, since there was no longer an intermediate position.

Reanalysis of Anacrusis

Classical B and C verses gave rise to late verses which formally mirrored classical A verses with anacrusis, as seen in the following comparisons:

Classical form	Corresponding late form
xx/Sxs	xx/SxSx
xx/Ssx	xx/SxSx

The difference between (xx)Sx/Sx and xx/SxSx may have been difficult for late poets and audiences to attend to, and since three, four, or even five unstressed syllables were not especially unusual at the start of classical B and C verses, the limitation to two unstressed syllables before two-stress verses no longer seems to have had any force in the late verse tradition. Presumably as a result of this sort of metrical overlap, we find syllables in anacrusis in late Old English verse in a variety of contexts not allowed in the classical tradition.[9] A rule for extrametrical elements in late verse that would account for the kinds of changes to anacrusis described here might be articulated as follows: unstressed (extrametrical) syllables may precede any foot. As this formulation indicates, unstressed syllables before the first stress of a verse were reinterpreted as being equivalent to unstressed syllables before the second foot of a classical verse.

Given these changes to the late Old English verse system, we can articulate the following rules for the system as a whole.

P4 (late): In late Old English verse, inherited (classical) verses and verse types continue to be metrical.

The highly traditional and formulaic nature of Old English verse ensured that older forms were not simply superseded at some watershed moment in the tenth century. Instead, older forms and verses continued to be composed and transmitted, and they must have continued to be perceived as metrical. The presence of even a large number of classical verse types in a poem, then, cannot prove that it belongs to the classical period, as a very late poem like *The Death of Edward* should remind us. P4, it should be noted, simply defines inherited verse-types as metrical; it does not assert that later poets and audiences interpreted the structures of such verses in the same ways as classical poets and audiences had. Indeed, it seems likely that they did not. However, the only way to understand late verse is to examine the innovative forms that were not previously allowed, and in the following discussion, I will generally focus on the innovative forms.

P5 (late): Resolution, anacrusis, and compound like metrical subordination were non-functional in late Old English verse. All s-clusters alliterate with one another and with s-.

The reasoning behind most of the elements of P5 has been presented above; I include it here because these changes represent basic, foundational changes from the classical system. The change in the alliteration patterns concerning the letter 's-' is seemingly unrelated to the the other changes, but it is clear from numerous examples that this feature of classical alliteration has changed in the late period.

FS3 (late): Late Foot Structures

Changes to perceptions of initial unstressed syllables and to subordinated syllables led (in straightforward ways) to extensive revisions in available foot-structures. The x-feet remained unchanged, with x, xx, and xxx being common, and (as in classical verse) xxxx standing as a very uncommon, but probably necessary, fourth x-foot. Table 3.1 shows classical and late equivalents for S-feet.

The forms underlined in Table 3.1 were essentially new, while the rest remain largely unchanged from the classical tradition. Significantly, there no longer remains a separate category for the scansion of finite

TABLE 3.1
Late Stressed Feet

Classical foot form	Late foot form
s	S, Sx
sx[10]	Sx, Sxx
S	S, Sx
Sx	Sx, Sxx
Sxx	Sxx, <u>Sxxx</u>
Ss	SS, SxS, SSx, <u>SxSx</u>
Sxs	SxS, SxxS, <u>SxSx</u>, <u>SxxSx</u>
SxxS	SxxS, <u>SxxxS</u>, <u>SxxSx</u>, <u>SxxxSx</u>
Ssx	SSx, <u>SxSx</u>, <u>SSxx</u>, SxSxx

verbs, which tend in late verse to be scanned as S-positions, although some finite verbs (especially 'wesan' and verbs tending towards auxiliary function) are often scanned in late verse as x-positions.

Note that seven new foot-structures appear in Table 3.1; it is this increase that gives late Old English verse such a different subjective 'feel' in comparison to classical verse. But also, one can readily see that any lingering perception that foot-structures correspond to word-stress contours must no longer apply in late Old English verse.

FC4 (late): Late Verse Forms

In its most general form, a metrical late Old English verse can be defined by the following simple rules. Any verse must take one of these two forms:

> x-foot + S-foot
>   or
> S-foot + S-foot

and unstressed extrametrical elements are allowed before either foot.

While the simplicity of this system obviously allows some verse types which cannot be directly derived from classically authorized ancestors, it has the dual advantages of ease of expression and great variety in the specific authorized types. While the number of possible feet has been greatly increased, the rules for combining feet into metrical verses have been correspondingly simplified, and the system itself remains useful in its flexibility and versatility.[11] Because late Old English verse evolved from classical verse, however, we ought to expect that the earliest examples of late verse should include the fewest numbers of such radically new types and that their numbers might well increase with time, and this does, in fact, seem to be the case.[12]

Note, of course, that this new descriptive system does little to support any notion that the late Old English verse system features two-stress verses. Since foot forms are no longer closely associated with word-level stress patterns, any and all stressed positions within these verses are conceptualized as having full metrical stress. Verses, then, have from one to four full stresses, and while they continue to be made from two metrical feet, they cannot be said to feature two stresses with any truly descriptive validity.[13]

In the metrical transformation that led to late Old English verse, a number of verse forms were authorized that had previously been excluded from the classical Old English verse tradition, and the most frequently occurring sorts of these newly authorized types can stand as diagnostic types for late Old English verse, in the sense that the clustering if such types in a single poem provides strong evidence that that poem belongs to the late tradition. A sampling of such diagnostic types (by no means exhaustive) is given in Table 3.2.

Clusters of these diagnostic verses in poems such as *The Metrical Psalms*, *The Judgment Day II*, *Durham*, and *The Death of Alfred*, I believe, confirm that each of these poems belongs to the late Old English poetic tradition.[14] Further, such evidence also suggests that my analysis of this tradition as having descended from 'classical' Old English verse must be substantially correct. Such a conclusion, of course, is buttressed by the fact that each of these poems also includes numbers (sometimes large numbers) of verses which would be metrical in classical Old English metre as well. In a poem like *The Battle of Maldon*, where classical forms greatly outnumber the late forms, we see such conservatism in its most powerful mode. Of the poems considered so far, only in *Durham* and *The Death of Alfred* do we really see late forms outnumbering classically metrical forms; the notably late date of these two poems offers strong evidence for the evolutionary development of late Old English verse away from classical norms.

TABLE 3.2
Diagnostic Late Old English Verse Forms

Type	Classical Ancestors/Examples	Specific Scansions
xx/SxSx	xx/Ssx, xx/Sxs	
	PPs 61.9 4b: on þam ilcan fremmað	xx/SxSx
	Mald 75b: se wæs haten Wulfstan	xx/SxSx
	PPs 64.4 3a: and on his eardungstowum	xx/(x)SxSx
	MCharm2 10b: ofer þe fearras fnærdon	xx/(x)SxSx
	Dur 20a: ðær monia wundrum gewurðað	(x)xx/SxxSx[15]
xx/SSxx	xx/Ssx	
	PPs 71.4 1a: on his soðfæstnesse	xx/SSxx
	DAlf 25a: on þæm suðportice	xx/SSxx
Sx/SxSx	Sx/Ss, S/Ssx, S/Sxs	
	JDay II 81a: lifes læcedomas	Sx/SxSx
	PPs 66.1 1a: Miltsa us, mihtig drihten	Sx/(x)SxSx
	Dur 15a: and breoma bocera Beda	(x)Sx/SxxSx[16]
xx/SxxxS	xx/Sxxs	
	JDay II 18a: and synfulra gehwam	x/SxxxS
	PPs 57.7 3a: hi sunnan ne geseoð	x/SxxxS
	PPs 74.5 1a: Ne ahebbað ge to hea	xx/SxxxS
	DAlf 7a: and his geferan he todraf	xx/(x)SxxxS
	Dur 17b: and he his lara wel genom	xx/(x)SxxxS
SSx/Sx	Ssx/S, Ss/Sx	
	Mald 282a: Sibyrhtes broðor	SSx/Sx
	PPs 145.7 7a: soðfæste drihten	SSx/Sx
	Dur 4a: ea yðum stronge	SSx/Sx[17]
SSxx/S	Ssx/S	
	PPs 84.9 2a: mildheortnesse mod	SSxx/S
SxSx/Sx	SS/Sx, Ssx/S	
	PPs 98.1 2b: ungemete swiðe	SxSx/Sx
	JDay II 194b: ungemetum wepað	SxSx/Sx
SxSx/S	Ssx/S	
	PPs 67.1 1b: ungeleafe menn	SxSx/S
	JDay II 102b: ungerydre sæ	SxSx/S

VC4 (late): Late Verse Combination Rules

Late Old English verses are still generally linked by alliteration into full lines. However, in contrast to classical verse, alliteration may link any S-position in the a-line to any S-position in the b-line. In addition, some forms of linkage that had been secondary in the classical tradition may serve as the primary linkage in the late tradition, including verse rhyme that links half-lines and lines with only AA- or BB-alliteration.[18] *Occasionally, full lines appear to show no linkage at all.*

Somewhat surprisingly, all of the varieties of linkage identified in VC4 seem to have made their appearance in the late verse tradition at an early point. The *Chronicle* poem from annal 975DE, called *The Death of Edgar II* in Robinson and Stanley's facsimile volume, provides an especially valuable example:

Her Eadgar gefor, Angla reccend,	x/SxxS[19]	Sx/Sx
Wesseaxena wine, 7 Myrcna mundbora.	SSxx/Sx	(x)Sx/SSx
Cuð wæs þæt wide geond feola þeoda,	Sxx/Sx	x/SxSx
þæt afaren Eadmundes ofer <ganetes> beð	(x)Sxx/SSx	xx/SxxS
cynegas hine wide wurðodon swiðe,	Sxx/(xx)Sx	Sxx/Sx
bugon to þam cyninge swa him wæs gecynde.	Sx/(xx)Sxx	xx/(xx)Sx
Næs <se> flota swa rang, ne se here swa strang,	xx/SxxS	xx/SxxS
þæt on Angelcynne æs him gefætte,	xx/SxSx	Sx/(x)Sx
þa hwile þe se æþela cyning cynestol gerehte.	(x)Sx/(xx)SxxSx	SxS/(x)Sx

(975D, cited from Cubbin; relineated)

I provide late Old English scansions here for clarity. Line 2, of course, features AABB-alliteration, while line 4 has only AA-alliteration. Rhyme provides the only link in line 7, while rhyme (or off-rhyme) and alliteration both appear in line 5. Alliteration falls on S-positions that would be unusual or unmetrical in classical verse in 5a, 6b, and 9a. Line 3 has either no link at all or else relies upon off-rhyme to link 'wide' and 'þeoda.'[20]

As an example such as this one suggests, it is still clear that alliteration remains the dominant mode of verse linkage in late Old English poetry, but there is a great deal more variety available in the linking strategies used by late Old English poets than was available to their classical predecessors. Modern readers, primarily accustomed to the standards of classical verse, may well feel like these innovative linking strategies are too unfamiliar to be acceptable, but they seem to have been normal and acceptable to late Old English poets and audiences. One final rule is needed, however, to accommodate the variety of observed rhymes in the late verse traditon.

S3 (late): Late Old English Rhyme. For late Old English verse, rhyme must be defined as the repetition of any phonetic element within a stressed syllable, not including the initial consonant or consonant cluster. Off-rhymes may include near-phonetic repetitions, and inflectional rhyme may sometimes be functional.

While I treated only full root-rhymes as productive in my analysis of rhyme in classical Old English verse, it is clear that in late Old English verse, 'rhyme' was a much broader and various category than that, and almost certainly broader than modern conceptions of rhyme allow. The following examples of rhyme-pairs from late Old English poems show the breadth of late rhyme:

DAlf 13: syþþan Dene comon   and her frið namon
WC 8: þæt swa hwa swa sloge heort oððe hinde.   þæt hine man sceolde blendian
WC 15: gif hi woldon libban.   oððe land habban
WC 18: hine sylf upp ahebban.   7 ofer ealle men tellan[21]
SB 3: buton hyo me selle   hire agenes willes[22]

Clearly, the notion of phonetic repetition underlies such rhymes: we sometimes see repetition of vowels only (WC 18, although inflectional rhyme may apply here as well), while repetition of consonants only is somewhat more frequent (repetition of both root-vowel and root-final consonants continues to be the norm, however). Frequently, inflectional syllables are allowed to differ if rhyme links roots. But, significantly, 'rhyme,' even as broadly defined as is necessary here, continues to be distinguished from the phonetic repetition involved in alliteration, because alliteration is allowed to link any two stresses, but rhyme is allowed as a linking strategy only between the final stresses of each verse. Rhyme may be used in other positions ornamentally (as in classical Old English poetry), but it does not seem to serve as a primary line linkage unless it is verse rhyme.

Finally, as the scansions provided above for *The Death of Edgar II* suggest, the process of scanning late Old English verse is, in general, relatively straightforward, although ambiguities of scansion often seem to abound. But, as with ambiguous scansions in the classical tradition, the metricality of such ambiguous verses is rarely, if ever, in doubt, and once a passage has been identified as late Old English verse, the process of scanning its lines is not especially difficult. The following chapter addresses the issue of properly identifying examples of late Old Englsh verse, by reexamining a set of texts conventionally identified as prose: the corpus of Ælfric's so-called rhythmical prose.

Ælfric and Late Old English Verse

The rules for late Old English verse given in chapter 3.1 were derived strictly from poems generally acknowledged to be late Old English verse: poems already included in the *ASPR* and the passages printed as verse in Plummer's edition of the *Anglo-Saxon Chronicle* in particular. An important feature of the analysis that led to those rules, of course, was the assumption (justified by the results, I believe) that the metrical forms of these late poems descended from the forms used in classical Old English poems. The articulation of a descriptive metrical system for late Old English verse has long been a *desideratum* in the field of Anglo-Saxon studies, and, initially, my only intention in describing late Old English verse was to provide such a description for these late – and unjustly neglected – poems.

Surprisingly, however, the rules for late Old English verse as expressed in chapter 3.1 above appear also to describe the most regular of the 'rhythmical' texts of Ælfric, although the latter have long been called prose by contemporary scholars.[1] The reason why Ælfric's rhythmical works have been identified as prose, however, seems simply to be that they are too good to be bad verse.[2] Long-standing critical dependence on Sieversian formalism certainly seemed to leave no other option, but (as I believe I have shown) late Old English verse operated by rules identifiably distinct from the rules of classical verse described by Sievers. In this chapter, I will discuss the very real possibility that Ælfric was a poet (or, at least, a versifier), frequently using a verse system indistinguishable from that described in chapter 3.1.

What we, as modern readers and critics, call Ælfric's works clearly makes a difference, and in formulating the question of the generic identity of Ælfric's rhythmical works as a choice between 'prose' and 'verse,'

I realize that I am running against the tide of a recent critical trend that prefers to identify Ælfric's rhythmical compositions as – quite literally – occupying some sort of middle ground between the two genres. 'Rhythmical prose,' of course, is the most common term for this third entity, but Norman Blake's 'rhythmical alliteration' also has adherents, especially as it includes a somewhat broad spectrum of forms that seem to fall between unambiguous examples of verse and 'normal' prose. Faced with the problem of understanding the development of Layamon's verse form (a topic I will take up in detail in chapter 4.1), a number of critics have found this middle ground to be a more plausible origin for Layamon's metre than 'classical' Old English verse.[3] The implied historical development – from classical Old English verse, to rhythmical prose (or rhythmical alliteration), to rhyming and alliterating early Middle English verse has nevertheless remained troublesome, both because of the suggested verse-prose-verse sequence and because of the difficulty of deriving Layamon's frequent use of rhyme from Ælfric's almost purely alliterative style.

By offering an argument for identifying Ælfric's rhythmical works as verse, however, I believe I can ameliorate both difficulties: a progression from classical Old English verse to late Old English verse (including Ælfric) to Layamon's form obviously allows us to see all of the relevant changes as evolutions in verse form. Further, if we see Ælfric as a late poet who happened to favour alliteration over rhyme (a stylistic choice that other late poets did not always make), we would be able to derive Layamon's use of rhyme from the practice of other late poets. Indeed, the possibility that Ælfric's vast preference for alliteration was idiosyncratic opens the door for a straightforward origin for Layamon's rhyme in the general use of rhyme in late Old English verse.[4]

At this point, however, it is worthwhile to begin the examination of Ælfric's so-called rhythmical prose; I will start with a passage from the *Life of Cuthbert*, generally acknowledged as Ælfric's first extended composition in the rhythmical style.[5] The following passage, taken from Godden's edition, has been relineated, however, according to its rhythmical structure:

	Sum eawfast man. eac swilce hæfde.	x/SxS	xxx/Sx
	micele cyððe. to ðan halgan cuðberhte.	Sxx/Sx	(xx)Sx/SSx
	and gelomlice his lare breac.	xx/Sxx	x/SxS
	þa getimode his wife. wyrs ðonne he beðorfte.	xx/SxxxSx	Sxx/(xx)Sx
5	þæt heo ðurh wodnysse. micclum wæs gedreht;	xxx/SSx	Sxx/(x)S
	Þa com se eawfæsta. to ðan eadigan cuðberhte.	(x)S/(x)SSx	(xx)Sxx/SSx
	and he wæs on ðam timan. to prafoste geset.	xxx/(xx)Sx	x/SxxxS

on ðam munuclife. þe is lindisfarnea gehaten.	xx/SxSx	(xx)SxSx/(x)Sx
þa ne mihte he for sceame. him openlice secgan.	(xx)Sx/(xx)Sx	(x)Sxxx/Sx
10 þæt his eawfæste wif. on ðære wodnysse læg.	xx/SxxS	xxx/SxxS
ac bæd þæt he asende sumne broþer.	(x)Sx/(xx)Sx	Sx/Sx
þe hire gerihta. gedon mihte.	xxx/(x)Sx	x/SSx
ær ðan ðe heo of life. gelæd wurde;	xxx/(xx)Sx	x/SSx

(Godden, *Second Series* 85)[6]

As the scansions I have provided suggest, there is no difficulty at all in interpreting the individual verses of this passage as belonging to the sort of late Old English verse described in chapter 3.1. In terms of linking strategies used by Ælfric, we see alliteration in lines 2–4, 6, 8–11, and 13, including the coalliteration of 's-' and 'sc-' (a feature often seen in the *Metrical Psalms*).[7] Verse rhyme is clearly used as a primary linking strategy in line 12 here, and the lack of alliteration in the remaining three lines may not be as serious a deficiency as it first seems. Ælfric, for example, frequently appears to allow alliteration to fall on prepositions (line 7; see the discussion below) and the alliteration of 'eawfast' and 'hæfde' in the first line is also quite likely; we might recall that 'Holofernes' is used to alliterate with vowels several times in *Judith* (cf. the discussion of initial 'h-' below). Likewise, although no alliteration joins the halves of line 5, 'wodnysse' continues the w-alliteration that joined the halves of line 4 together.[8] Such continued alliteration is at least occasionally seen in late poems, such as the *Metrical Psalms*.[9]

Virtually all of the metrical, alliterative, and rhyming features of this passage, then, can clearly be paralleled in poems from the late Old English period, and as far as formal features are concerned, there seems to be little difficulty in identifying a passage such as the one quoted above as verse – apart from the inertia of the critical position which has conventionally seen Ælfric as a prose writer. Similar examinations of passages from Ælfric's rhythmical works yield similar results, and it is difficult not to conclude that Ælfric's verses and lines are built in much the same way as verses and lines from the late Old English poetic tradition. To identify Ælfric as a poet on this basis seems, at the least, plausible. But the case for Ælfric as poet or versifier does not rest on the formal features alone: the evidence of scribal activity also suggests that at least some contemporary readers (perhaps even including Ælfric himself) may have associated this style with verse.

The most important such scribal or manuscript evidence comes from the pointing seen in a passage such as the one quoted above. Of the twenty-six verses printed from the Cuthbert homily, only two lack points, and such a high pointing percentage would be quite remarkable even in classical verse texts. As Godden notes in his edition (from which the above passage was quoted), 'The punctuation and capitalization are those of the manuscript [Cambridge University Library Gg. 3. 28]' (*Second Series* xciv), and such regular pointing as we see here must surely call to mind the tradition of metrical pointing which Katherine O'Brien O'Keeffe has so ably described in Old English poetic texts.[10] And as Godden further notes, it is well recognized that such pointing constitutes 'a system clearly distinct from the normal punctuation' (*Introduction* xxxvii). Although he does not say it explicitly, the implication seems to be that the punctuation seen in a passage such as this one marks out structural units, rather than syntactic ones.

Of course, O'Brien O'Keeffe's study concludes that eleventh-century scribal practice involved the pointing of both a-lines and b-lines of verse (as here), while tenth-century scribes frequently pointed only the b-line (*Visible Song* 137). Her further comment, 'It is to the late tenth century that we should look for the development of new visual information in the writing of Old English verse' seems especially relevant in the current context (*Visible Song* 137). CUL Gg. 3. 28 dates from just around 1000, and if we identify Ælfric's rhythmical works as verse, we would seem to have precisely the manuscript evidence that O'Brien O'Keeffe suggests that we seek for this development.[11]

One hesitates to make too much of the connection, but it is difficult not to associate the development such verselike pointing in Ælfrician texts with the increasing textualization (and decreasing 'orality') of classical verse in the manuscript record of the tenth century. We might recall O'Brien O'Keeffe's conclusion that 'the appearance, in the late tenth century, of a trend toward apparently metrical punctuation at the b-line coincides with the diminishing of 'formulaic' reading in these records' (*Visible Song* 192). It is at least possible that the development of metrical pointing in the latter tenth century (in Ælfric's works and in the poetic tradition as a whole, both classical and late) might have arisen as a need to visually indicate verse boundaries after the metrical late Old English verse developed. That is, the new verse forms typical of late Old English poetry were less easily identifiable to readers (both because they were new and unfamiliar and because they were more varied and variable), and the pointing tradition may have developed as a way of marking such newly confusing boundaries. Certainly the simultaneity of the metrical changes and the change in pointing practice is striking, and the development of late Old English verse (and the regular pointing found in some Ælfric manuscripts) appears to have important implications for our understanding of the process of textualization in this period. It seems clear that late Old English verse was an essentially literary form (as Ælfric's works are clearly literary in origin and outlook). The basic forms of the late verse tradition descended from classical verse types, but otherwise both late verse and Ælfric are easily distinguishable from the formulaic, compound-filled, orally derived standards of classical verse.[12] The evidence of pointing in Ælfric manuscripts such as CUL Gg. 3. 28, then, may well stand as a clear indicator that Ælfric (or his earliest scribes) was using pointing to clarify structure at a moment when poets and audiences were confronted with a variety of newly authorized verse types.[13]

Besides pointing, however, the scribal treatment of the transitional points between 'normal' prose and the rhythmical style provides additional evidence. *The Life of Edmund*, for example, begins with a (non-rhythmical) prose account of the textual transmission of the Edmund material, first to Abbo of Fleury and thence to Ælfric, followed by the beginning of the 'rhythmical' remainder of the text. On folio 203r of Cotton Julius E. vii (Skeat's base manuscript), we see that the scribe has included a large (three-line) initial 'E' to mark the beginning of the rhythmical portion, which is also set off from the preceding 'plain' prose by nearly a full line of unused text space.[14] As I have argued elsewhere, such blank space and *litterae notabiliores* often seem to mark boundary points between prose and verse.[15] While the shift from prologue to *vita* may be sufficient to result in such a heavily marked textual boundary, the similarity of the treatment of the boundary point here to some prose-verse boundaries seems important as well.

Finally, it is worthwhile to consider one further possible hint as to Ælfric's own perceptions of his form. At the beginning of the Cuthbert homily (which seems to have been, we should recall, Ælfric's first extended composition in the rhythmical style), we read about Bede's treatment of the Cuthbert material in a passage of regular prose: 'Beda se snotera engla ðeoda lareow þises halgan lif. endebyrdlice mid wulderfullum herungum. ægðer ge æfter anfealdre gereccednysse. ge æfter leoðlicere gyddunge awrat' (Godden, *Second Series* 81).[16] The distinction Ælfric draws here is an intriguing one: in Latin, at least, verse is contrasted to an 'anfealdre gereccednysse': a simple narrative. Of course, immediately after his comment that Bede wrote his second version of the *Life of Cuthbert* in the form of a song or poem, Ælfric shifts from the unornamented prose of this introductory matter to his rhythmical style. In this context, it seems difficult not to associate the conspicuous rhythmical and alliterative ornamentation of this style with verse; further, the fact that Bede's verse *Life* is more of a direct source for Ælfric than the prose *Life* may well suggest that Ælfric's first explorations in the rhythmical style were associated with Bede's own poem.[17]

What I am suggesting, of course, is that the formal similarities seen between late Old English verse and Ælfric's rhythmical prose are supported by scribal treatment, which clearly identifies these works as different from normal prose and demanding precisely the same sorts of distinctive spatial/textual treatments otherwise used for poetry. When differing types of evidence all point to a single conclusion, that conclusion normally carries some conviction; the evidence of pointing, textual space, and formal analysis all supports the possibility that Ælfric was working in verse. The oxymoronic nature of the conventional label 'rhythmical prose' should remind us of just how unusual Ælfric's prose is *as prose*: but in its forms, linking strategies, and presentation, it is not at all unusual as late Old English verse.

In order to assess the consequences of identifying Ælfric's rhythmical style as a verse style, I will turn, in the remainder of this chapter, to a consideration of *The Life of St. Sebastian*, the fifth selection in Ælfric's *Lives of Saints*. I chose this text on the basis of its length (at 474 lines in Skeat's edition, it is substantial enough to suggest that conclusions about frequencies have some validity), but it turns out to offer a great deal for our assessment of Ælfric's particular understanding of the metrical requirements and expectations of his form. Just as poets (such as the *Beowulf* poet) clearly had their own unique and individual habits and practices within the classical tradition, Ælfric, while working within the late Old English verse style, nevertheless seems to have also had his own unique characteristics.

Before beginning to assess Ælfric's habits, however, it is important to note that reading Ælfric's *St. Sebastian* as late Old English verse leads to the conclusion that the text has only 473 full lines. Skeat's lines 106–7 appear in his edition as follows:

Eadige synd þa þe þinum wordum gelyfað.
and þa beoð awyrigde þe þises twyniað.   (*Lives* 1:122; ll. 106–7)

As they stand, neither line features any clear sort of alliteration or rhyme, and one might even be uncertain about half-line divisions. Clearly, Skeat lineates this passage as two lines because of its length, but the pointing here (Skeat prints the points from his base manuscript, Cotton Julius E. vii) suggests that we have only two half-lines. Each can certainly be scanned as an acceptable verse of late Old English poetry:

Eadige synd þa þe þinum wordum gelyfað.	SxxS/(xxxx)SxxSx[18]
and þa beoð awyrigde þe þises twyniað.	(xxxx)Sxx/(xxx)Sxx.

Doing, so, of course, also allows us to see the line as linked by alliteration; here, the very act of reading the passage as late Old English verse allows us to understand both Skeat's error in lineation and the actual structure of the passage.

After discounting Skeat's line 392 (in Latin), a simple count of the work's remaining 472 full lines identifies no fewer than 395 as being clearly linked by alliteration across the caesura. Three lines also appear to feature rhyme as the only link:

109: and manna eagan onlyht   þe blinde wæron on niht
281: Nis þæt clæne herigendlic.   ne þæt gale tallic.
393: Eala hu mycel god is.   and hwylc wynsumnys

Rhyme linking the suffixal '-lic' syllables together (as in line 281) would seem to be unusual, but perhaps it is possible for Ælfric.[19] Certainly, there is no difficulty in scanning the rhyme-syllables in lines 109 and 393 as falling on stressed positions. The overall percentage of lines with verse rhyme in Ælfric is low, but he does seem to use them occasionally, as here and as in the example given above from the *Life of Cuthbert*.

A number of other lines (and types of lines) suggest additional features of Ælfric's practice. For example, it seems clear that alliteration is achieved in some lines by considering some proper names as either having two stresses or following Latin patterns of word-stress:

2: se wæs lang on lare   on mediolana byrig.
263: on þan cræfte aspende   tranquillinus min fæder.
339: Þa be-laf sebastianus   on þære byrig mid þam papan.
349: sebastianum he ge-sette.   him eallum to mund-boran.

Also, a number of lines suggest that initial 'h-' can be ignored for purposes of alliteration:

56: for þam earmlican swæsnyssum.   þissera heofiendra
92: hire spræce be-næmed.   and heo hnah adune
103: and heold ane boc.   æt-foran his eagum.
134: het lædan of þan hæftum   ealles sixtyne.
142: þa wearð he ge-hæled.   fram eallum his sarnyssum.
146: ac hi wurdon gehælede.   fram heora untrum-nysse.
259: þe his hæle hremde   þurh reðe wiglunga.

This alliterative feature, of course, occurs even in some classical Old English poems. As in other late Old English poems, Ælfric also allows AA- or BB-alliteration, including (here) one example of AABB-alliteration:

7: on godnysse scinende.   and on eallum þeawum arwurðful.   (BB)
128: mid his wif. Zoe.   and þrym and ðrittigum mannum   (BB)
188: ne moste syllan wið sceattum.   oþþe swa ge-bicgan.   (AA)
246: gewurðe godes willa   and eower eac æt þysum.   (AA)
267: Chromatius cwæð.   hwæt derað þis ænigum.   (AA)
287: He ge-þafode ða.   þæt hi þæt weorc to-wurpon.   (AABB)
300: and arn to þam engle.   wolde his fet gecyssan.   (AA)
334: and wunige se þe wille.   mid me on þyssere byrig.   (AA)
373: þa ða he ne mihte þa menn.   gebigan fram criste.   (AA)
466: PETRVS and PAVLVS   ærest bebyrgede wæron,   (AA)

With ten such examples, it is difficult not to conclude that this feature of late Old English verse is also a regular feature of Ælfric's alliterative practice. So far, then, no fewer than 419 of Ælfric's 472 lines have a linkage of the sort we expect to see in late Old English verse.

Still, however, this number leaves more than ten percent of the lines in the *Life of St. Sebastian* seemingly without any sort of poetic linkage. While unlinked lines do occur in late Old Engish verse, this percentage seems high. Remarkably, though, it seems to be the case that Ælfric employs two additional types of alliterative linkage to maximize the alliteration in these works. First is his widely acknowledged use of alliteration on prefixes and prepositions,[20] as in the following examples:

13: He ge-sette hine to ealdre.   ofer an werod.
46: heora wif awurpon.   and wiðsocon heora bearn   (AA)
80: lætað hi nu faran.   to ðam forestihtan kynehelme.
84: on þam ge sylfa moton   mid him æfre wunian.

119: þæt hi æfre þa martyras   mis-læran woldon.
127: Þa wearð gefullod   se fore-sæda nicostratus.   (BB)
147: mid þam þe se mæsse-preost.   hi mid þam fulluhte aþwoh.
185: anne gyldene wecg.   wið þam þe he him tæhte.
191: þe hine gefullode.   and fram þære coðe gehælde.
194: to þam heah-ge-refan.   and he cwæð him to.
208: hi ða begen bædon   binnon þam fyrste god.   (AA)
247: Hi þa sona begen   be-gyrndon hi caflice.
341: marcus. and marcellianus.   mid heora fæder tranquilline.   (AA)
367: mid feower his ge-ferum.   and toforan þam deman gebroht   (AA)
416: and for ðe þingode.   and for þinum folce.
468: Lucina þa ferde   to ðam fore-seadan seaðe   (BB)[21]

As my marginal notations indicate, six of these sixteen lines would have AA- or BB-alliteration even if we rejected the possibility of alliteration on prefixes and prepositions, but the other ten examples may well suggest that alliteration on these normally unstressed particles is an acceptable feature of Ælfric's practice.[22] Likewise, Ælfric seems to allow lines which themselves feature no alliterative link to stand, especially when they share an alliterator with a neighbouring line.[23] A passage such as the following seems especially illuminating:

and for-leton hine   swa licgan for deadne.
þa com sum wudewe.   þe wæs anes martyres laf.
on þære ylcan nihte.   þær he læg forwundod.
wolde his lic bebyrigan.   and gemette hine libbendne.
heo lædde hine þa   to hire huse cucenne.   (*Lives* 1:144; ll. 429–33)[24]

As they stand, lines 430, 431, and 433 have no alliterative linking to join their verses. But both lines 429 and 432 have l-alliteration, and Ælfric's use of 'laf,' 'læg,' and 'lædde' in the other three lines must serve to make this an alliteratively linked passage. Including these three examples, I find a total of twelve of the remaining 'unlinked' lines feature this sort of alliterative link to a preceding line, to a following line, or both.[25]

Taking these two additional types of alliterative structure into account leaves some twenty-five lines of the total 472 unaccounted for. Such a percentage is small (about 5 per cent), and probably within the range we see in other late Old English verse examples. While it may be possible that alliteration is sometimes functional on other 'minor syllables' besides prepositions and prefixes, it is somewhat difficult to be certain; since some lines that exhibit no clear linkage are apparently allowed, it seems best not to assume too much in the way of alliteration of additional minor syllables.

What this examination of the *Life of St. Sebastian* has allowed, I believe, is an opportunity to see exactly how much the alliterative (and other) linking strategies used by Ælfric correspond to those seen in the late Old English verse tradition as a whole. Besides alliteration that joins two verses into a line, Ælfric also uses AA- and BB-alliteration, occasional rhyme, and has occasional unlinked pairs of verses. All of these are found in the late Old English verse tradition. But further, Ælfric seems to use two additional strategies that are not as frequently seen in other late Old English verse: the alliteration of prefixes and prepositions and the use of continued alliteration across two lines to support a single alliterator in one of the two. These strategies, I think it is worth pointing out, would be unnecessary in a genre such as rhythmical prose is understood to be. Rhythmical prose uses rhythm as its primary formal structure, and alliteration is used more or less ornamentally to link numbers of rhythmical units into pairs (while many may remain unlinked by alliteration). Ælfric's use of continuing alliteration over multiple lines has no clear function in rhythmical prose, but it can clearly serve to limit the numbers of unlinked verse lines. Likewise, there is no clear motive for the promotion of prefixes or prepositions to positions of stress in prose, but the rules of even classical verse allowed prepositions to be stressed under certain circumstances and hence to take alliteration. Ælfric seems to have at least partially understood that feature of classical verse and used it in his own compositions.

My examination of *St. Sebastian*, then, adds additional support to the conclusion that Ælfric was writing verse. Not only is the evidence of verse form and scribal treatment relevant, but certain patterns of alliteration in Ælfric's work seem to be understandable only in a verse context, since those patterns are not well explained by the hypothesis that Ælfric was working in prose, no matter how rhythmical. The conclusion that Ælfric's rhythmical compositions are, indeed, late Old English verse seems impossible to avoid.

The Poetics of Late Old English Verse

Not only did the very metrical basis of Old English poetry change in the transition to late Old English verse, but the available poetic tools and how they were used for poetic effect also seem to have changed. To take only the most obvious examples, hypermetric verses and lines were no longer available, and verse rhyme was an allowed alternative to alliteration; such changes had poetic consequences as well as metrical ones. The general scholarly neglect of late Old English verse (conditioned, I believe, by the continuing reliance on Sieversian formalism) has resulted in a lack of appreciation for the poetic possibilities available in the late Old English period, and (as discussed above) late poems are frequently associated with pejorative terms such as McIntosh's 'late "debased" Old English verse' ('Wulfstan's Prose' 112). This chapter will explore at least some of the poetic changes that accompanied the transition to late Old English verse, attempting to address some of these works on their own poetic terms without drawing implicit or explicit qualitative comparisons to the standards of classical Old English verse, standards which clearly do not apply.

It is worthwhile to begin the examination of the poetics of late Old English verse with a passage that has generally been disparaged or condemned on the basis of its supposedly poor quality, *The Death of Alfred*, from the *Chronicle*'s annal 1036 (manuscripts C and D).[1] I quote the verse portions of annal 1036 as they appear in the *ASPR*:[2]

Ac Godwine hine þa gelette and hine on hæft sette,	(x)SSx/(xxxx)Sx	(xxxx)S/Sx
and his geferan he todraf, and sume mislice ofsloh,	(xx)x/SxxxS	(x)xx/SxxxS
sume hi man wið feo sealde, sume hreowlice acwealde,	xx/(xxx)SSx	xx/SxxxSx
sume hi man bende, sume hi man blende,	xx/(xx)Sx	xx/(xx)Sx

10	sume hamelode, sume hættode.	xx/Sxxx	xx/Sxx
	Ne wearð dreorlicre dæd gedon on þison earde,	xx/SxxS	x/SxxxSx
	syþþan Dene comon and her frið namon.	xx/SxŚx	xx/SSx
	Nu is to gelyfenne to ðan leofan gode,	xx/(xx)Sxx	xx/SxSx
	þæt hi blission bliðe mid Criste	xx/Sxx	Sx/(x)Sx
15	þe wæron buton scylde swa earmlice acwealde.	(x)xx/(xx)Sx	x/SxxxSx
	Se æþeling lyfode þa gyt; ælc yfel man him gehet,	(x)Sxx/SxxxS	SSx/SxxS
	oðþæt man gerædde þæt man hine lædde	xx/(xx)Sx	xx/(xx)Sx
	to Eligbyrig swa gebundenne.	x/SxSx	xx/Sxx
	Sona swa he lende, on scype man hine blende,	Sx/(xx)Sx	(x)Sx/(xxx)Sx
20	and hine swa blindne brohte to ðam munecon,	(x)xx/(x)Sx	Sx/(xx)Sxx
	and he þar wunode ða hwile þe he lyfode.	xx/(x)Sxx	(x)Sx/(xx)Sxx³
	Syððan hine man byrigde, swa him wel gebyrede,	xx/(xxx)Sxx	xx/SxSxx
	ful wurðlice, swa he wyrðe wæs,	x/Sxx	xx/SxS
	æt þam westende, þam styple ful gehende,	xx/SSx	x/SxxxSx
25	on þam suðportice; seo saul is mid Criste.	xx/SSxx	x/SxxSx (6–25)⁴

Thirteen of these twenty lines feature alliteration, according to the scansions given, and seven are linked only by rhyme.[5] Two of the rhyming lines (12 and 24) also feature stressed words in their respective a-lines that continue the alliteration of the previous line. If we accept off-rhyme and inflectional rhyme, at least six lines feature both rhyme and alliteration (lines 9, 10, 16, 19, 21, and 22). Unlike both classical Old English poems and some other late Old English poems, however, the author of *The Death of Alfred* seems to have an especially strict sense of rhyme: although allowing rhyme to link words with different root-vowels ('todraf'/'ofsloh'; 'comon'/'namon'; 'scylde'/'acwealde'; 'gyt'/'gehet'),[6] this poet seems especially concerned to match the inflections of rhyme words, also seemingly allowing disyllabic inflections to serve as rhyme-links on their own.[7]

It is also worth pointing out the degree to which this poet seems to intentionally balance paired verses. Verses with single S-positions are paired in lines 9, 10, and 17; those with two S-positions are paired in lines 7–8, 11–12, 19, and 24–5. The two heaviest verses of the entire poem are paired with one another in line 16. With some frequency, a verse with one stress in the a-line is paired with a two-stress verse in the b-line, but this seems clearly preferable (six examples) to having the single-stress verse in the b-line (one example).[8] Note also that in lines 9 and 17, the parallelism and the balance involves b-verses which would have been disallowed in classical Old English verse. The implication of these observations, I believe, is that for this poet, at least, the proliferation of forms allowed in the late poetic tradition is brought under a degree of control by a general principle of balance within the full line.

But there are also other ways in which the forms employed in this poem are poetically effective. The rhyming catalogue passage from early in the poem is especially remarkable:

> and sume mislice ofsloh,
> sume hi man wið feo sealde,   sume hreowlice acwealde,
> sume hi man bende,   sume hi man blende,
> 10   sume hamelode,   sume hættode.

Here, lines 7 and 8 each pair two-stress verses, while lines 9 and 10 pair one-stress verses: this passage is especially balanced. But at the same time, each line is conspicuously shorter than the last, while the poem's weakest rhyme (line 7) is followed by a line with pure rhyme, followed by two lines with both rhyme and alliteration. In short, throughout this 'sume-catalogue,' the linking devices become progressively more effective, while the lines and verses themselves grow shorter. It is hard not to read this as a formal 'tightening' of verses, lines, and links, providing a nice formal parallel to the tightening bonds and other tortures dispensed by Godwine and his men.

The poet of The Death of Alfred also has a fine ear for paronomastic connections, where the phonological similarity of words hints at an etymological or semantic connection.[9] The paronomastic links between 'dæd' and 'gedon' (line 11) and between 'wurðlice' and 'wyrð' (line 23) are, perhaps, neither subtle nor especially effective, but in lines 13-14, the paronomastic effects of 'gelyfenne'/'leofan' and 'blission'/'bliðe' certainly seem to heighten the power of the lines.

In the end, then, our reading of The Death of Alfred is certainly improved by understanding the possibilities and structures of the late Old English verse form. The poet uses complex linking strategies while also, it seems, employing metrical structures for poetic effects. Likewise, the poet continues a long-standing tradition in Old English verse of employing paronomasia. Rather than simply being an example of 'late "debased" Old English verse,' as McIntosh has described it, The Death of Alfred works on its own terms as a poem, written in a system decidedly different from the classical verse system, but a poetic system, nevertheless. An understanding of that system is crucial to even a preliminary understanding of The Death of Alfred's poetics.

In the context of The Death of Alfred, it is worthwhile to turn our attention to the Chronicle's 1086 poem, William the Conqueror, preserved

only in the Peterborough manuscript, although almost certainly com-
posed before 1100:

```
        castelas he let wyrcean.   7 earme men swiðe swencean.      Sxx/(x)SSx        (x)SxS/SxSx
        Se cyng wæs swa swiðe stearc.   7 benam of his underþeoddan man
                                                                 (x)Sxx/SxS        (xx)S/(xx)SxxxS
        manig marc goldes.   7 ma hundred punda seolfres.        Sx/SSx            (x)SSx/SxSx
        Ðet he nam be wihte.   7 mid mycelan unrihte             (xx)Sx/Sx         (xx)Sxx/SSx
  5     of his landleode,   for litte[l]re neode.                xx/SSx            x/SxxSx
        he wæs on gitsunge befeallan.   7 grædinesse he lufode mid ealle.
                                                                 xx/(x)SxxxSx      (x)Sxxx/(x)SxxxSx
        he sætte mycel deorfrið.   7 he lægde laga þær wið.      (x)SxSx/SS        (xx)SxSx/SS
        þæt swa hwa swa sloge heort oððe hinde.   þæt hine man sceolde blendian.
                                                                 (xxxx)Sx/SxxSx    (xxxx)Sx/Sxxx
        he forbead þa heortas.   swylce eac þa baras.            xx/SxSx           xx/(xx)Sx
 10     swa swiðe \he/ lufode þa headeor.   swilce he wære heora fæder.[10]
                                                                 (xxxx)Sxx/(x)Sx   (xxx)xx/(xx)Sx
        Eac he sætte be þam haran.   þæt heo mosten freo faran.  (xx)Sx/(xx)Sx     (xx)Sx/SSx
        his rice men hit mændon.   7 þa earme men hit beceorodan.(x)SxS/(x)Sx      (xx)SxS/(xx)Sxx
        Ac he [wæs] swa stið.   þæt he ne rohte heora eallra nið.xx/(x)SS          (xxx)Sx/(xx)SxS
        ac hi moston mid ealle   þes cynges wille folgian        (xx)Sx/(x)Sx      (x)SxSx/Sxx
 15     gif hi woldon libban.   oððe land habban.                xx/SxSx           xx/SSx
        land oððe eahta.   oððe wel his sehta.                   Sxx/Sx            xx/SxSx
        Wala wa.   þæt ænig man sceolde modigan swa.             SxS               (xxxx)Sx/SxxS[11]
        hine sylf upp ahebban.   7 ofer ealle men tellan.        xx/SxxSx          (x)xx/(xx)SSx
        Se ælmihtiga God   cyþæ his saule mildheortnisse.        (x)SSxx/S         SxxSx/SxSx
 20     7 do him his synna   forgifenesse.                       (x)Sx/(x)Sx       SSx/Sx
```
                                        (Plummer, 1:200; my lineation) [12]

In terms of the forms of individual verses, this poem allows us to see
just how far late Old English verse could depart from the standards of
classical Old English poetry. Rhyme (perhaps including inflectional
rhyme: e.g., lines 1 and 12) almost entirely supplants alliteration as the
primary poetic device for connecting half-lines, although such exten-
sive use of rhyme should probably be seen as idiosyncratic rather than
typical.[13] Rhyme, it should be noted, may even link full lines, rather
than half-lines (19-20).[14] But note also that alliteration is far from aban-
doned in *William the Conqueror*. In lines 3, 5–6, 8–9, 12, 15, and 19, allit-
erative linking works across the caesura; in lines 1–2, 7, 11, and 17, we
see AA-, BB-, or AABB-alliteration as well: thirteen of the twenty lines
here have functional alliteration in the late verse style, and at least
eight lines have both rhyme and alliteration.[15] While rhyme is surely
the most outstanding formal feature of this poem, we should also be
careful to note the poem's extensive use of both types of linkage.

It might well be worth noting in terms of poetics that the line with the
greatest metrical problem here (line 17) exhibits both AABB-alliteration

and verse rhyme. It is tempting to hypothesize that the alliteration and rhyme function to counteract the problems caused by the unusual or unmetrical trisyllabic a-line. We might note as well the dense use of alliterative and rhyming effects in lines 5–8 (all rhyming lines, where lines 5, 6, and 8 also have alliterative linking acorss the caseura). Line 7 has both BB-alliteration and one of the most remarkable rhymes in the poem, where the two syllables of the compound 'deorfrið' are rhymed with 'þær wið.' Line 8 has not only linking alliteration (between 'sloge' and 'sceolde') but also double alliteration on 'h-' in the a-line. Such a concentration of effects is remarkable, and I believe we should conclude that the *William the Conqueror* poet was deeply concerned to use these formal possibilities. The beauty or power of such effects has rarely been appreciated, however, because of a lack of understanding of the form.

In the alliterative works of Ælfric, too, we can find numerous similar passages that move beyond merely competent versifying into the realm of powerful and effective poetry, passages where the formal features of the compositions become a contributing factor to both their meaning and their effect. A nice example of one such passage can be found at the end of Ælfric's *The Life of Oswald*:

	Eft se halga Cuðberht, þa þa he git cnapa wæs,	xx/SxSx	xx/(xx)SxS
280	geseah hu Godes ænglas feredon Aidanes sawle,	(x)Sx/SxSx	Sxx/SxxSx[16]
	þæs halgan bisceopes, bliðe to heofenum	x/SxSx	Sx/(x)Sxx
	to þan ecan wuldre þe he on worulde geearnode.	xx/SxSx	(xxx)Sxx/(x)Sxx
	Þæs halgan Oswoldes ban wurdon eft gebroht	(x)Sx/SxxS	xx/SxS
	æfter manegum gearum to Myrcena lande	xx/SxxSx	x/SxxSx
285	into Gleawceastre, and God þær geswutelode	xx/SSx	(x)Sx/(x)Sxxx
	oft fela wundra þurh þone halgan wer.	S/SxSx	x/(xx)SxS
	Sy þæs wuldor þam Ælmihtigan a to worulde. Amen.	(xx)Sx/(x)SSxx	Sx/Sxx
			(Needham 42)[17]

Of these nine lines, it is remarkable to note that no fewer than five feature 'cross alliteration' (lines 280–3 and 287), including a remarkable stretch of four consecutive lines.[18] Such a dense use of secondary alliteration is exceptional, even in the classical verse tradition, although (as I have argued elsewhere) classical verse does sometimes make use of such ornamental effects.[19]

Godden, of course, has suggested that 'one of the functions of [Ælfric's alliterative] style was evidently to produce a concluding flourish' citing the final paragraphs and doxologies from a handful of the *Catholic Homilies* (*Introduction* xxxvi). In *The Life of Oswald*, where the alliterative 'style' is used throughout, a similar concluding rhetorical flourish is here provided by the use of ornamental secondary alliteration. A comparable use of secondary poetic effects occurs, I believe, at the end of the classical poem *The Order of the World*: Ælfric's use of poetic effects here corresponds to that found within the classical tradition.[20] Here, then, we see Ælfric employing the possibilities of the form for literary effect, in a manner paralleled within the classical poetic tradition. And given the connections drawn between Ælfric's forms and late Old English verse forms, it seems likely that Ælfric here drew on the poetic tradition.

Because Ælfric (like other late Old English poets) makes less use of poetic compounding than classical verse, the *Lives of Saints* feature fewer of the sorts of figurative and imaginative effects we associate with classical compounds. Of course, this should not be taken as evidence that Ælfric's works are comparatively prosaic: in the passage from the end of *The Life of Oswald* quoted above, the 'rhetorical flourish' resulting from the extensive use of cross alliteration does have a powerful poetic effect.[21] Not only does the density of the alliteration itself insist on a series of powerful imaginative links (epsecially in lines 281–2), but the 'interlace' effect of cross alliteration, which involves two alliterative links across the caesura, suggests a formal wholeness or completeness, a tidying up of loose ends, that is eminently appropriate for both concluding doxologies and for the final movement of a poem.

In other passages, Ælfric sometimes seems to use alliteration for a different kind of poetic effect, as in the following passage from the second homily in Pope's *Supplementary Collection*:

220	(God ge)sceop his gesceafta on syx dagum ealle,	SxS/(xx)Sx	(x)SSx/Sx
	and geswac (on þone) seofoþan, swa þæt he syþþan ne gesceop		
		(xx)S/(xxx)Sxx	xx/(x)SxxxS
	nane oþre gesceafta, ac þa sylfan geedniwað	xx/SxxSx	(xx)Sx/(x)SSx
	on mannum and on nytenum mihtiglice oþ þis.	(x)Sx/(xx)Sxx	Sxxx/(x)S
	He gesceop þa twegen men, and (ealle tida gesette,)	(xx)Sx/SxS	(x)xx/SxxSx
225	ac he ne gesceop na syþþan seldcuþe (gesceafta,	xx/(xx)SxSx	SSx/(x)Sx
	of þam ealdan) dihte þe he æt fruman gesette;	xx/SxSx	xx/(x)SxxSx
	ac he gescipð ælce dæge edniwe sawla	(xxx)S/SxSx	SSx/Sx
	and on lichaman geliffæst, (swa swa we leorniað) on bocum,	(xx)SSx/(x)SS	xx/(x)SxxxSx
	and þa sawla ne beoð na(hwær gesceapene	xx/SxxS	Sx/(x)Sxx
230	æ)r þan þe God hi asent to þam gesceape(nan lichama[n]	xx/(x)SxxS	(xxx)Sxx/SSx
	on he)ora moddra innoþum, and hi swa men (wurþað.)	x/(xx)SxSxx	xx/(x)SSx

(Pope, *Supplementary Collection* 1:240)[22]

The remarkable nature of this passage is clarified when we recall that Ælfric allows 's-' and 'sc-' to alliterate with one another, an alliterative peculiarity that is shared with the late Old English poets in general, but perhaps especially with the author of *The Metrical Psalms*. Ælfric also shares with the *Psalms* poet a tendency to use the same alliterating sound in a sequence of lines: eight of Ælfric's twelve lines in this passage have primary alliteration on the 's' sound.[23] In three lines (220, 221, and 225) there are four syllables alliterating on this sound, and three lines (222, 224, and 227) have cross alliteration. The only line in the passage without alliteration linking its verses (226) has 'gesette' on its final stressed position, and both the preceding and following lines have s-alliteration (the preceding with four 's-' words; the following with cross alliteration).

Such an extensive use of alliteration on a single sound, combined with 'quadruple' alliteration and cross alliteration is, from a purely statistical perspective, most probably intentional. Ælfric here uses alliteration to lend poetic and rhetorical power to this narrative of the Creation. The fact that similar extended passages using a single alliterating sound were used in *The Metrical Psalms* may suggest a possible source for Ælfric's alliterative usage here; once again, however, such a circumstance (as with the coalliteration of 's-' and 'sc-') suggests that Ælfric does indeed use late Old English poetic models for his own practice.

For a final example, we can look at the form and effect of Ælfric's first alliterative paragraph from *The Life of Edmund*:

Eadmund se eadiga Eastengla cynincg	SS/(x)Sxx	SSx/Sx
wæs snotor and wurðful. and wurðode symble	x/SxxSx	x/SxxSx
15 mid æþelum þeawum þone ælmihtigan god.	x/SxxSx	(xx)SSxx/S
He wæs ead-mod. and geþungen. and swá an-ræde þurh-wunode		
	(xx)SS/(xx)Sx	(xx)SSx/(x)Sxx[24]
þæt he nolde abugan to bysmorfullum leahtrum.	xx/SxxSx	x/SxxxSx
ne on naþre healfe he ne ahylde his þeawas.	xx/SxxSx	xx/(x)SxxSx
ac wæs symble gemyndig þære soþan lare	xx/SxxSx	xx/SxSx
20 [gif] þu eart to heafod-men ge-set. ne ahefe þu ðe.	xx/(xx)SxxxS	xx/SxxS
ac beo betwux mannum swa swa an man of him.	xx/(xx)Sx	xx/(x)SxS
He wæs cystig wædlum and widewum swa swa fæder.	xx/SxSx	(x)Sxx/(xx)Sx
and mid wel-willendnysse gewissode his folc	(xx)S/SxSx	x/SxxxS
symle to riht-wisnysse and þam reþum styrde.	Sx/(x)SSxx	xx/SxSx
25 and gesæliglice leofode on soþan geleafan.	(xx)Sxxx/Sxx	x/SxxSx

(Skeat, *Lives of Saints* 2:314–16)[25]

Here, an intense concentration of various sorts of wordplay and alliterative emphasis combine for a powerful rhetorical effect, precisely at the beginning of the alliterative passage. Twice (lines 13 and 16) Ælfric reuses the morpheme 'ead-' from Edmund's name, and three of the first four lines share vocalic alliteration, the first line having four alliterating syllables. The second line (the only one of the first four without vocalic alliteration) has cross alliteration, as do the two final lines of the paragraph. Consecutive alliteration also appears twice in the final four lines, and three consecutive verses (23a–4a) may be linked by rhyme (on the syllables '-nysse,' '-wissode,' and '-nysse'; we might recall the possible rhyme on similar syllables in *William the Conqueror* 19-20). Paronomasia is probably to be understood in lines 14, 20, and 25; a further paronomastic linkage probably connects the words 'geþungen' and 'þeawas' in lines 15, 16, and 18. Together, these features of wordplay and formal sound patterning give the passage a poetic feeling of artistic wholeness and linguistic density.

What these examples from Ælfric suggest, I believe, is that the late Old English verse tradition provides the most appropriate sort of context for understanding the various sorts of sound patterning and word play used by Ælfric. In this sense, the comparative and contextual evidence gathered here serves as a valuable confirmation of the surprising conclusion drawn in chapter 3.2 that Ælfric's rhythmical works appeared to operate on the same metrical principles as late Old English verse. Indeed, intense alliterative patterning is at least occasionally seen in both Ælfric's works and in a poem like *William the Conqueror*, just as effective uses of paronomasia are found in both Ælfric and *The Death of Alfred*. Both of these poems from the *Chronicle*, of course, postdate Ælfric's compositions, but it seems appropriate to say that the poetic similarities identified here (especially considering the metrical similarities) support the likelihood that Ælfric and the *Chronicle* poets were working within a continuing poetic tradition.[26]

But further, it is important to recognize that these late works were anything but poetically clumsy or 'debased.' While the poets of these works clearly did not obey the rules of classical Old English verse, they were, nevertheless, poets capable of exploiting the possibilities of their form for their own ends. It is in these kinds of examples that we see where the failure of metricists to understand the form of these works has had its most powerful consequences: by not addressing these works on their own terms as poems, literary readers as well as metricists have failed to appreciate their artistry through a simple failure to appreciate their form. An improved understanding of late Old English verse has the potential to open up a new world of Anglo-Saxon poetic expression for modern readers.

Layamon and Early Middle English Verse

It has long been supposed that Layamon's verse form descended from the alliterative genres of the late Old English period.[1] Older scholarship from the twentieth century tended to hypothesize a popular tradition of late Old English verse from which early Middle English verse descended. N.F. Blake has usefully summarized this line of thinking: 'There was a popular poetry which has not survived as well as the extant poetry which is literary [and] it was from this type of poetry that the early Middle English poets, particularly Laʒamon, learned their craft' (118). Blake, however, imagined an alternative genealogy, based upon the observation that 'the popular poetry is invented to explain Laʒamon's *Brut*; its existence is assumed from the continuity of the alliterative tradition' (118). Rather than invoking a largely hypothetical 'popular' verse tradition, Blake identified the alliterative works of Ælfric as a more plausible ancestor to the early Middle English alliterative poetry, sidestepping the question of how 'rhythmical prose' could influence verse by inventing a new taxonomic category: 'rhythmical alliteration.' More recently, Blake's interpretation of this line of descent has been powerfully seconded by Stephen Brehe.[2]

My position, of course, is that Ælfric's works – along with other late Old English poems – were in fact a powerful influence on the works of Layamon and his contemporaries, either as direct sources or as ancestors in a shared tradition; the difference is sometimes quite difficult to sort out, although in chapter 4.2 I will at least attempt to do so. But, crucially, Ælfric's works influenced early Middle English not through some notion of 'rhythmical alliteration' but through their essential identity as poetic works; other late Old English poems (possibly including some that no longer survive) may have been equally influential on Layamon and his contemporaries. In this chapter, I will attempt a description of the rules operative in Layamon's *Brut* (and, by extension, in other poems with similar metrical forms, such as *The Soul's Address to the Body* or *The Proverbs of Alfred*). And just as the rules for late Old English verse seem to have clearly derived from the rules of classical Old English verse, the early Middle English rules discussed here can be seen as an evolutionary development from the late Old English verse described above in chapter 3.1.

Before beginning my description, however, it is important to note that several problems must accompany any effort to address the metre of the *Brut*. First, the very length of the *Brut* means that just about anything one looks for can be found, from hyper-short three-syllable verses to lines with the most complicated sorts of linkings imaginable, such as a line with linking alliteration across the caesura *and* with (additional) AABB-alliteration *and* with rhyme (e.g., line 2326). The task of the metricist attempting to describe Layamon's metre, then, becomes identifying the rules that account for his normal and typical verses, rather than trying to deal with every single one of his (sometimes clearly exceptional) verses and lines. But in addition, I believe, we must recognize that any attempt to describe the metre of Layamon's *Brut* is fraught with a further uncertainty, since there may well be three sets of metrical understandings at work: that of Layamon himself, and those of the Caligula and Otho scribes.[3] To take just one example of possible conflicts among these understandings, we might consider the following corresponding passages from the two manuscripts:

þa he bezst wende to halden his lond.~
þa hafde Hengest hit an his hond.   (Caligula manuscript, ll. 7189–90)[4]

The corresponding passage in the Otho manuscript is markedly different:

þo he best wende .~   to holde his cunde.
þo hadde hit þe cwene.~   and Hengest imene.
(Otho manuscript, ll. 7189–90)[5]

Although Brook and Leslie print the Caligula version as two lines, the scribe's pointing (and the alliteration and rhyme) seem to suggest that it is either intended as or interpreted as a single line, while the Otho version is pointed (and printed) as two poetic lines. Which version might represent Layamon's intended text is very far from clear; it is possible, of course, that neither version is Layamon's.[6]

In a number of other cases, we can usefully compare single verses from Caligula and Otho, as in the following examples:

Caligula verse	Otho verse
6210b: lette beoden his ferde uorð-riht	6210b: bed his ferde forþriht
6460a: Lauer[d] king cum uorð-riht	6460a: Louerd king forþ-riht
6901b: ne sæh ich nauere ær swulche cnihtes	6901b: ne seh ich soche cnihtes
12970a: and þa six swin he gon æten alle	12970a: and alle þe six swin he eat
13096a: þe oðer hehte Beof <of> Oxene-uord	13096a: þe oþer was Beofs of Oxeneford
13096b: welle wide sprong þæs eorles word	13096b: wele wide sprang his word
13101a: Þe king nom þas þreo cnihtes hende	13101a: Þ(o) .... nam þis cnihtes hen(de)
13789a: Riwadðlan braid ut his sweord sone	13789a: Ridwalþan his sweord droh

In these examples (and more can be found), verses that might demand scansion with five stresses in the Caligula manuscript are presented as four-stress verses (or, in some cases, as three-stress verses) in the Otho manuscript.[7] Do we have here a case where the Otho scribe has 'shortened' verses due to a perception that five-stress verses are unmetrical? If so, then we probably ought to conclude that Layamon at least allowed occasional five-stress verses himself, and the Otho scribe's sense of metre differed from Layamon's.[8] But it may also be possible that, in these cases, the Caligula scribe has lengthened verses to a degree that Layamon would have found unmetrical (and thus the Caligula scribe's sense of metre differed from Layamon's). Once again, choosing between these alternatives may be impossible. The metrical divergences between the Otho and Caligula versions are so extensive that many more such examples could be brought forth; there can be little certainty that describing the metre of either manuscript's version of the poem will describe the metre employed by Layamon.

Nevertheless, it seems that an attempt to describe Layamon's verse ought to be made. In the remainder of this chapter, I will make such an attempt, using a formalism parallel to and deriving from the formalism used in other sections of this book. Specifically, my formalism directly derives from that used in the analysis of late Old English metre presented in chapter 3.1; to this degree, I also claim that Layamon's verse form derives directly from the verse forms of preceding centuries. Finally, however, because of the clearly exceptional nature of some of Layamon's verses and lines, I will admit that the system described below will not, in fact, serve to scan all of Layamon's verses: but it does seem likely that such a system underlies the basics of Layamon's form.[9]

MEP1. Either alliteration or rhyme normally links half-lines together into lines.

Already during the postclassical Old English period, rhyme could substitute for alliterative linking. In the early Middle English alliterative verse used by Layamon, this substitution is actually quite common. For a more detailed account, see MEVC1.

MEP2. Metrical verses are formed by simple rules for combining metrical feet.

This 'simplicity' rule merely attempts to codify the notion that a useful metrical system (such as that which allowed Layamon to compose over 16,000 lines of verse) must not be of excessively high complexity. The idea of metrical feet appears to be inherited from postclassical verse, although the particular forms of feet differ (see MEFS1).

MEP3. Metrical feet are derived from the syllabic patterns of stressed words.

This rule is actually parallel in form and content to the classical Old English P3, although no such rule could cover the variety of metrical feet observable in late Old English verse. As such, this rule represents the primary conceptual simplification which took place as late Old English verse evolved into early Middle English verse.

Foot Structure Rules

MEFS1: There are four 'stressed-feet'; they can be listed as:

S, Sx, Sxx, and Sxxx.

Compound words (including lengthy proper names) are frequently scanned as two S-feet, but if they are short enough, they may also be scanned as a single foot, depending on the metrical circumstances. Alliteration on secondary elements confirms the possibility of scanning compounds on two feet. There are no 'x-feet' in early Middle English verse; the verse-combination rules indicate that unstressed words and syllables generally fit into verses in extrametrical positions (see below).

Generally, metrically stressed elements are words of high semantic import (nouns, adjectives, adverbs, and many verbs) and unstressed elements are generally conjunctions, prepositions, determiners, pronouns, and some common adverbs (e.g., 'þa'). Some adjectives, for example, may be variably stressed (e.g., 'muchel'; cardinal numbers), and many finite verbs and adverbs seem to be similarly variable.[10] Words which are linguistically unstressed may undergo metrical stressing (as in the earlier verse systems), and thus even words of very low semantic value may be stressed at the end of a verse, as in the following:

Brut 10321: 7 þere weoren mid him.	(xxx)Sx/(x)S	(rhyme with 'Colgrim')[11]
Brut 11740a: Leouere me. weore.~	Sxx/(x)Sx	(rhyme with 'neore')
Brut 417b: al þat him beforen wes.	(xxxx)Sx/S	(alliteration on 'f')

The foot-combination rules ensure that the final elements in these verses receive metrical stress, regardless of their 'natural' stress categories.[12]

Foot Combination Rules

MEFC1: Metrical verses may have from one to four S-positions.

Generally, previous attempts to scan early Middle English verse have taken the two-stress verse as a given (Oakden, Friedlander, Cable). There seems to be little or no motivation to do so, however, except to preserve this feature of Sieversian formalism. Three-stress verses are, in fact, very common in the *Brut*, and they can be easily derived from post-classical Old English forms (as above).[13] Four-stress verses in Layamon are somewhat rarer, but it seems clear that they must be allowed (see examples in the essay by Noble and also in Brehe, 'Reassembling').[14]

At least one verse-type seems to have been allowed by this rule in early Middle English alliterative verse that was probably unmetrical in late Old English verse: verses that end in a series of stressed (mono)syllables, such as (xx)S/S/S. It would seem that such verses were possibly allowed in late Old English verse, but they are rare in that tradition, since the classical ancestors of such verses would have compound words in the final two syllables.[15] Nevertheless, such verses do appear in Layamon, perhaps most frequently in verses like the following:

Brut 1397b: þat þe king dead lai.   (alliteration on 'k' and rhyme)[16]

Another verse type excluded from late Old English verse but present in Layamon involves three trisyllabic stressed sequences within a single verse. These verses, too, are somewhat uncommon, but there are clear examples, as in the following cases:

Brut 5503a: 7 Custance hauede Ælene
Brut 8303a: auere he hatede Ierusalem
Brut 14809b: þene stude he cleopede Cernele
Brut 15293b: he warnede æuere Ædwine king

These verses, although rare, appear to support the claim that Layamon's verse form does indeed differ from late Old English verse, because these verses cannot be scanned as having two metrical feet (as defined for late Old English). Instead, it seems appropriate to scan each of the trisyllabic items as a separate S-foot, and to scan with three S-positions in a verse (or, in cases such as *Brut* 15293b, with four S-positions).[17]

MEFC2: Metrical verses must have at least four syllables.

This rule remains unchanged from classical Old English verse to early Middle English verse.[18] Cable notes that four-syllable verses are very frequent in classical Old English verse but rare in Layamon (*Alliterative Tradition*); this observation only shows what we should expect, since it is not especially surprising to find that the shortest possible and longest possible verse-forms are both relatively rare in this system. The classical Old English system, operating on completely different principles, accommodated four-syllable verses easily and frequently; the rule stated here merely defines four-syllable verses as metrical for early Middle English as well. The rarity of such short verses in Layamon's *Brut* is probably best understood as a consequence of their status as the theoretical minimum.

MEFC3: Extrametrical syllables are allowed before each foot.

This rule is essentially unchanged from the corresponding late Old English rule. It appears that extrametrical sequences may be as long as five syllables, although such sequences are relatively rare. Long extrametrical sequences are most frequent before the first foot; verses rarely have more than one extrametrical sequence longer than two or three syllables. Note that the allowable positions for extrametrical syllables result in (or, at least, are related to) the assignment of metrical stress to the final word of any verse, as indicated above.

Verse Combination Rules

MEVC1: Alliteration can link any two S-positions in the two verses of a full

*line. Rhyme (as in late Old Engish verse, including any types of phonetic rep-
etition exclusive of the initial consonant or consonant cluster in stressed sylla-
bles)[19] may link final S-positions of two verses in a line ('verse rhyme').[20] Lines
may be linked by alliteration, rhyme, or both. AA-, BB-, and AABB-alliteration
are all allowed. Occasionally, full lines have neither rhyme nor alliteration.*

As should be clear, the specifics of how rhyme and alliteration work in
Layamon are virtually identical to how rhyme and alliteration worked
in late Old English verse, as described above in chapter 3.1. Although
Layamon's rhymes often strike modern ears as unusual or even
unlikely, virtually all of the types of rhyme he employs are paralleled
in late Old English poems such as *William the Conqueror* and *The Death
of Alfred* and on the Sutton Brooch. Likewise, the fact that alliteration
links any two positions (often including AA- or BB-alliteration) while
rhyme must be verse rhyme is clearly paralleled in the late Old English
verse tradition. The foot-structure and verse-structure rules, then, can
be seen as the major innovations in early Middle English verse; the
verse-linking strategies employed by Layamon and his contemparies
remained largely the same.

It is important to note, however, that rhyme in Layamon does have
some interesting and innovative features, the most important of which
is the fact that, in general, purely inflectional rhyme seems to be non-
functional in the *Brut*. It is somewhat difficult to pin down the issue of
inflectional rhyme, because when the only possible linkage lies in
matching inflections, it may be tempting to label such lines as featuring
inflectional rhyme, but it is also possible that such lines simply have no
linkage at all. Certainly, Layamon does allow some lines without any
sort of linkage. When we can be relatively certain that inflectional syl-
lables do participate in the rhyme, however, they are almost always
paired with syllables that receive full stress, as in the following kinds
of examples:

> *Brut* 2271: he clupede to his dringes: Nu forh nu niðinges.
> *Brut* 4412: 7 eoden to þon kaisere.   þer he wes i þon here.~
> *Brut* 6313: þat is on Latin fuliwis.~   þat me sæið Pax vobis.
> *Brut* 6468; 7 he bah to þan kinge.   alse mon dæð of runinge.~[21]

All of these examples are taken from the Caligula manuscript, but the
pattern seems clear, as the rhymes in these examples are the only possi-
ble linkages (although there may be an alliterative link between 'fuli-
wis' and 'vobis' in *Brut* 6313). Further, rhymes linking 'kaisere' and

'here' are formulaic in Layamon, being used repeatedly, so the likeli-
hood seems to be that all of these are examples of functional rhyme in
the *Brut*. The following examples, however, are somewhat less clear,
although they may feature unstressed or inflectional rhymes:

> *Brut* 17: An-oþer he nom on Latin.~   þe makede Seinte Albin.
> *Brut* 18: 7 þe feire Austin.~   þe fulluht broute hider in
> *Brut* 7030: Þu sæide Hængest.~   cnihten alre fæirest.

Here, alliteration may provide the linkages, but it seems possible that
the rhymes are also functional. The best account of these kinds of
examples, however, seems to relate to the fact that verses of these types
feature proper names, almost without exception. While we might not
be otherwise inclined to scan 'Hængest,' 'Austin,' or 'Albin' as com-
pound words, it seems possible that Layamon could do so, and (if so)
these examples would work identically to those in my first group,
rhyming a stressed syllable with an unstressed syllable. The best candi-
dates for purely inflectional rhyme seem to involve cases like the fol-
lowing:

> *Brut* 3941: 7 swa heo þer boȝeden.~   þe wile þe heo luueden.

Here the rhyme is disyllabic, and we might recall lines such as *Maldon*
42, 'Byrhtnoð maþelode, bord hafenode,' from the late Old English tra-
dition, where disyllabic inflectional rhymes seemed to be allowed.[22]
But it may be the case that such a line as 3941 is simply a line without
a functional link. More work needs to be done, I believe, in sorting out
when such inflectional rhymes can be proved to be effective and func-
tional.

By far, the most important feature of my analysis of Layamon's metre
is its complete abandonment of the principle of two-stress verses. Vir-
tually all of the most influential treatments of Layamon have insisted
on a two-stress model, almost certainly because of Sieversian scansions
of classical Old English poems.[23] The reliance upon the principle of
two-stress verses, I believe, has in fact led to serious misunderstand-
ings of Layamon's method, especially in his use of alliteration and
rhyme. Consider the following passage from near the end of the *Brut*,
where an unnamed messenger proposes a marriage alliance between
Penda and Cadwalan:

ane <u>sus</u>ter he haueð <u>hende</u>.~   in þan <u>æst</u> <u>ende</u>.
nis nan <u>fei</u>rure <u>wif</u>mon.~   þa <u>whit</u> sunne scineð <u>on</u>.
þe king of <u>France</u> <u>Leou</u>wis.~   <u>3irn</u>eð hire ful <u>iwis</u>.

(Caligula manuscript, ll. 15516–18)[24]

Here, I have underlined the syllables that would probably be inter-
preted as stressed in a two-stress system; as such a mark-up indicates,
such a system identifies these lines as rhyming lines with weak rhymes
(because the rhyming syllables in two cases do not match in stress) and
only 15517 has linking alliteration. But in the scansion system I pro-
pose here, we have quite a different understanding of such lines
(again, marking stresses with underlining:

ane <u>sus</u>ter he <u>haue</u>ð <u>hende</u>.~   in þan <u>æst</u> <u>ende</u>.
nis nan <u>fei</u>rure <u>wif</u>mon.~   þa <u>whit</u> <u>sun</u>ne <u>scin</u>eð <u>on</u>.
þe <u>king</u> of <u>France</u> <u>Leou</u>wis.~   <u>3irn</u>eð hire <u>ful</u> <u>iwis</u>.

The first of these three lines can now be seen as having AABB-allitera-
tion in addition to rhyme, while line 15517b shows ornamental double
alliteration that is supplementary to the line's linking rhyme and allit-
eration. Line 15518 now shows both alliteration and rhyme, and the
possibility that 'Leouwis' might be scanned as a compound (see the
discussion of rhymes and names above) opens up the door for a line
with both cross alliteration and rhyme.[25]

As this sort of example suggests (and numerous similar cases could
be found in the *Brut*), the very ways in which we think about Laya-
mon's use of rhyme and alliteration depend upon our scansion system,
and our appreciation of Layamon's artistry might well be altered by
thinking about his metre in new ways. A full reassessment of a major
poem like the *Brut* is, of course, impossible here, but we might look at
the following passage in order to begin such a reassessment. Here,
Arthur taunts Baldulf in a well-known speech:[26]

3urstendæi wes Baldulf.~   cnihten alre baldest.
nu he stant on hulle.~   7 Auene bi-haldeð.
10640   hu ligeð i þan streme.~   stelene fisces.
mid sweorde bi-georede.~   heore sund is awemmed.
heore scalen wleoteð.~   swulc gold-fa3e sceldes.
þer fleoteð heore spiten.~   swulc hit spæren weoren.
Þis beoð seolcuðe þing.~   isi3en to þissen londe.

10645   swulche deor an hulle.~   swulche fisces in wælle.
          ʒurstendæi wes þe kaisere.~   kennest alre kingen.
          ne he is bicumen hunte.~   7 hornes him fulieð.
          flihð ouer bradne wæld.~   beorkeð his hundes.
          he hafeð bihalues Baðen.~   his huntinge bilæfued.
10650   freom his deore he flicð.~   7 we hit scullen fallen.
          and his balde ibeot.~   to nohte ibringen.
          and swa we scullen bruken.~   rihte bi-ʒæten   (ll. 10638–52)[27]

In terms of poetics, this passage is remarkable in a number of ways. Arthur begins with a pair of rhymes on the first element of Baldulf's name, noting that yesterday he was bold, but today he is merely an onlooker ('bi-haldeð'). Then he moves into a series of at least five full lines (10640–4) all linked by alliteration (in both halves of each line) on the 's'-sound, with most of the lines actually alliterating on different s-clusters: 'st-,' 's-,' 'sc-' 'sp-,' and 's-.'[28] Such cluster alliteration is not mandatory in the *Brut*, but (as here) it seems it can be used to heighten the poetic effect (and we might recall that the poet of *Judith* also seemed fond of such cluster alliteration). The s-cluster lines are, significantly, linked thematically, as well as through alliteration, as they together make up Arthur's development of the image of the mail-coated fishes in the stream.

The rhyming line in 10645 follows this development, suggesting that Baldulf, too, is now more closely aligned with the animal kingdom ('swulche deore an hulle') like the steel fishes in the stream. That line is then followed by another group of lines that primarily feature alliteration, including alliterative links between lines. If we tabulate the initial sounds of the stressed syllables in 10646–9, we see the following pattern:

    10646a: ʒ D K   b: K vowel K
    10647a: K H   b: H F
    10648a: F B W   b: B H
    10649a: H H B   b: H L

As such a tabulation reveals, each of the first three b-lines here is alliteratively linked to the following a-line, and we see three sections of three verses each with continued alliteration: 10646a–7a (alliterating on 'k'); 10648a–9a (alliterating on 'b'); and 10648b–9b (alliterating on 'h').[29] The complex alliterative linkages in this section allow Arthur to develop a second comparison, in which Baldulf is now identified as a hunter, first apparently followed by horns and hounds, but ultimately fleeing from his prey – prey that Arthur claims he and his men shall fell. This brings Arthur to his conclusion, in which he returns to b-alliteration (and to punning on Baldulf's name) to note that he will bring Baldulf's 'bald ibeot' to nothing by his victory.[30]

As this analysis makes clear, I believe, Arthur's speech here is remarkably constructed, with different kinds of alliterative sound-play usefully and functionally paralleling the rhetorical structure of the speech. The only truly rhyming line in the passage (10645) provides the linkage between the two movements; the 'steel fishes' section quite appropriately dominated by the sibilant s-alliteration, and the 'hunter' section perhaps equally effectively characterized by the dense and swift alternation and repetition of alliterating sounds. Alliteration on 'b' and punning wordplay on 'bald'/'Baldulf' tie the beginning and end of the speech together. And while not every section of the *Brut* features this degree of attention to issues of poetics, Layamon does at least occasionally reach such heights, and it is only with an appropriate understanding of his metrical practice that we can hope to follow him.

Layamon's Old English Poetics

In his influential study 'Laʒamon's Antiquarian Sentiments,' E.G. Stanley articulates his view of Layamon as an 'archaistic' poet: 'We may wonder if archaizing accords with Laʒamon's sentiments as they emerge from his work: I believe it does. Of course, the wish to archaize is rooted in a love of the archaic; the archaistic is merely imitative of the archaic, and derives from it by a deliberate act of recreation' (25). The mode and methods of Layamon's 'deliberate act of recreation,' however, continue to demand our examination. Recent scholars, indeed, have been inclined to identify the sources of Layamon's verse form in the manuscripts of Old English works. Carolyn VanDyke Friedlander, writing in 1979, suggested that Layamon and his contemporaries were able to imitate certain forms of Old English poetry from observing 'the [OE] manuscripts' skeletal features – two half-lines, each with two stresses, joined into a couplet' (229). More recently, S.K. Brehe, citing Ælfric's so-called rhythmical prose as a source for Layamon, suggests that in Layamon's day, 'Ælfric's alliterative compositions would have been perceived as verse, or as something very close to verse' ('Rhythmical Alliteration' 76). As my arguments throughout this book suggest, of course, I am in general agreement with these scholars that the forms of early Middle English verse descend from those of late Old English verse, including the rhythmical compositions of Ælfric; what I hope to show in this chapter is the degree to which Layamon relied directly on the late Old English verse tradition, including his apparent familiarity with the poems of the *Anglo-Saxon Chronicle*.

In thinking about how Layamon (or other early Middle English poets) might have been influenced by the late Old English verse tradition, we can identify two most likely modes of such influence. On the one hand, we might hypothesize a continuing tradition of versifying, exemplified by poems such as *William the Conqueror, Durham,* and *The Grave,* extending right through the twelfth century until Layamon's time: a living tradition that early Middle English poets simply inherited, as late Old English poets inherited the tradition of classical Old English verse. The relative rarity of surviving examples, however, has often been taken as evidence against this possibility (cf. Blake, 'The popular poetry is invented to explain La3amon's *Brut'* 118). On the other hand, though, we might suppose that Layamon and his contemporaries attempted to 're-invent' Old English poetry (which this line of argument assumes to belong to a moribund tradition), basing their metrical forms on what they could observe of the 'skeletal features' of Old English verse from the manuscript record.

It seems to me, however, that a middle ground must be identified in order to properly place Layamon in context. First, there does appear to me to be some evidence that Layamon practised within a living tradition, even if his archaizing served to announce the degree to which he found that tradition to be distastefully innovative. But second, I think there is solid, if unrecognized, evidence to suggest that Layamon actually did know some works of late Old English verse directly, such as a number of the poems from the *Anglo-Saxon Chronicle.* It is worthwhile to explore both sorts of evidence in some detail.

Layamon and a Living Tradition?

Certainly, one of the most powerful pieces of evidence that there was a continuing tradition of poetic composition in the twelfth century and into the thirteenth lies in the fact that Layamon was not alone in the type of verse he wrote. As many other writers have pointed out, the metrical system used by Layamon also seems to have been used in *The Soul's Address to the Body* and the *First Worcester Fragment,* as well as in the *Proverbs of Alfred* and in portions of the Middle English *Bestiary.* The paucity of clear twelfth-century examples seems to be intriguingly counteracted by this flowering of thirteenth-century poems.[1]

Further, however, it is useful to recall the ways in which the rules for Layamon's verse (as I articulated them in chapter 4.1) seem to have developed in an evolutionary manner from the rules of late Old English verse. In particular, those metrical features of the *Brut* which have been only poorly understood by modern readers are hard to understand as developing out of Layamon's readings of late Old English verse manuscripts. To look at one kind of example, I have suggested that a scansion rule causes the last word of every verse to be stressed, and that such a rule persisted from classical Old English poetry straight through to Layamon. As far as I am aware, no such rule has been clearly expressed by metricists before, and for Layamon to have simply derived it from the evidence available to him seems fairly unlikely. Far more probable is the likelihood that he simply composed in a verse-form familiar to him, where such a rule was implicit.

Other features seem equally hard to understand as having been 'discovered' by Layamon in either classical or late Old English verse, such as the rules for what sorts of phonetic repetition can be used as rhyme, or the rule that extrametrical syllables can precede any foot. Excepting the significant changes to foot-structure and foot-combination rules, the other rules of late Old English verse are reflected too perfectly in Layamon to lend credibility to the hypothesis that Layamon derived them inductively – unless we grant that Layamon must have been a metricist superior to those of the nineteenth and twentieth centuries. Even if we grant that, we would probably justify it by noting that Layamon is closer in time to Old English verse – which is only an advantage, of course, if we assume some sort of poetic continuity, so even this line of argument seems to work out in favour of a continuing poetic tradition.

Further, of course, the activities of the Otho scribe must be noted. Although modern readers have been quick to discount the Otho text as reflecting a rather radical scribal intervention, in which the most interesting formal feature of Layamon's poem, its archaism, has been systematically downplayed, reduced, or edited out, it is necessary to recall that the Otho scribe must have had an operative understanding of metre to accomplish his revision. That is, the existence of the Otho revision suggests how unlikely it was that Layamon was working in a poetic vacuum: Layamon may have wanted to inject a species of Anglo-Saxonism into his work, but the Otho reviser's purpose seems to have been to return the poem to a more familiar form. Because we know that Layamon was interested in archaizing, the Otho text may give us an even clearer picture of the metrical forms current in the early Middle English alliterative tradition than Layamon's own text. At the very least, it clearly seems to suggest that there was indeed a fairly extensive tradition that the Otho reviser could draw upon.

But if there is evidence that can clinch the case for the continuity of the poetic tradition from late Old English verse to Layamon, we might expect it to lie in Layamon's use of poetic formulas derived from Old English. Perhaps because the poetic tradition in the late Old English period was notably less formulaic than classical Old English verse was, however, we find surprisingly few formulas shared by Layamon and Old English poems. But some of the parallels that can be seen do seem significant.

We can note, for example, that Elizabeth Sklar has argued that Layamon's rhymes involving 'broðer' and 'oðer' and those linking 'stunde' with 'wunde,' 'grunde,' or 'sunde' all should be taken to 'suggest that the *Maldon*-poet and Layamon were drawing on common poetic stock' (413). Sklar's argument, however, is weakened by the small number of clear examples she finds; numerous lines in the *Brut* do, indeed, rhyme 'broðer' with 'oðer,' but the rhyme is obvious enough that it need not evidence any continuous tradition: it might simply have been reinvented by Layamon, and by many another poet since then.[2] As far as the actual identity of individual verses, Sklar points only to the following pair:

Mald 271a: æfre embe stunde   *Brut* 3250a: and auer umbe stunde

Certainly, such a pair is remarkable, but more close parallels of this sort are necessary to make the conclusion that Layamon shares a tradition with *Maldon* (or any other late Old English poems) persuasive.

Fortunately, such evidence can be found. J.S.P. Tatlock, for example, has usefully collected what he identifies as 'epic formulas' in the *Brut*, a number of which seem relevant here:

Tatlock's Formulas	OE Examples:
Brut 2697b (etc): daies and nihtes	*Phoen* 147a, 478a; *Beo* 2269a
Brut 873b (etc): fæie þer feollen	*Beo* 1755a; *Brun* 12a.
Brut 7687b (etc): widen 7 siden	at least sixteen examples
Brut 8296a (etc): and he is an hæðene hund	*Jud* 110a

Tatlock only considers as formulas items occurring at least three times in the *Brut*; we might supplement his account with a few less-frequent items:

Brut 2908b ure wine-mæies (also 8783b)   *Mald* 306a: hyra winemagas[3]
Brut 6076b: gumene ælder (also 9263b)   *GenA* 1863b; *Daniel* 548a[4]

Brut 5996b: vnimete wide   PPs 72.5.1b: ungemete swyþe[5]
Brut 446a: Þa ansuereden (4710a; 15767a)   Satan 51a, 673a, 689a

Tatlock, writing in 1923, suggested that, of the formulas he collected, 'none is likely to have been handed down only by poetic tradition, have consciously passed from one poet to another, unless the formula *fæge feollon*' (515). Given the formulas under his consideration, such a conclusion was surely justified, as Tatlock suggests that most of the other examples can be identified as commonplaces of one sort or another. The fact that the Otho scribe eliminates or rewrites all of the Caligula verses with 'wine-mæies' or 'gumene' suggests pretty clearly that these were archaic or archaistic features of Layamon's poem, so they, perhaps, offer little clear evidence on the question of whether Layamon was participating in a living tradition. At least one formulaic verse type, however, may suggest that Layamon's poetic understanding was inherited, rather than invented: Layamon almost exclusively uses the formulaic rhyme-pair 'wide and side' as a b-line, just as it was almost exclusively used as a b-line in Old English poetry.[6] It seems unlikely that Layamon would use 'wide and side' so consistently as a b-line if doing so were not simply traditional.

But as even this example should make clear, the formulaic evidence for a truly living tradition of alliterative verse during Layamon's time is troublingly slim. While a number of verses (and, indeed, repeatedly used verses) in the *Brut* are closely paralleled by verses in the classical and late Old English verse traditions, such verses too frequently seem like commonplace collocations not limited to the realm of verse expression. 'Fæie þer feollen,' may indeed be sufficiently poetic to support the existence of a continuing tradition, and the fact that the Otho scribe preserves this no fewer than four times suggests that this verse was not perceived as troublingly archaic.[7] Likewise, the association of 'wide and side' with the b-line seems likely to be a traditional association, rather than anything else. The evidence of formulas, though slim, nevertheless does support the possibility of continuous and direct metrical development, as it also supports the likelihood of there having been a thirteenth-century tradition known by other poets and by the Otho reviser. However, as I will argue in the following section, Layamon almost certainly did not rely only on this tradition; he also knew at least some Old English poems directly: the poems of the *Anglo-Saxon Chronicle*.

Layamon and the *Chronicle* Poems

Françoise Le Saux's important commentary on Layamon's sources finds precious little, if any, evidence that Layamon directly consulted Old English works of any sort.[8] I believe there is clear evidence, however, that Layamon knew the poems of the *Anglo-Saxon Chronicle*. On the one hand, a surprising number of Layamon's verses are precisely paralleled by verses from poems found in the *Chronicle*, but the most compelling evidence derives from unique (or nearly unique) usages in the *Brut* and passages with clear parallels beyond the level of individual verses.

While there are relatively few of Layamon's verses that can be traced directly to classical Old English exemplars (see the previous section) some of those, as well as a handful of others, can be found in the poems of the *Chronicle*, as the following list suggests.

Verses from Layamon	Related *Chronicle* Verses
Brut 7687b, etc: widen 7 siden	Annal 959DE: wide. 7 side[9]
Brut 873b, etc: fæie þer feollen	*Brun* 12a: fæge feollan
Brut 7823b: cuð hit wes wide[10]	Annal 975DE: Cuð wæs þet wide[11]
Brut 1629b: þe while þe he leouede[12]	Annal 959DE: þa hwile þe he leofode[13]
Brut 12202b: þa him wes icunde	Annal 975DE: swa him wæs gecynde[14]
Brut 14381a: swa alse þe boc us suggeð	*Brun* 68b: þæs þe us secgað bec
Brut 13716a: swa al swa suggeð writen	*CEdg* 14b: þæs ðe gewritu secgað
Brut 906b: Godes wiðer-saka[15]	Annal 975D: Godes wiþærsacan
Brut 7672b: 7 Godes laȝen breken	Annal 975D: Godes lage bræcon
Brut 9310b: þe king wes swiðe steorc[16]	Annal 1086E: Se cyng wæs swa swiðe stearc
Brut 5055b: þat him God uðe.	Annal 1057D: swa him God uðe[17]
Brut 16015b: þurh mihte of ure Drihte	Annal 1067D: mihtigan drihtne[18]

As these examples indicate, the number of verses in the *Brut* that closely parallel recorded Old English verses increases substantially when the *Chronicle* poems are considered. The total number of overlapping verses is still small, no more than a couple of dozen, but in at least one case, the likelihood of direct borrowing is significant. The use of the word 'wiðer-saka' in *Brut* 906b and 6298a is notably archaistic, and the *MED* lists only the *Brut* and two twelfth-century collections of (probably originally Old English) homilies as using this word (Otho keeps this word in 906b, but has no line corresponding to 6298). As the word is one of the words typically considered characteristic of Wulfstan the homilist, it seems probable that Layamon derives it from some Wulfstanian source; given the parallels between other *Brut* verses and other *Chronicle* material, it seems likely that Wulfstan's contribution to annal 975D is Layamon's direct source for this verse.

At the level of the full line (and slightly longer passages) there appears to be additional evidence for Layamon's use of poems from the *Chronicle*. I will address three relatively compelling examples, all involving the *William the Conqueror* poem in annal 1086E; each deserves at least brief comment. The first such parallel is the following:

> *Brut* 14221–2:
>
>   he hehten heom to cume all anan.~   þat wolde lond habben.
>
>   oðer seoluer oðer gold.~   o[ð]er ahte o[ð]er lond[19]
>
> *William the Conqueror*:
>
>   gif hi woldon libban.   oððe land habban
>
>   land oððe eahte.   oððe wel his sehta.[20]

In the passage from the *Brut*, we hear about how Modred coerced his followers to come to him, while the 1086E poem describes how William the Conqueror persuaded his followers to do his bidding. The lexical, syntactic, and contextual parallels are striking, I think, and it seems likely that this is a case of fairly direct influence. A second remarkable parallel occurs in the following passages:

> *Brut* 9796: Wa la wa.~   þat hit sculde iwurðen swa.
>
> ('Alas, alas, that it should happen so.')
>
> *William*: Wala wa.   þæt ænig man sceolde modigan swa.
>
> ('Alas, alas, that any man should [be] so wilful.')

In both poems, the trisyllabic a-line is exceptional. But the combination of the exceptional a-lines with the degree of verbal repetition in the b-lines ('þæt,' 'sceolde,' 'swa') is remarkable enough to, once again, suggest the possibility of a fairly direct relationship. Striking as these two examples are, however, the third such case is even more notable:

> *Brut* 159: he wende to sceoten þat hea der.~   7 ihitte his aȝene fader
>
> ('He went to shoot that stag and hit his own father.')
>
> *William*: swa swiðe 'he' lufode þa headeor.   swilce he wære heora fæder.
>
> ('So greatly he loved the stags, as if he were their father.')

Here the only parallels are the rhyme words, but they themselves are quite remarkable. 'Heahdeor' for 'stag' is not a common word in Old

English (Bosworth-Toller lists two examples, including this one), and it is even rarer in Middle English, with the passage from the *Brut* being the only cited example in the *MED* (Otho has 'he wend. sceote an deor'). The rhyme itself (involving a compound and a simplex) is unusual enough to raise doubt, I think, about whether this can be anything but a direct borrowing. Taken together with the two preceding passages of parallels between the *Brut* and *William the Conqueror*, I think we have sufficient similarities to conclude that there is a direct relationship.[21]

Three further passages from the *Brut* seem to explicitly invoke books of history as providing the basis for superlative historical comparisons, as I have discussed elsewhere in relation to *The Battle of Brunanburh*, *The Death of Alfred*, and the *Chronicle* poem in annal 979DE (*Textual Histories* 101–6, 110–11). It is useful to quote each of these:

> *Brut* 10313–14: Nis hit a nare boc idiht.~   þat æuere weore æi fiht.
> inne þissere Bruttene.~   þat balu weore swa riue.[22]
> *Brut* 13716–17: Swa al swa suggeð writen.~   þæ witeʒe idihten.
> þat wes þat þridde mæste uiht.~   þe auere wes here idiht.[23]
> *Brut* 15576–8: nas hit nauere isæid.~   no on bocken irad.~
> þat æuer ær weore.~   æi swa muchel ferde.
> æuere in Ængelonde.~   þurh ænie king to-gadere.[24]

The use of books as authorizing such historical comparisons is one of the most striking historiographic features of the *Chronicle* poems as a group, and it seems very possible that Layamon has adopted this strategy from the *Chronicle*. Le Saux discusses the second of these passages in some detail in her examination of the 'triadic' passages in the *Brut* that have sometimes been seen as being due to Welsh influence. In particular, Le Saux suggests that a somewhat complicated Welsh textual history may underlie the 'very gross error' (150) by which *Brut* 13717 suggests that Arthur's battle with Luces took place 'here.' A simpler explanation, I believe, may lie in the fact that this historiographic strategy in the *Chronicle* (and in the other two examples from the *Brut*) is always associated with some explicit reference to the island of Britain (and in *The Death of Alfred* 12b, 'her' is explicitly used). That is, while the 'triadic' nature of this passage is undeniable, the error involved in 'here' may result from an essentially formulaic association between the historical superlative and British or English events.

A final example of apparent borrowing from or reference to the

Chronicle appears in the following extended passage where Vortimer describes his father Vortigerne and his policies; the key portions come near the beginning and end of the passage:

> Vortigerne hehte ure fader.~   him uulieð unrædes.
> He hafð ibroh[t] i þis lond.~   hæðene leoden.
> ...
> 7 hæðene laȝen.~   luuede to swiðe.
> þa we sculleð sceonien.~   þa while þa we luuien.
>
> (*Brut* ll. 7402–3, 7420–1; Caligula version)[25]

A number of verbal parallels suggest that Vortimer's negative characterization of his father's tolerance of heathen peoples and customs is based on the similar condemnation of Edgar in the 959DE *Chronicle* poem:

> Ane misdæda he dyde þeah <u>to swiðe</u>.
> *þæt* he ælþeodige un sida <u>lufode</u>.
> 7 <u>hæðene</u> þeawas,   <u>innan þysan lande,</u>
> <u>gebrohte</u> to fæste.   (Plummer 1:115; abbreviation expanded)[26]

For ease of comparison, I have underlined the items in the *Chronicle*-text that seem to correspond to those in Vortimer's speech. Further, the final verse in the *Brut* passage, 'þa while þa we luuien' seems to be a clear formulaic variation of a verse from earlier in 959DE, 'þa hwile þe he leofode,' a verse used twice in the *Chronicle* poems and (as noted above) used at least five other times in the *Brut*.[27] While the lexical similarities may not be precise enough to prove the relationship beyond a shadow of a doubt, they are nevertheless striking, especially given the contextual similarities involved, in that in both cases we are told of kings' problematically accepting actions in relation to heathen peoples and practices. When the other sorts of evidence for a relationship between the *Chronicle* poems and the *Brut* are taken into account, it does seem likely that Layamon here borrowed some of his phrasing from the the portions of the 959DE poem that were on a similar topic.

In the end, I believe there are important similarites between the *Brut* and the *Chronicle* poems at a variety of levels. We have seen examples of individual rare words, unusual rhymes, and full-verse formulas shared between the two, as well as parallels in phrasing at the level of the full line. Both the *Chronicle* poems and the *Brut* share the historiographic strategy of making superlative historical comparisons by direct reference to the authority of books, and Vortimer's speech seems to echo Wulfstan's 959DE poem about Edgar. With such a variety of lexical, formulaic, historiographic, and contextual parallels, I believe the case is secure for identifying the *Chronicle* poems as a direct source for Layamon.

The identification of the *Chronicle* poems as a source for Layamon is surprising in some ways (especially since no one seems to have noticed a link before), but in other ways it is exactly what we should have expected from a poet interested in both history and in archaic English verse. Although the *Chronicle* would have provided little British history to Layamon, it is natural, perhaps, to suspect that he would have consulted the *Chronicle* during his researches, and he would have found poems there that would almost certainly have caught his attention, especially given his apparent wish to archaize his own poem. Surely it is also worth noting that (with the exceptions of *Cædmon's Hymn* and *Bede's Death Song*), the *Chronicle* poems are our best examples of widely distributed (and hence widely read) poems from the Old English period; in this respect, too, they are the mostly likely candidates to have reached and influenced Layamon.

For my purposes in this book, it is especially important to note that Layamon seems to have, in fact, identified the late Old English *Chronicle* poems as poems. Of equal importance is the observation that, unburdened by any Sieversian notions of scansion, Layamon seems to have borrowed more extensively from examples of late Old English verse in the *Chronicle* than from the *Chronicle*'s classical poems. If my list of verse-parallels above has any validity, he apparently recognized verse in annals corresponding to the surviving annals 959DE, 975D, 1057D, 1067D, and 1086E. This recognition, then, stands as corroborative evidence for my analysis of these same works as verse: Layamon's use of these works confirms that they were, in fact, perceived as poems, at least by this thirteenth-century reader.

It is, I believe, appropriate to conclude my work on early English metre and poetics here, as Layamon's use of material from the *Chronicle* poems confirms what so many scholars have long asserted: that his antiquarian archaizing was designed to give his work a specifically Anglo-Saxon flavour. To the degree that he was successful we might identify Layamon as the last Old English poet: an important part of his poetic expression derived from the attempt (at least sometimes successful) to literally use the language and forms of Old English poetry. Further, I believe I have also suggested a clear genealogy for his verse-form in general, a direct descendent of the late Old English verse used from the mid-tenth century to the end of the Anglo-Saxon period. In a very real sense, my project in this book has been simultaneously a reassessment of Old English metrical form and a reassessment of early English literary history. As I hope to have suggested here, a detailed investigation of both classical and Old English verse has led me directly to new discoveries and new understandings of Layamon and the *Brut*. In every sense, the early Middle English alliterative verse of Layamon and his contemporaries is part of a continuous poetic tradition that begins with the classical verse of Cædmon and *Beowulf*. Much work, I believe, remains to be done to understand the full extent of this tradition and how its very continuity must inform our understandings of the works which survive, but I hope that this book of mine at least outlines both the form and extent of the tradition.

Notes

Chapter 1.1: Introduction

1 Summaries of the 'five-types,' for example, frequently indicate that they might be better characterized as being six or even seven types. See, for example, Cable, *Alliterative Tradition* 7 for a listing of six Sieversian types (distinguishing D from D4), and Kendall 21, n. 24, for a listing of seven 'realizations of the basic Sievers types' (distinguishing also A3 from A). These distinctions are, in fact, well recognized and have been persuasively defended by Pope (distinguishing D from D4) and Bliss (distinguishing A from A3). Yet teachers and metricists continue to refer to 'five types' and to take the Sieversian exposition of Old English metre as fundamental, although there is good reason to believe that types A and D (at least) include forms which ought not to be grouped together.

2 In general, Sieversian A3 verses are scanned with a first stress notably lighter than the second stress, and with alliteration generally on the second stress. Bliss argued that some A3 verses had, in effect, only a single stress, and it seems likely that line 1a of *Cædmon's Hymn* would qualify as one of these. One might note that Fred C. Robinson's interesting essay on the accentuation of 'nu' in the first verse of *Caedmon's Hymn* turns on precisely the claim of two stresses per verse, arguing that 'nu' is the first accented syllable. The formalism I propose in this book will offer a different interpretation of this verse (and similar ones).

3 Worse, the statistical arguments which are generally employed in studies of Old English metre – going back at least to Bliss – often do not prove what they claim to prove. Bliss claims that 'in practice it will be found that a metrically signficant difference between two types of verse generally causes a marked variation' in two types of criteria: '(1) the proportion of a-verses to

b-verses; (2) the proportion of a-verses with double alliteration' (*Metre* 4). Hutcheson employs statistical criteria that are essentially identical, replacing Bliss's two proportions with three positions: 'off-verse, on-verse with single alliteration ... and on-verse with double alliteration' (*Poetic Metre* 2, n. 4). The claim made by both Bliss and Hutcheson is that patterns showing statistically different distributions are therefore *metrically* different. Of course, this is not necessarily true: the differences in distribution do presumably point to a significant poetic difference in the patterns in question, but not all poetic differences are metrical differences. Syntactic, morphological, or other differences may explain the distributions. To take just one simple example, we might look at Sieversian D-verses of the form / / \ x: in such verses, one can show (for many poems, at least) a statistically different distribution regarding single and double alliteration in the a-line depending solely on whether or not the verse is filled by a full-verse compound. Full-verse compounds in such D-verses generally exhibit only single alliteration, while D-verses with two-word expressions show a real preference for double alliteration in the a-line. Bliss and Hutcheson would thus define the difference as a 'metrical' difference. A difference there is, but the reason why full-verse compounds usually feature only single alliteration lies in the rarity of self-alliterating compounds, not in a 'metrical' difference. As such examples show, the reliance on Bliss's statistical criteria has led only to a nightmarish multiplication of supposedly distinct metrical entities. Note that Fulk (181–2) expresses similar reservations about conclusions drawn from Bliss's statistics, although generally accepting most of those conclusions.

4 To take just one recent example, note the following 'transformational rule' invoked by Calvin Kendall for scanning certain lines: '*Sentence particles in a clause-initial half-line which lacks stressed elements acquire metrical stress from right to left in accordance with the stress and phrase rules of the metrical grammar until the first valid metrical contour emerges*' (24; italics in original). I want to point out that Kendall's book does make valuable contributions to our understanding of the metre of *Beowulf*, but the very task of integrating those contributions into a Sievers-based formalism seems to lead Kendall to complex and nonobvious rules. Examples of rules or conclusions of similar complexity can be found in many of the recent books on Old English metre.

5 The ascendancy of formulaic analysis during the second half of the twentieth century may have contributed to the lack of attention paid to Old English poetics. Although few scholars working through the oral-formulaic approach would claim that the tradition was the master of the poets rather than the reverse, nonmetrical studies of form in Old English verse have nevertheless tended to focus on formulas, formulaic systems, and themes

(i.e., poets' adherence to tradition) far more than on the effects of individual poetic choices.

6 Pope, for example, in *Seven Old English Poems*, employs Sieversian scansion, including Sievers's account of metrical feet, though he claims, 'In my opinion, this feature of the system has been an obstacle to the understanding of the basic rhythms of Old English verse' (108). Fulk addresses the implications of using Bliss's system on pp. 54–5, writing 'Of course, that the considerable majority of recent metrical studies have employed this system does not mean that it is correct, or even the most appropriate system for uses such as this. But certainly the use of any other system would require more detailed justification' (54).

7 B.R. Hutcheson has recently gone even further in arguing for some normal verses that have three full stresses.

8 That is, Sievers takes the principle that each verse has two stresses as one of his basic descriptive and analytical points, and his notions of scansion clearly depend upon this principle (see 25, §8). Bliss's 'vindication' of Sievers is therefore rather problematic, since Bliss himself undermines one of Sievers's key starting positions.

9 See Cable's fine discussion of the parallels between the construction of a (mental) grammar in a language learner and the construction of a metrical system in a poet, and the suggestion that we should expect to see 'changes in the metrical tradition' over time (*Alliterative Tradition* 105).

10 Fulk himself is clearly aware that such concerns are the primary focus of his *History*: 'The former type of variation [i.e., variation in the metrical values of individual words] has been far more intensively studied than the latter [i.e., changes in allowable verse-types], and the considerably greater part of this study will be devoted to it' (1).

11 Those who make some statement about the increased frequency or variety of anacrusis in later verse include Fulk 257, and Russom, *Old Germanic Meter*, 157, n. 100; the frequency and variety of anacrusis in *Maldon* is acknowledged by virtually all commentators. See Cable ('Metrical Style;' *Alliterative Tradition*) for comments about the frequencies of various verse-types across time. Cable does argue that the distributional changes at the end of the Old English period do actually signal a change in the underlying metrical principles.

12 Fulk notes the problem with such a perspective, but cannot seem to avoid it himself: 'It is sometimes difficult not to portray late aberrations from classical norms as representing decline rather than simple change. This is admittedly a jaundiced view ... But because we tend to regard apparently earlier verse as representing a metrical standard, it has not always been possible in this chapter to characterize metrical change impartially' (256, n. 10).

13 Readers should note my especially extensive debt to the formalism of
Geoffrey Russom. In its inception, the formalism I propose here began as
an attempt to integrate Calvin Kendall's observations about initial finite
verbs into Russom's word-foot formalism. The result of the attempt, of
course, was not so simple, and I believe my formalism has much to offer
that is new. Nevertheless, my debts to Russom and Kendall deserve spe-
cial mention.

14 Standard discussions of both processes can be found in Campbell's *Old
English Grammar.* For contraction, see sections 234–9; for parasiting see sec-
tions 360–7. Fulk's *History of Old English Meter* discusses both (and their
metrical implications) in detail.

Chapter 1.2: Sieversian Formalism

1 The conventional names for the various basic Sieversian types will be
described in full below.

2 Citations of individual verses will be taken from Krapp and Dobbie's
ASPR, as far as possible. Verses from other sources will be cited more fully
as they come up. In citations of individual verses, short titles for Old Eng-
lish works will be taken from Mitchell, Ball, and Cameron, 'Short Titles' as
supplemented by 'Addenda and Corrigenda.'

3 It is important to note that many of these conclusions (especially the con-
clusion about the stress level of finite verbs) derive wholly or in part from
Sieversian scansion. The Germanic word-stress rule is well recognized and
strongly supported from nonmetrical evidence, but contemporary evi-
dence for Old English sentence-level stress patterns is almost entirely
derived from verse. While the summary of Old English stress presented
here is fairly traditonal and widely agreed upon, it is important to realize
that a new understanding of Old English verse may involve a reassessment
of some of these conclusions about sentence-level stress.

4 The portion of the rule about free sentence elements is essentially a sum-
mary of the effects of Kuhn's first law. Compare, however, the similarity of
the effects of displacement in the two examples below:

Beo 2642b: þeah ðe hlaford us	xx/x/	(free sentence particle displacement: 'us')
Beo 2588a: grundwong þone	/ \ /x	(proclitic displacement: 'þone')

5 Note that, in Old English, no word ends with a short stressed vowel, which
means that the two resolved syllables will always fall within a single word:
there can be no resolution across word boundaries.

6 The principle of resolution demands a degree of attention, then, to where
syllable boundaries fall in Old English words. When a single consonant

falls between two vowels, it is considered to belong to the latter syllable; the preceding syllable can thus be long only if it has a long vowel. Likewise, any syllable with a vowel followed by two consonants can be identified as long, since the syllable boundary between such a syllable and the next is considered to fall between the consonants. Occasionally, of course, morpheme boundaries may take precedence over these general rules in determining syllable boundaries.

7 Especially since Modern English makes virtually no phonemic use of syllable length, modern readers of Old English verse have little or no intuitive feel for the syllabic equivalence implied by resolution, which demands that we scan as similar verses which (to modern ears) have completely distinct stress contours. For us, at least, scanning Old English verse is a discipline of the eye and the mind, far more than of the ear.

8 In Sievers's own formalism, type A3 has a stress in the first foot, although one that is weaker than that in the second foot. Bliss argues for one-stress A3 verses, and I consider this type to be a regular component of Sievers-Bliss formalism.

9 Types A3 and D4 are here given their conventional names, which derive from Sievers's original taxonomy. One of the most compelling arguments against Sieversian scansion lies in the lack of precision of this taxonomy which asssociates types A and A3, D and D4. The work of Pope, Bliss, and Russom has (in different ways) strongly suggested that the Sieversian taxonomic associations essentially misrepresent the relationships between various verse types.

10 Note that here, a word with full linguistic stress ('cyn') is mapped onto a position in the metrical contour with secondary stress; such mismatches are allowed, especially when one word can be considered as semantically subordinated.

11 There are two primary limitations on this possible replacement: (1) Sieversian scansion does not allow / \ to replace /(x): that is, a compound may not be placed in a position where its second element is an 'optional' element of the verse contour; and (2) this replacement is not allowed in the second foot of a C verse.

12 In particular, see the growing literature on the interactions between Old English metre and syntax, which suggests ever more clearly that there is often a syntactic basis to metrical forms which cannot simply be boiled down to stress patterns.

13 Problems with the standard account of 'half stress' (in Campbell's *Old English Grammar*) are described by Cable, who concludes; 'The problem with Campbell's analysis is that he took a structure of the literary metre to be a structure of the ordinary, non-metered phonology' (*Alliterative Tradition* 25).

Campbell's account of half stress includes discussion of those syllables metricists often designate as bearing 'tertiary' or 'reduced' stress.

14 Fulk discusses the strictly phonological evidence for the existence of tertiary stress on pp. 171–9, suggesting on 178 that 'the most important indication of the existence of tertiary stress remains – the difference between the phonological developments of unstressed vowels and those with tertiary stress ... Without tertiary stress there is no way to explain why we find, for instance, *-full* rather than *-foll*, and *–dom* rather than *-dam*' (87). In these and equivalent examples, Fulk fails to consider the very real possibility that at the point when the relevant phonological changes occurred, such words may well have had secondary stress on these elements; his initial assumption that these words do not have secondary stress thus perhaps affects his own analysis.

15 Cf. Bliss: 'Tertiary stress is also found on all long or disyllabic derivative or formative endings' (*Metre* 26). Thus, since '-ade' in 'gefrætwade' is disyllabic, it has tertiary stress in Bliss's account of things. Fulk repeatedly suggests that Bliss pretty much discards tertiary stress (e.g., 'Bliss rejects Sievers' assumption of stress at the tertiary level': Fulk 171), but Bliss's scansion of verses like 96a as type d1b implies tertiary stress: 'Type d1 (Sievers's Types C1 and C2) ... must be divided into two varieties, one with secondary and one with tertiary stress' (*Metre* 64).

16 It is important to note that, of all of the potential chronological indicators discussed by Fulk, the issue of tertiary stress generates (by far) the most extensive commentary. The problems of tertiary stress are unavoidable from any Sievers-Bliss perspective, but the difficulties caused by these problems are undoubtedly complex and extensive – extensive enough to call the formalism which generates them into question, in my opinion.

17 Note that I also exclude A3 verses (since they have only a single stress) and the 'maðelode' verses which, as has frequently been noted, are excluded from the double-alliteration requirement by virtue of the fact that this useful verb should not be limited to characters whose names begin with 'm.'

18 To be more precise, the numbers for *Beowulf* work out as follows:

Double alliteration rates in Sieversian types, excluding verses with compounds

Type	Percentage of Double Alliteration in a-line
D4	96.0%
A (excluding two-word /x /x)	92.7%

E	80.0%
D	78.6%
C	49.3%
B	34.0%

If I had excluded proper names (and there seems to be evidence supporting such an exclusion; see below, chapter 2.1) the numbers would be even more impressive in the top group. The simplest A-type, where the two Sieversian feet are occupied by two words of the form '/x,' features only optional double alliteration; possible reasons for this fact are also discussed in a later chapter.

19 See Campbell, *Old English Grammar*; this observation about proper names is, in fact, related to the issues discussed above in relation to tertiary stress.

20 The scansions given here reflect those of Bliss, although I give them the more familiar Sieversian type-names.

Chapter 2.1: A New Formalism for Classical Old English Metre

1 At the risk of repeating my comments from chapter 1.2, the standard interpretation of long and short syllables suggests that a syllable is long if it has a long vowel (or long diphthong) or is 'closed' by having a final consonant. A consonant which is sometimes syllable-final (as in an uninflected root) is, when followed by another vowel in the same word, usually syllabically identified with the second of the two syllables, although morphological considerations occasionally take precedence, as in '*eorðærn*' which should be considered as self-alliterating compound, rather than being syllabically split '**eor-ðærn.*'

2 Generally, however, I do not accept conclusions about linguistic stress which are based in Sieversian metrics. For example, I scan compound proper names as equivalent in stress to other compounds. Further, linguistic stress is sometimes to be distinguished from metrical stress, in that alliteration patterns prove that words with no appreciable linguistic stress can nevertheless sometimes have metrical stress. See below.

3 Note also that unpaired verses sometimes seem to be alliteratively linked to either the preceding or following lines. Such cases raise the possibility that verses are at least sometimes linked in triplets, rather than always in pairs. In his discussion of unpaired verses, Alan Bliss notes this possibility and suggests that 'short lines occurring in the manuscript may have been intended as such by the poet, particularly if a short line has either double or continued alliteration' ('Single Half-Lines' 449).

4 As noted above, there are 'exceptions' of one sort or another for virtually

every general principle which can be suggested for Old English verse. We should perhaps expect such from poets, but (of course) exceptions are generally infrequent, and they are allowed precisely because they do not endanger the overall coherence and consistency of the basic system. Likewise, the mere existence of exceptions should not invalidate an otherwise coherent descriptive metrical system. Our task as metricists is not to provide an account of every single verse, but rather to provide an account of the underlying system which defines metrical and unmetrical verses. Cf. Cable's comments on tendency statements and the problems of trying to account for every single verse (*Alliterative Tradition*, 13f).

5 Some recent theorists have disputed the existence of resolution as a feature of Old English versification, notably David Hoover, in *A New Theory of Old English Meter*. Yet resolution accounts for certain distributional patterns in classical verse which are otherwise difficult or impossible to explain. For example, if there is no resolution, then the pattern / \ x /x is seemingly allowed: yet this pattern is really only attested in classical verse with any frequency when either the last stress or the half stress is filled by a short syllable. Similarly, the 'dip' in classical B-type verses is generally trisyllabic only when the first stress is held by a short syllable (a few apparent exceptions can be seen where elision of adjacent vowels operates). These varied distributional features can all be explained by the equivalence principle called resolution, in which short-stressed plus unstressed equals long-stressed.

6 It does not seem likely to me that a principle of isochrony applied in Old English verse; Cable's recent argument that Old English metre was a syllable-counting metre certainly captures a great deal of the structure of the verse, although my formalism suggests that Cable's conclusions on this count are simply a derivative consequence of other more basic principles and that the level of abstraction they represent may not have been operative for Old English poets. See Cable, *Alliterative Tradition*.

7 Note that Russom allows only x and xx as x-feet, writing: 'there are no xxx feet because Old English has no trisyllabic unstressed words' (*Linguistic Theory* 14). Presumably, Russom interprets syncopation as being mandatory in words like 'nænigne' and 'hwæþere.' 'Nohweðere' would presumably also be separated by Russom, as well as treated as subject to syncopation.

8 This sentence thus stands as a partial statement of Kuhn's law of sentence particles. Cf. Calvin Kendall's observation that weak-onset verses (i.e. those with initial unstressed elements) frequently are clause-initial.

9 Examples are from *Beowulf*, where auxiliary verbs appear to be limited to 'wesan' and 'weorþan.' See the next chapter for more detailed discussion of the main verb/auxiliary verb distinction.

10 Weak Class II verbs which tend to have trisyllabic forms, it turns out, are not included in the s-foot category. Such verbs are scanned as Sxx; see S-feet, below.

11 Two other nice examples of subject pronouns which are phonologically attached to preceding verbs can be seen in *Christ and Satan* 57b and 64b. Momma asserts that 'this kind of enclisis is limited to combinations of particular finite verbs and subjective pronouns in Old English: manuscripts may attest *wenic* but not, for instance, **wenstu* (from *wenst þu*) or **hyrdic* (from *hyrde ic*)' (*Composition* 46). Orthographically, Momma's claim is generally correct, but the possibility of elision and/or enclisis in cases like 'hyrde ic' may well be indicated metrically, even if not orthographically. See below for a case where I believe 'hyrde ic' is, indeed, to be interpreted as a disyllabic sx sequence in the metre.

12 See the foot combination rules below for an account of the numbers of 'metrical positions' in Old English verse.

13 Words with monosyllabic suffixes like '-lic' (as well as '-leas' and perhaps '-ful') can be shown to demand scansion as Sx because they do not demand double alliteration when they occur in four-syllable A-type lines, while Ss words do tend to demand double alliteration. Nevertheless, the distinction between suffix and secondary compound constituent is not always clear in scansion.

14 Alliteration patterns confirm that there is no sxx foot, and thus both finite and non-finite weak Class II verbs are generally scanned with an Sxx foot. The alliterative confirmation is that such trisyllabic verbs in the first foot appear to alliterate mandatorily, as would be expected if they were placed on S-type feet, while s-type feet would demand only optional alliteration. Cf. Russom, who also notes that such a trisyllabic verb 'always corresponds to Sxx' (*Linguistic Theory* 106). See below for rules on alliteration.

15 In most metrical theories, compound names are scanned with 'tertiary stress' or 'reduced stress' on the second element. This practice appears to stem solely from the use of Sieversian formalism, and I believe there is clear evidence for secondary stress in compound names. Note that Bliss groups compound names among words with 'tertiary stress,' on the basis that 'the individual elements have no independent significance' (*Metre* 26); as late as the eleventh century, however, the pun on Æthelred's name which yielded the by-name 'Unræd' clearly demonstrates a continuing ability to (correctly) analyse the elements of such compound proper names. In poems of classical metre, it seems perfectly appropriate to imagine that poets and audiences had just as much sensitivity to name elements, at least when they did correspond to current lexical items.

16 The s-position of an Ssx foot must either have secondary stress or be a long

syllable. Trisyllabic words with neither (such as 'fultuma') are to be scanned as Sxx. This rule simplifies a great deal of confusion over Old English scansion; compare Fulk's conclusion about so-called tertiary stress: 'ictus at the tertiary level has nothing to do with stress, but with syllable length only' (233).

17 Geoffrey Russom makes a powerful argument for the remarkable conclusion that prefixes should often be scanned as separate words; his treatment of the subject in *Old English Meter and Linguistic Theory* is very much worth examining, and I cannot improve upon it (8–9). Nevertheless, I depart from Russom in adopting s-feet, where prefixes, in fact, determine the very foot-forms which are allowed, since verbal prefixes are limited to one or two syllables.

18 Cf. Bliss's typical formulation: 'particles and proclitics are not stressed unless they are displaced from their normal position in the clause' (*Introduction* 7).

19 Russom, too, allows mismatches, but notes that they come at the cost of complexity. This claim is undoubtedly correct and is related to the poets' urge to keep mismatches to a minimum. More complex verses, of course, are those more difficult for poets, listeners, and readers to scan, and thus more complex verses are generally rarer than less complex verses. I will discuss some other cases of mismatching in the next chapter.

20 Previous metrical theories have often asserted that metrical verses must have exactly four positions; this was usually accomplished by asserting that a sequence of unstressed syllables corresponds to one metrical position. A verse of the form xx/Sx or xx/Sxx, however, would thus seem to result in verses with three 'positions' but they clearly have at least the minimum number of syllables. In my formalism, verses may have between four and eight metrically counted syllables; counting 'positions' in the traditional fashion does not seem to improve the descriptive account of my formalism in any way. Cf. Cable, who has claimed that Old English verse is essentially a syllable-counting verse (*Alliterative Tradition*).

21 Note that resolution is often mandatory in classical verse when a foot would otherwise be ill-formed. For example, in *Beowulf* 3005a: 'æfter hæleða hryre,' resolution must operate on 'hryre' to avoid an Sxsx foot, and the first two syllables of 'hæleða' are likewise considered to be resolved, by analogy to verses with feet which would otherwise have to be scanned *Sxxxs. Such cases suggest that resolution is generally to be considered as applying unless blocked or suspended, rather than only applying as an exception to the typical case.

22 See Fulk's discussions of Kaluza's law for an interesting account of what

sorts of syllables and sequences were originally subject to resolution, and
for historical developments in this case. Geoffrey Russom's essay 'Con-
straints on Resolution' also offers a fine account of how frequently or rarely
resolution is suspended, and his larger conclusions, as far as I can see, are
not in conflict with my overall claim here. Russom does, however, claim
'resolution on a deeply subordinated s position after two alliterating ele-
ments also seems necessary in *sellice / sædracan* 1426a and *eahtodan / eorlscipe*
3173a, which would otherwise represent patterns of unparalleled length'
('Constraints' 162, n. 38). The bold-faced type in the preceding quotation is
Russom's, used to indicate the potentially resolved sequences. In my for-
malism, these sequences are not, in fact, resolved; Russom's concern about
lengthy sequences adopts too quickly hypothetical constraints on the
expansion syllables of so-called D* verses. Such long verses are rare, but
they appear to be perfectly well formed. The troublesome Beowulfian verse
'fyrdsearu fuslicu' (*Beowulf* 232a; also discussed by Russom) has, in my for-
malism, resolution on '-searu' but not on '-licu' and is also a rare formation,
but one that is perfectly well formed: Ss/Ssx.

23 Chiefly, extrametrical elements are limited to one syllable in E verses, and
are so rare in SB verses as to be possibly excluded on principle. Cf. Russom:
'One would expect a strong bias against extrametrical words in very long,
very heavy verses [e.g., SB, SC]; but this need not have taken the form of a
categorical prohibition' (*Linguistic Theory* 37). One SB verse which appears
to have an extrametrical element is *Daniel* 634a: 'mætra on modgeðanc,'
although (of course) this verse may be subject to elision. See FC3 below for
names of verse types used here.

24 Note that the possibility of an xxxx initial foot plus an xxxx extrametrical
sequence gives a theoretical maximum of eight unstressed initial syllables
in a verse. In fact, such verses are quite rare (as we would expect), but one
good example is *Soul and Body II*, l. 90a (corresponding to *Soul and Body I*, l.
97a): 'Þonne ne bið nænig to þæs lytel lið.' The word boundaries here
would allow a scansion of xxxx/(xxxx)Sxs.

25 It would technically be possible to scan this verse as Sxx/(xxxx)Ss,
although the large extrametrical element is far more typical of sA verses
than of SA verses, especially those with Sxx as the first foot. Other cases of
similar elision do appear in *Beowulf* supported by manuscript spelling, and
the pronoun is almost certainly to be interpreted here as being part of the
first foot. Despite the orthography, then, it seems that sequences like
'Hyrde ic' could (at least sometimes) count as sx in the metre.

26 Just as the limit of the number of extrametrical syllables in E-type verses
may derive from rhythmic similarities between E verses and SB verses.

Consider the following types:

SB: S/Sxs   S/Sxxs
CS: Ssx/S   Ssx/(x)S

Although it is difficult to be sure, such parallelism may suggest that the limit of one extrametrical syllable in CS verses may have originated from the fact that B-feet larger than Sxxs are disallowed. My comment about b-feet is intended to suggest that CS verses may have been 'reanalysed' as S/sxS and S/sxxS, thus authorizing the b-feet seen in xb verses.

27 Note that xb verses thus correspond quite closely to Sieversian B3 verses, which are B verses in which the alliteration is limited to the second 'lift.' It is possible that b-feet arose in Old English only after the process of contraction was complete, as alliterating monosyllables would then be acceptable in the final syllable of the line. That is, an xA verse, such as xx/(xx)Sx, where the Sx portion is held by a contracted form, would be available for reanalysis as an xx/sxS verse (and such a form would seem preferable to xx/(xx)S by the four-syllable rule). As specific examples, consider *Riddle 6*, 5a: 'þonne mec min frea' and *Seafarer* 9a: 'wæron mine fet.' In the former, contraction yields a classical scansion like xx/(xx)Sx, although it might be possible to scan it, post-contraction, like xx/sxS. In the *Seafarer* verse, scansion as xx/sxS seems to be demanded (alliteration is on 'f'), since treatment of 'mine' as extrametrical would result in a verse with three metrical syllables. Verses which might appear to be of the form xx/S are, in fact, very rare (see *Beowulf* 262a, 'Wæs min fæder' for one candidate), and are generally scanned as xx/Sx, with suspended resolution to preserve the four-syllable rule. See below for a similar argument suggesting that Sxx/S verses may also have originated after contraction.

Note also that a number of verses which Momma (*Composition*) identifies as syntactically unusual or anomalous can be regularized by scanning them with b-feet, rather than treating them (in Blissian fashion) as light 'e' verses. Consider the following:

Verse	Scansion	Momma's page number
LPrII 104a: And na us þu ne læt	xx/(x)sxS	99
PPs 121.1 1: Ic on ðyssum eom	xx/sxS	110
Instr 221a: Þu ful gearo þe na wast	xx/sxxS	141
Finn 144a: Ða him sona frægn	xx/sxS	144

In each case, Momma identifies these verses as either anomalous or unique.

Note that some of these appear in verse that might be described as late, even postclassical (see chapters 3.1–3.3), where structures corresponding to classical b-feet are even more common. But for the classical examples, the fact that syntactic anomalies identified by Momma here correspond to an unusual metrical form which (by putting many of the supposedly 'detached unstressed elements' onto stressed positions) resolves the syntactic anomaly seems to provide powerful support for the existence of b-feet.

28 Specifically, the following types are allowed in my formalism: Ss/Sxx, Ss/Ssx, Sxx/S, and Sxs/S. All of these types are rare but there are examples for each. Also, this formalism would presumably allow Ss/Sxs verses, although I have found none in the surviving corpus: such verses would presumably be rarer than Ss/Ssx verses, which are themselves quite rare. The rarity of Ss/Ssx and Ss/Sxx is well accounted for by their weight; although Russom disallows these verse types on account of their weight, I would prefer to suggest that their weight explains their rarity without casting them into the realm of unmetricality. The rarity of Sxx/S and Sxs/S verses may arise from some other basis, such as the possibility that they became allowable only late in the classical period. Note that (as I suggested for sxS feet above) Sxx/S verses may have become acceptable only after the historical process of contraction had finished its course: a verse like *Beowulf* 3097b: 'beorh þone hean' (scanned Sxx/Sx, with contraction in 'hean'), would have then become eligible for reanalysis as Sxx/S. The rarity of Sxx/S verses in classical metre might thus be explained because they simply represented a relatively new form, without a stock of formulaic examples. If this analysis is correct, we would expect to see the frequency of such verses increase in later poems. Sxs/S verses may well have been originally authorized by analogy to Ssx/S verses and Sxx/S verses; Sxs/S verses are the rarest of the E types.

29 It is worth considering just how many specific types were available to the poets. If we look just at xB verses, we have three potential initial feet (x, xx, xxx; note that here I exclude xxxx as a viable x-foot), five potential extrametrical sequences (Ø, x, xx, xxx, xxxx), and two final feet (Sxs, Sxxs). The number of possible specific types of xB verses, then, is 3 x 5 x 2, or 30. Fifteen of these thirty types appear in *Beowulf* (the 'missing' types include all six possible types with four extrametrical syllables and five of the six possible types with three extrametrical syllables). These types, of course, ought to be rare, and the fact that they do not appear in *Beowulf* is not surprising. The very multiplicity of available specific types has often seemed problematic for metrical theorists; one advantage of my formalism is to suggest a set of simple rules which account for the observed types, including many rare types.

30 James Keddie has recently claimed that resolution should not be blocked in all Sieversian C verses, and that we should scan many such verses as something like xx// (i.e., with a resolved stress at the very end). The lack of parallelism that results between verses of the structure x/Ssx (e.g., *Beowulf* 1b: 'in geardagum' and xx/Ssx (e.g., *Beowulf* 1a: 'Hwæt, we Gar-Dena,' which Keddie would allow to resolve to xx/Ss) seems like a serious difficulty, and I prefer the parallelism implied in my formalism here.

31 That is, resolution of these Sx-feet to S-feet would not only constitute a class change (and is blocked on these grounds), it would constitute a class change to an unmetrical class.

32 The simplest explanation for the Sx/Sx exclusion may be that the 'typical' verse form in classical Old English verse is Sx/Sx, and that more complex types with two S-positions must have double alliteration to minimize their complexity. That is, an SS a-line with double alliteration is metrically less complex than one with single alliteration. Evidence for this possibility can be found in Sx/Sx verses that feature a 'bracketing mismatch' (see Russom, *Linguistic Theory*, 15ff.) in which the syntactic boundary fails to match the foot-boundary (i.e., the x-position of the first foot is proclitic to the S-position in the second foot). In *Beowulf*, Sx/Sx verses with such a bracketing mismatch have double alliteration 90 per cent of the time, while two-word Sx/Sx verses without such a mismatch have double alliteration only optionally (29 per cent of cases). The bracketing mismatch adds to the complexity of the Sx/Sx verse, and thus demands double alliteration. Note that not all poems have mandatory (or quasi-mandatory) double alliteration in all SS verses; see the next note.

33 Double alliteration is not always mandatory in SS-type a-lines in all poems. Thus, in *Elene*, double alliteration is not mandatory in Ss/Sx (although most poems show mandatory double alliteration in this type), and in *Beowulf*, double alliteration is, in fact, not mandatory for the specific type S/Sxx (note that double alliteration in this type is clearly mandatory in *Andreas*, however). In poems where double alliteration is not mandatory for specific a-line types with two S-feet, it is optional. Such cases of nonconformity with the general principles outlined here might allow us to 'profile' the practices seen in different poems, allowing us to determine at least some of the features of differing poetic practices. Here and elsewhere, I resist the temptation to assert that the practice of the *Beowulf* poet is the norm to which all other classical poetry should be compared.

34 Unless otherwise noted, all further comments or statistics about double alliteration rates will concern only verses featuring none of the 'exceptional' forms discussed in this note and the three other types of exception to

be discussed below. To give just one example of the appropriateness of this method, consider the rates of double alliteration seen in my count of S/Ssx verses in *Beowulf*:

Total S/Ssx verses in the a-line of *Beowulf*:	153
Full-verse compounds	47
Verses with proper names	34
Remaining verses with double alliteration	67
Remaining verses with single alliteration	5

That is, 93 per cent (67/72) of applicable S/Ssx verses have double alliteration, and in *Beowulf*, I consider S/Ssx to have mandatory double alliteration, in that it seems best to consider the five verses with single alliteration as exceptions to a general rule requiring double alliteration. The existence of categorical exceptions to the requirement for double alliteration makes the counting of double alliteration rates in all examples of a specific type a pointless exercise.

35 Here I will give a couple of examples of verses employing traditional doublets: *Andreas* 1122a: 'duguðe ond eogoðe,' *Beowulf* 72a: 'geongum ond eardum,' and *Phoenix* 37a: 'Wintres ond sumeres.' Examples of lines where rhyme or cross alliteration replaces double alliteration can be found in chapter 2.3. It is worth noting that there may be other formulaic exceptions to the requirement for double alliteration, such as Sx/(x)Sx verses ending in 'gehwylcum' (or in an inflectional variant). In *Beowulf*, I count 242 Sx/(x)Sx a-lines with double alliteration and 19 without; of these 19, six end with a form related to 'gehwylcum.' This high proportion of exceptions to the general rule may mark these verses as an authorized 'formulaic exception.' This same exception can, in fact, be seen in other poems as well.

36 Kendall suggests that some syntactic subgroups of xB verses (for example) may sometimes require double alliteration (cf. Kendall 140–1, for one example). But it nevertheless seems significant that whole classes of SS verses generally require double alliteration, while the same is not true of xS verses.

37 Cf.Kendall's formulation: 'Wherever a fully stressed compound appears, whether in the a-verse or the b-verse, its first stressed element will alliterate' (161). Proper names, as I have noted above, stand as an exception to this general rule.

38 Note that this logic also neatly explains the rarity of SB b-lines where the second foot is filled by a single word: there are few Sxs names and no Sxs words without secondary stress. SB verses with the second foot filled by

more than one word are, on the other hand, relatively common in the b-line, despite Bliss's argument that the D4 verse (corresponding to SB) is excluded from the b-line.

39   I count 158 S/Ssx b-verses in *Beowulf* with second feet scanned as single words. Of these, 73 have long penultimate syllables without secondary stress; 68 have proper names; 17 have compounds, one of which participates in cross alliteration. That is, just over 10 per cent have the unexpected form in which a compound fails to alliterate. The exceptions are clearly allowed, but I believe the general trend to avoid such verses is clear; if a parallel can be drawn to rates of double-alliteration, the exclusion of compounds for S/Ssx verses in the b-line is approximately 'mandatory,' but not without exception.

40   At this point I might also note that all five of the a-line S/Ssx verses with single alliteration in *Beowulf* noted above (note 34) featured Ssx words in the second foot without secondary stress. That is, such Ssx words are not only allowed in the second foot of S/Ssx verses in the b-line, they are allowed in S/Ssx verses in the a-line with single alliteration.

41   It is worth noting that this same evidence has previously been used to support the existence of 'tertiary stress.' That is, the rule allowing S/Ssx verses in the b-line if the second foot has either a name or no secondary stress has been interpreted as a single rule: three-position names and Ssx words without secondary stress have been lumped together as words with 'tertiary stress' on the medial syllable. My account, I believe, explains the same observations without invoking the suspect linguistic category. It is worth noting that many of the b-line compounds in the second foot of S/Ssx verses are identified by Kendall as 'class II compounds.' Those listed by Kendall on p. 176, however, may be better considered as having variably-stressed prefixes (as is '*un-*'); cf. Kendall's later comment: 'If the base word is a simplex, the combination proclitic + simplex evidently forms a compound or quasi-compound phrase which belongs to class II' (184), which seems to imply that class II compounds in the second foot of b-lines may in fact behave much like prefixed forms. The details of these compounds and verses would appear to repay more detailed study. Likewise, there remains the possibility that at least some of the Ssx words I feel have secondary stress may merely have been perceived as Ssx words with long medial syllables by the *Beowulf* poet.

42   Because Russom's formalism involves treating initial finite verbs which alliterate as S-positions, triple alliteration in such verses is excluded in his account since the third alliterating element therefore appears to be doubly subordinated. In my account, such verses are allowed in the general case

(although perhaps excluded in particular poems, such as *Beowulf*) as the double subordination requirement seems not to hold in some poems.

43 Or it may be possible to suggest that exceptions to the rule such as these are equivalent to b-line verses with double alliteration. That is, both types of verse may count as exceptions to the same rule.

44 In *Andreas*, we see Ss alliteration in Ss/Sx (1549a, 1596a) and in Ssx/S (226a, 532a, 728a).

45 See the *Meters of Boethius* 13.50a, 17.15a, 24.23a, 29.18a.

Chapter 2.2: Scanning Old English Verse

1 Fulk examines verses with inflected forms of 'earfoþ' in the first foot, and concludes that they 'nearly always fill three metrical positions' (225). That is, Fulk claims that verses like *Genesis A* 180a ('earfoða dæl') should be scanned as Ssx/S, while a verse like this one from *The Wanderer* is the exception to the general treatment of this word. Yet the longer poems in which verses similar to *Genesis A* 180a are found (*Christ III, Juliana, Guthlac A*) all seem to allow the Sxx/S verse-form in other cases, suggesting that scanning 'earfeþa' as Sxx is the norm, rather than the exception. One might note that spelling the medial vowel as 'e' (as in *The Wanderer*, and frequently elsewhere) suggests no stress on the medial syllable, which has a short vowel. In short, it seems that 'earfeþa' corresponds to Sxx according to the description of foot forms in the previous chapter, and I scan it thus here.

2 'So speaks the wanderer, mindful of difficulties, of cruel slaughters, the fall of dear kinsmen: "Often I must alone, before each dawn, speak my care. Now there is no one of the living to whom I dare clearly speak my mind. I know in truth that it is a princely custom in a man that he bind fast his spirit, hold tight the hoard of his words, however he thinks. The weary-minded one may not withstand fate, nor the troubled thought accomplish much help."' Throughout, translations from Old and Middle English are my own.

3 Pope (*Seven Old English Poems*) suggests this verse might be scanned as an expanded E verse, on the basis that 'the first two words go together' (116). I disagree, and I prefer to scan verbal complements and modifiers as linked most closely to the verb, rather than to preceding nouns. See below, note 5.

4 Although no examples appear in these lines, my system, like most others (as I have noted above), makes conventional use of the dual forms brought about by the historical linguistic processes of contraction and parasiting. For a clear discussion of these issues, see Fulk, chapters 1 and 2. Russom's 'prosodic rules' for the dual forms permitted by these processes (basically

allowing poets to optionally disregard the results of contraction and paras-
iting) will serve my system as well as Russom's, and I will assume them
throughout. See Russom, *Linguistic Theory*, 39–43.

5 I use syntactic closeness to disambiguate E-class verses from SB verses even
in the b-line; Bliss excludes SB verses from the b-line by claiming they must
feature double alliteration (and hence must appear only in the a-line; *Metre*
72–3). It is only possible for him to do so because such verses may be
scanned as E verses; I prefer to allow SB in the b-line and to distinguish
between SB and E on the basis of the relationships between the elements.

6 Alternatively, we could say that resolution occurs in 9a simply because
there is no prohibition against resolution in this position. As noted else-
where, it seems clear that, for classical Old English verse, resolution always
occurs, except under circumstances where it is prohibited. In further analy-
sis and scansion, I will generally not discuss cases of resolution that operate
normally, but I will discuss circumstances in which resolution is prohibited
or blocked.

7 In general, we should probably note that extrametrical syllables always
add complexity to a verse and are thus often avoided when possible.
Simultaneously, however, it appears that the complexity of an extrametrical
element must sometimes have been less than the complexity caused by an
unusual or rare foot-form.

8 So far as I am aware, the observation that the final word of any Old English
verse must be stressed has not been made before, but it is of central impor-
tance in scanning verses. Indeed, the 'last word stressed' rule virtually rep-
licates the rule of 'displacement,' where 'particles and proclitics are not
stressed unless they are displaced from their normal position in the clause'
(Bliss, *Introduction*, 7), but since particles and proclitics are generally dis-
placed to the end of the verse, it seems more efficient to identify the rule in
question as a strictly positional 'last word stressed' rule. If previous metri-
cists have not articulated a 'last word stressed' rule, that probably stems
from a commitment to the notion of stress-through-displacement.

   According to my reading of Old English verse, virtually the only excep-
tions I can find to the general claim that the last word of a verse is stressed
are verses like the following: *Beowulf* 426b, 'Ic þe nu ða' (to be scanned x/
Ssx) and *Judith* 86b, 'Þearle is me nu ða' (Sx/(xx)Sx). The 'nu ða' collocation
is fairly frequent in the final position, and both of these verses suggest that
'ða' does not receive stress (since that would entail double alliteration in
the b-line). I strongly suspect that 'nu ða' functioned as a semi-compound
('nu-ða') with the second syllable always unstressed. Note that the *OED*
lists the *Beowulf* example as a single word, the first citation given under the

headword 'Nowthe'; it seems likely that 'nu' and 'ða' were considered as a single lexical unit quite early, and that the 'last word stressed' rule applies to 'nuða,' not to 'ða' in such verses. We might also compare the equally frequent (and equally redundant) collocation 'þa gyt' in which the second element is always stressed. These adverbial pairs may have existed as metrical alternants of the forms sx (or Sx) and xs (or, possibly, xS).

One might be inclined to conclude that a 'last word stressed' rule is a modern artefact of conventional (lineated) presentations of Old English verse, and that no such rule could apply in the context of continuing streams of aurally or visually received poetry that would have been available to listeners or readers of surviving manuscripts, since the manuscripts do not consistently mark verses. Yet, although John Miles Foley finds no clear analogue to 'right justification' in Old English verse (202) such a rule may be related to the phenomenon of 'right justification' that Foley has described in other Indo-European orally derived verse, although here applying in the domain of the verse, rather than the line. Such right justification is an increased rigidity of form in the 'right hand' portion of a metrical unit, combined with relative freedom of form in the beginning or 'left hand' portion. Fulk also discusses right justification in his discussion of the rule of the coda: 'The effect of the rule is to demand more rigid structure in the latter part of the verse than in the former' (201). It seems likely that such increasing rigidity aids listeners or readers in identifying verse boundaries, supporting the possibility that a rule might make explicit reference to verse-endings.

9 Note that my explanation of these verses differs from standard accounts, which identify 'minne,' and 'durre' as stressed because they are 'displaced' from their normal syntactic positions (cf. the preceding note). According to standard accounts, 'minne' ought to precede 'modsefan,' and the finite verb 'durre' ought to be in the initial dip of the clause. ('Hycge' and 'wille' are usually explained as stressed only because they must be to make their verse scan; they are not displaced.)

10 In *Beowulf*, I count 538 verses with the specific scansion Sx/(x)Sx; virtually all such verses have an extrametrical syllable that is proclitic to the second foot. By contrast, I find 91 verses which demand scansion as Sxx/Sx. The conclusion that the use of a normative foot (Sx) with an extrametrical syllable was less troublesome for audiences than the rare Sxx foot alone seems difficult to avoid.

11 See Kendall 33f. See also Bliss's discussion of nonfunctional alliteration in his examination of stress on finite verbs (*Metre*, chapter 2, 6–23).

12 That is, scansion systems frequently treat finite verbs as unstressed if they

do not alliterate, but fully stressed if they do alliterate. Russom's treat-
ment of these verbs makes the clearest move towards consistency: 'We
conclude that the root syllable in an unemphatic verb corresponds to met-
rical S in some verses and to metrical x in others. That is exactly what we
would expect if such syllables bore reduced stress and could occupy any
type of metrical position' (*Linguistic Theory* 104). By dispensing with the
linguistically suspect category of 'reduced stress,' s-foot formalism also
allows a consistent treatment of these verbs that can explain their allitera-
tive characteristics.

13 That is, scanning finite verbs on s-positions is merely a notational conven-
ience reflecting their secondary alliterative status. This formalism should
not be interpreted as indicating that finite verbs themselves have 'second-
ary stress.' See the following note.

14 We might note that verses like 391a and 264a contain the sequence xsS, and
thus may seem to stand as counterexamples for Cable's claim that 'there is
a proscription against three rising levels of stress' (*Alliterative Tradition* 148).
We must recall, however, that scansion of finite verbs on s-feet should not
be taken to imply that such verbs must have secondary stress. Neverthe-
less, it may be the case that Cable's conclusion stems from his use of Siever-
sian formalism and its systematic confusion of stress and ictus.
Linguistically, it seems very probable that the verb 'het' in 391a is more
prominent (and hence more heavily stressed) than the pronoun 'Eow,'
while the alliteration on 'secgan' suggests that it (in turn) is more promi-
nent than 'het.' The impossibility of equating metrical prominence, linguis-
tic prominence, and stress, however, makes the value of Cable's claim
uncertain, and s-foot formalism takes an agnostic position on such matters
while still accounting for the alliterative qualities of finite verbs.

15 We can probably specify the rule here more precisely. In b-lines without a
'naturally stressed' word before the penultimate syllable, primary stress
will fall on any finite verb within the verse (e.g., *The Wanderer* 14b: 'hycge
swa he wille' or *Beowulf* 1265b: 'Þanon woc fela'); it seems likely that in
such cases, the fact that finite verbs are 'naturally' stressed elements (even
when scanned on s-feet) plays the determinative role. If no finite verb is
available before the last word, the penultimate word receives stress, as in
the following verses from *Beowulf*:

Beo 1875b: on þa healfe	x/Ssx	(alliteration on 'þ')
Beo 2490b: þe he me sealde	xx/Ssx	(alliteration on 'm')
Beo 543b: no ic fram him nolde	xx/(x)Ssx	(alliteration on 'h')
Beo 251b: Nu ic eower sceal	xx/Sxs	(vocalic alliteration)

In each case, we have sequences of naturally unstressed elements preceding a finite verb, and in each case, the penultimate word is stressed. None of these particles is displaced; they apparently receive stress simply by preceding the final word of the b-line. The effects of the scansion rule under discussion here mirror the effects of Kendall's 'transformational rule' discussed above in chapter 1.1, n. 4.

16 We might supplement the argument made in the previous note with the following observation: it appears that if the 'last word stressed' rule results in a potential nonmetrical verse, even in the a-line, the next to the last word is promoted to full stress, as in the following examples:

Beo 197: on þam dæge þysses lifes	x/Ssx	Sx/Sx
Beo 2047a: Meaht ðu, min wine	sx/Ssx	
Beo 736a: ðicgean ofer þa niht	Sx/(xx)Ss	

In *Beowulf* 197 (and related lines); 'þysses' is stressed in the b-line by the combination of the 'last word stressed' rule and the exclusion of xA and sA from the b-line. *Beowulf* 197a, by the rule proposed in this note, may have stress on 'þam' because stressing 'dæge' results in a problematic potential verse form: *xx/S, and so 'þæm,' as the preceding syllable, is promoted to full stress so that 'dæge' can remain unresolved. Similar logic appears to explain *Beowulf* 2047a, with 'min' scanned on S, to prevent the possibility of *sx/(x)S. Likewise, stressing 'niht' in 736a would result in *Sx/(xxx)S unless, again, the word preceding 'niht' was promoted to an S position. The scansion of these lines has long been understood because of their alliteration, but the rule posited in this note seems to offer a relatively clear explanation of just how these (nondisplaced) elements manage to receive stress. In each case, the key elements are stressed in order to remove the possibility of an unmetrical scansion raised by the 'last word stressed' rule.

17 That is, verses like '*ne ofercom mid þy campe' are unmetrical because of the available s-feet, although accounts of anacrusis which focus on the nature of the negator and the verbal particle cannot exclude them. The limitation of anacrusis to two syllables has frequently been observed, but the use of s-feet appears to show the logic behind the limitation.

18 One might suppose that b-lines like *The Wanderer* 14b, 'hycge swa he wille' might have suggested to poets that these types of verses were, in fact, also acceptable in the a-line, but verses like *The Wanderer* 14b are not nearly as unusual in the b-line as the quoted examples are unusual in the a-line. The disparity does seem to suggest that the a-line examples and the b-line examples may have different scansions, as I suggest here.

19 The 'enta geweorc' verses are clear examples of sB verses, since the s-foot is sx (that is, they cannot be scanned as E verses); the following two verses may also be sB verses with a similar alliterative mismatch in the b-line:

> *And* 904b: wat æfter nu
> *Met 1* 75b: Breac longe ær

In both cases, the finite verbs carry the alliteration, and traditional scansion treats these as E-type verses (Ssx/S), but the adverbs in each verse seem most clearly linked to one another, and a scansion like s/Sxs is at least possible. The relative rarity of such verses may make certainty about their scansions impossible, but s-foot formalism can at least explain their rarity as a result of their alliterative mismatch.

20 Indeed, it might even be possible to scan *Beowulf* 756a as Sx/Sxs and *Soul and Body I* 104a as Sx/Sxs. Consider *Andreas* 999a: *'godes dryhtendom'* (S/Sxs). In the verse from *Andreas*, we have a seemingly unambiguous scansion (since the first element is a noun, not a verb), but note that the line alliterates on 'd.' It might be necessary to scan *Andreas* 999a as xx/Sxs, but I prefer to treat it as an alliterative irregularity, in which the self-alliterating compound outweighs the first S-position (note that *Andreas* also substitutes Ss alliteration in the first foot for double alliteration in Ss/Sx and Ssx/S verses). However we treat this verse, it is likely to remain somewhat anomalous.

21 It is very much worth noting that many of the verses that Momma identifies as violations of both Kuhn's first and second laws have the structure of SA verses with anacrusis (*Composition* 74f.). In this respect, these verses (in my formalism, originally patterned after sA verses) continue to behave syntactically like sA verses, in which free unstressed particles are clustered before the second foot. This circumstance regarding many SA verses with anacrusis would seem to support the connection I draw here between (x)SA verses and sA verses. For clarity's sake, I use the term 'anacrusis' only for S-type verses which include initial unstressed elements by analogy to s-type verses. In the s-type verses, the initial unstressed elements are not anacrustic, since they are an integral part of the first foot.

22 Again, when such verses appear in the a-line, double alliteration is mandatory, and seems to lessen or clarify these verses' complexity. It is the scansion of SA-type verses with anacrusis in the b-line (such as *Beowulf* 93b, here) which accounts for a remarkable feature of anacrusis in the classical verse. When SA-type verses with anacrusis appear in the b-line in classical verse, they rarely feature finite verbs in the (alliterating) first foot. Nonfi-

nite verbs are frequent, as are nouns, but finite verbs are very rare. This statistic seems to support the scansion of such b-lines as (x)Sx/Sx – i.e., as SA verses with a syllable in anacrusis. Note that in later verse, finite verbs do begin to appear in this position. The likelihood of an (x)Sx/Sx scansion in the b-line may also have opened the door for similar scansions in the a-line. Further work needs to be done to determine whether or not such scansions are in fact operative in the a-line, or whether these verses should be considered as sA verses with a scanning mismatch.

23 The further restriction which limits anacrusis to one syllable in the b-line will be discussed in chapter 3.3.

24 Cf. Russom's comment regarding 'edwitlif' from Beowulf 2891b: 'The multiple compound edwit-lif ... seems to represent the pattern Sxs' (Linguistic Theory 70).

25 We might note that Sx/Sx verses without a bracketing mismatch correspond to Bliss's type 2A1, while those with a bracketing mismatch are scanned by Bliss as 1A1 (i.e., with caesura after the first stress). With the understanding that bracketing mismatches introduce complexity that is counteracted by a requirement for double alliteration, both my formalism and that of Geoffrey Russom can thus account for much of what Bliss describes with his theory of the caesura.

26 'Now you readily know what will seem best in mind for you to make known of this, if this queen asks us about that tree; now you know my thought and mind.'

27 Although not all poems which include b-feet use cross alliteration to support the unusual verse form, Elene, Andreas, and The Pheonix do seem to do so. Andreas's one xb verse has cross alliteration (534a), The Pheonix's xb verse also does (655a), and both of Elene's xb verses do likewise (532a, 1164a). Of course, if such a verse has double alliteration, it is always scanned as xB, as in Andreas 1481a: 'ofer min gemet.' Such a verse may, however, be better scanned as xb with double alliteration, but until further work is done on such rare verses, it seems best to treat doubly alliterating verses as B-type verses.

28 Gradon's edition appears to suggest that 'treo' may be a contracted form (46), but Fulk does not agree (188).

29 SB verses also begin with a stress and end with a monosyllable, but SB does not seem a likely candidate for this particular verse.

30 Compare Guthlac A 369a 'ær oþþe sið': this verse appears immediately after what Krapp identifies as a missing leaf, and so may not be a full verse, but if it is complete, it provides a very nice parallel to the Genesis A verse.

31 Momma suggests a Bliss-style scansion for Beowulf 183b and like verses as

'B3' (i.e., as '- | x x x –'; 'Gnomic Formula' 425); except for the use of a Blissian caesura, such a scansion corresponds fairly closely to my scansion of such verses as Sxx/(x)S.

32 Cf. Momma, who labels the examples with forms of *'wesan'* in the second position the 'gnomic formula,' indicates just how formulaic such usages are, citing twenty-two examples ('Gnomic Formula' 423–4). It seems plausible to treat *'eft'* as unstressed in *Beowulf* 603a, yielding an identical scansion; the alternative is to treat it as stressed and scan as CsS.

33 To this frequently emended verse, compare *Guthlac A* 313a: *'leofes gelong.'*

34 'It is a wonder to tell how the mighty God, through greatness of spirit, distributes wisdom, land, and position to the race of men; he has power over all. At times in love he allows the thought of some man of a great family to turn.'

Chapter 2.3: Additional Rules

1 The section on hypermetric verses is a somewhat altered version of an essay I published on the same topic in *Notes and Queries* ('The Three Varieties of Old English Hypermetric Versification').

2 This observation corresponds closely to Russom's rule 38: 'The second foot [i.e., the second and third feet, in my formulation] overlaps a normal verse pattern with an S position in the first foot' (*Linguistic Theory* 60). Russom's analysis is effective for the Type 1 hypermetric verses described here, but it does not fare as well with the Types 2 and 3 hypermetric verses discussed below.

3 Hypermetric a-lines do occur without double alliteration (e.g. *Judith* 9a), but double alliteration is mandatory (in the sense of occuring in over 90 per cent of cases) in hypermetric a-lines.

4 Hieatt makes a similar claim: 'Hypermetric verses in Old English poetry generally come in groups of at least six (i.e., three lines)' (6), as do others.

5 Although the following list is not exhaustive, we see unclustered hypermetric lines in the following places: *Genesis A* 913, 1523; *Andreas* 51, 303; *Dream of the Rood* 133; *Elene* 163; *Christ II* 621; *Christ III* 1546; *Guthlac A* 25, 510, 636, 740; *Guthlac B* 1110; *Phoenix* 630. So many lone hypermetric lines (in so many different works) would seem to suggest that they are allowed.

6 To put it another way, the frequency with which normal lines feature three consecutive alliterating feet explains the general tendency to avoid triple alliteration in Type 1 hypermetric a-lines: allowing double alliteration only in Type 1 hypermetric a-lines minimizes any possible confusion between

hypermetric and normal lines. In short, the rules for normal and hypermetric verses must be understood as complementary and features of one system may be best understood with reference to the alternative system, as here. For a further example, see the discussion of hypermetric verses and anacrusis in normal verses, p. 53 below.

7 Cf. Russom's comments about the xx/Sx/Sx structure, which he notes is 'rare even in the first half-line, and never appears in the second half-line outside of hypermetric clusters' (*Linguistic Theory* 62).

8 'Then came Wealhtheow forth, walking under a golden ring, where the two good men sat, nephew and uncle; then still was there peace together between them, each true to the other. Likewise there Unferth the spokesman sat at the feet of the Scylding lord; each one of them trusted his spirit, that he had a great mind, although he had not been kind to his kinsmen at the play of swords. Then spoke the woman of the Scyldings: "Receive this cup, my lord."'

9 Note that I scan 376a with the unusual xxx initial foot in order to prevent the extrametrical syllables from exceeding the theoretical limit of four.

10 'Never will you shift me from these words, while my wit supports me. Though you torment it with pains, you may not touch my soul, but you bring it to a better condition. Therefore I will endure that which my lord appoints for me. The sorrow of death is not mine.'

11 The *Guthlac A* poet does also use hypermetric verses which obey the Type 1 rules, but his usage of verses such as those quoted here is also typical for *Guthlac A*.

12 Additional examples of triply alliterating hypermetric a-lines include: *Christ III* 1162; *Rune Poem* 28a; *Solomon and Saturn II* 338a; *Maxims II* 3a; and *Against a Dwarf* 10a.

13 Each of these poems has two or more lines using Type 2 rules; some of these poems also contain lines that follow Type 1 rules, but since Type 2 rules supplement Type 1 rules (rather than replacing them), the use of verses following Type 1 rules is also to be expected from poets using Type 2 and Type 3 verses.

14 'A king must hold a kingdom; a city is seen from afar, a work of skill, the work of giants, of those that are on this earth, a marvellous structure of wall-stones. Wind is the swiftest in the sky; thunder, at times, the loudest. The powers of Christ are great; fate is strongest.'

15 To take just two examples, Mitchell and Robinson claim that 'rhyme had no functional role in Old English versification' (*Guide* 167). Likewise, see E.G. Stanley's disclaimer, 'I do not know if it is possible to have cross alliteration in addition to double alliteration' (*Foreground* 136, n. 43). The uncertainties

of scholars of such repute indicate just how poorly the secondary effects considered in this chapter are currently understood.

16 Andy Orchard's essay, 'Artful Alliteration in Anglo-Saxon Song and Story' addresses various sorts of supplemental alliteration at the level of the line and in larger structures, although his focus on ornamental alliteration allows him to include alliterative links between stressed and unstressed elements. As a catalogue and analysis of ornamental effects, Orchard's essay has a different purpose from what I undertake here, where I hope to address the degree to which supplemental alliteration patterns play a functional, structural role in the classical Old English versification system.

17 For the purposes of this investigation, I will use a relatively conservative definition of rhyme in Old English, considering only syllables that have identical vowels and identical final consonants (or consonant clusters) as examples of rhyme. Resolved sequences must match through both syllables. These guidelines exclude the possibility of rhyme in compounds like 'heorudreorig' and 'waroðfaruða'; the very real possibility that these compounds might have been perceived as featuring acceptable off-rhymes suggests that a broader understanding of Anglo-Saxon rhyme might be rewarding; nevertheless, my goal in discussing rhyme is to demonstrate that, with even the most restrictive definition, rhyme can be shown to be a functional part of Old English verse technique.

18 Note also that, according to S1, lines like *Maldon* 42: 'Byrhtnoð maþelode, bord hafenode' (cf. *Maldon* 309), are not considered to rhyme, as th e '-ode' suffixes occupy the 'xx' portion of Sxx feet. Again, a fuller consideration of rhyme in Old English verse may need to include such examples.

19 Similar examples include the following:

Jul 53b: ne meaht þu habban mec	xsx/Sxs
And 1272a: Heton ut hræðe	sx/Ssx
Ex 400a: Wolde þone lastweard	sx/(xx)Ss

The lists in this and the following four notes are intended to be illustrative, rather than exhaustive. Most of the examples under discussion could be paralleled by more, often many more, verses or lines.

20 Cf. the following examples:

GuthB 1015b: Meaht þu meðelcwidum	sx/Ssx
Gifts 93b: hafað healice	s/Ssx
GenA 1460b: Gewat se wilda fugel	xsx/Sxs

21 Cf. the following examples:

Hell 47a: heahfædra fela	Ssx/S
ChristC 1215a: orgeatu on gode	Ssx/(x)S
ChristC 1405a: Neornxawonges wlite	Sxsx/S (note anomalous scansion)

22 Cf. the following examples:

Dan 374a: nergend hergað	Sx/Sx
Phoen 216a: Bæl bið onæled	Sx/(x)Sx
Ruin 31b: Hryre wong gecrong	S/Sxs

23 Cf. the following examples:

Fates 81: sigelean secan, ond þone soðan gefean	Ss/Sx	xxx/Sxxs
And 1181: iren ecgheard, ealdorgeard sceoran	Sx/Ss	Ss/Sx
Jul 452: siþe gesohte, þær ic swiþe me	Sx/(x)Sx	xx/Sxs

Note that in the final example here, the rhyme links the same syllables linked by primary alliteration.

24 It does, nevertheless, seem to be the case that coalliteration of s-feet and S-feet in a-lines is often poetically functional; the cases of such double 'sS' alliteration in the b-line are quite infrequent in comparison to examples in the a-line, which suggests that poets often used such alliteration intentionally in the a-line, but generally avoided it in the b-line.

25 To this verse, compare *Lord's Prayer II*, 95a: 'Heofonwaru and eorðwaru,' which we might scan as Ss/(x)Ssx. Such a scansion suggests that the parallel elements differ in treatment ('-waru' is resolved in one case, unresolved in the other), but this poem probably ought to be considered as belonging to the late Old English verse tradition, in which resolution is nonfunctional (see chapters 3.1–3.3). The verse is a partial parallel, then, but from a different stage in the evolution of Old English verse.

26 Of course, the requirement for double alliteration in the verse from *The Pheonix* is suspended by the use of what is clearly a semantic doublet. This verse, then, does not stand as a significant nonoccurrence of double alliteration.

27 Interestingly, three of the four Ss/Ss verses listed from *Beowulf* allow the secondary element of the name to coalliterate with the primary alliteration of the line (cf. *Beowulf* 1884b: 'gifu Hroðgares'); these b-lines have two syllables linked to the primary alliteration, but it seems likely that these are allowed by the same principle that allows sS alliteration in b-lines (cf. the discussion of *Elene* 792b: 'Forlæt nu, lifes weard,' above, p. 58).

28 *Christ II* has double alliteration in the following a-lines:

   Ss/Sx: 670a, 811a, 853a
   S/Ssx: 472a, 493a, 534a, 540a, 554a, 644a, 660a, 681a, 860a
   Ssx/S: 515a, 529a, 566a, 579a, 727a, 730a, 741a, 835a, 845a.

29 It is worth noting that other Cynewulfian works do not always seem to fol-
   low this pattern. I hope to take up the issue of the metrical consistency of
   the works in the Cynewulf canon in a separate work.

30 The following are the remaining Sxx/Sx a-lines from *The Phoenix*; all have
   double alliteration: 39a, 58a, 51a, 258a, 294a, 371a, 542a, 588a, 590a, and
   641a. In *Guthlac B*, I count thirty-one Sx/Ssx a-lines with double allitera-
   tion, with no examples (other than 1014a) with single alliteration. In the
   same poem, there are fourteen Ss/Sx or Ss/(x)Sx a-lines besides those
   quoted above; all have double alliteration (878a, 952a, 993a, 1002a, 1074a,
   1102a, 1214a, 1244a, 1266a, 1279a, 1315a, 1357a, 1370a, and 1379a). Finally,
   in *Beowulf*, there are thirteen additional a-lines of types Ss/Ss and Ss/(x)Ss
   besides the one give above, all have double alliteration (61a, 193a, 330a,
   485a, 608a, 641a, 1017a, 1189a, 1698a, 1719a, 1722a, 1881a, and 2434a).
   Again, other poems may not always be so strict about double alliteration in
   these types, but in the cases under discussion, no exceptions seem to be
   allowed unless cross alliteration is employed.

31 In *Andreas*, we find the following examples of S/Sxx a-lines with double
   alliteration: 447a, 453a, 755a, 841a, 891a, 1116a, and 1589a; the rhyming
   example is the lone example with single alliteration. In *Beowulf*, I count
   ninety-five a-lines of the form Sx/Ssx, two of which have full-verse com-
   pounds and three of which have personal names: these are categorical
   exceptions to the rules for double alliteration, as described above in chapter
   2.1. Of the remaining ninety examples, eighty-nine have double alliteration
   and the quoted verse shows rhyme. Of the forty-nine a-lines of form S/Sxs
   that I count in *Beowulf*, one has a name, forty-seven have double allitera-
   tion, and the quoted verse has rhyme. Once again, the logic seems clearly to
   be that these poets do allow rhyming verses in places where double alliter-
   ation is otherwise required, although not all poems do so.

Chapter 2.4: Classical Old English Poetics

 1 Turning to the *ASPR*'s editor as a familiar example, we can note that Dob-
   bie's discussion of the metre of *Judith* identifies the use of hypermetric lines
   and verses as the poem's 'most striking feature' (lxii), while also suggesting

that its rhyme-lines are 'of greater significance' for determining a probable date for the poem.

2 Some of the specific observations I make here about *Judith* were anticipated in Mark Griffith's discussion of the poem's alliteration and metre, in his edition of *Judith*, 25–37, and in his discussion of rhyme (167–8).

3 Hypermetric lines in *Judith* include the following: 2–12, 16–21, 30–4, 59–68, 88–99, 132, 272–3, 287–90, 337–49. Regarding hypermetric lines, Griffith, in his edition, notes that 'the first half of the poem up to the beheading scene is densely packed with long clusters ... whilst the remainder of the poem, excluding its hypermetric conclusion, contains only seven expanded lines' (35).

4 I find cross alliteration in the following lines: 3, 20, 58, 61, 78, 83–6, 93, 98, 108, 112, 135, 137, 155, 165, 173, 215, 223, 235, 237, 253, 310, 325, 339, and 344.

5 Supplementary alliteration is seen in *Judith* in verses 68b, 91b, 111b, 243b, 290b, and 311b.

6 For examples of verse rhyme or off-rhyme in *Judith* (linking half-lines together) see lines 2, 29, 36, 60, 63, 110, 113, 115, 123, 153, 202, 293, and 304.

7 'He was not yet dead then, entirely soulless. The valorous woman then earnestly struck the heathen hound a second time, so that the head rolled away from him on the floor. Afterwards, the foul trunk lay dead, the spirit gone elsewhere, under some abysmal headland, and there it was brought low, sealed in torment, ever after entwined by worms, bound in tortures, harshly fettered in hellfires after the journey hence.'

8 The term 'verse rhyme' is that used by Steven Brehe in his consideration of Ælfric and Layamon ('Rhythmical Alliteration'), but it is eminently suitable for describing the rhyming of the final stresses of two half-lines of classical Old English verse as well.

9 Alliteration on the same sound in two or more consecutive lines is straightforwardly labelled as 'continued alliteration' by Orchard (433).

10 The notion of cross alliteration or other secondary effects providing a kind of linguistic interlace might seem odd at first. But if we mark primary and secondary poetic effects in the middle of this passage with P and S, respectively, we can see a pattern as follows:

þone hæðenan hund, þæt him þæt heafod wand	PP/S	PS
forð on ða flore. Læg se fula leap	PP	SPS
gesne beæftan, gæst ellor hwearf	PS	PSx
under neowelne næs ond ðær genyðerad wæs	PP/S	PS

The general alternation between stressed elements participating in primary and secondary poetic structures seems to me to offer a remarkable linguistic analogue to the well-known Anglo-Saxon artistic motif of interlace. That secondary effects like this could be ornamental seems clear; even if the Anglo-Saxon poet or audience might not have conceptualized the use of these secondary effects as interlace, it still seems a useful term for modern readers as it serves to remind us of the linguistic effect of these poetic devices. Leyerle's famous essay on 'interlace structure' examines interlace as a heuristic metaphor on a different level in Old English poetry.

11 'I wish to pray you, god of beginnings, spirit of comfort, and son of the all-ruler, for thy mercy in my need, the strength of the trinity. Very much now for me is [my heart inflamed].'

12 Although I did not make the calculation in my 'Estimating Probabilities' essay, it is possible to estimate how unusual such a sequence of lines really is. Using the estimated frequencies from that essay, we can note that any line which is a candidate for cross alliteration will be followed by three more such lines about one-quarter of the time; the probability for random cross alliteration in all three of these succeeding lines should be about one in 2744 cases. That is, we should expect one line with cross alliteration to be followed by three more in about one case in ten thousand if the cross alliteration were random. Since there are probably fewer than 1500 lines with cross alliteration in the entire corpus (including postclassical verse in the *ASPR*), the (random) chance that a case of four consecutive lines would have cross alliteration in the surviving corpus is about one in seven. Thus, although we might not be particularly surprised to see four lines with cross alliteration in sequence (we should be surprised if it happened twice in the corpus), we should also probably conclude that, when such a sequence appears at a moment of obvious rhetorical importance, random chance is not a compelling explanation for what we see.

13 Cf. Griffith's comments about the same passage: 'Its alliterations go well beyond the normal requirements: there is cluster alliteration in l. 83, and in verse 86a, crossed alliteration in ll. 83 and 85 and, possibly, in 84 ... and alliterative enjambement in ll. 85-6. There is also inflectional rhyme in l. 85 The density of these devices suggests artifice, and their use appears to be appropriate to the formality of the context, effecting a degree of stylistic heightening' (29).

14 As noted by Griffith, (166–7), this happens in the following lines: 5, 23, 29, 30, 37, 55, 57, 80, 83, 86, 88, 106, 125, 164, 199, 205, 214, 221, 240, 247, 282, 317, 321, and 337.

15 Cf. Griffith's comment: 'The battle scenes are devoid of hypermetric verse (apart from the statement in 289b-90 that the Assyrians threw away their

weapons) perhaps because the poet was concerned not to slow down the pace of the narrative by the use of a more leisurely form' (35).

16 'Bright were the city buildings, many a stream-hall, high horn-treasure, the army-noise great, many a mead-hall full of the joys of men – until fate the mighty changed that. Walls fell widely, pestilence days came, death took all of the valiant men. Their ramparts became wasted foundations; the citadel fell.' Here I have expanded (in square brackets) the *ASPR*'s (and the manuscript's) use of the runic abbreviation for 'mon.'

17 The alliteration of a line's final stress with the primary stress of the following line is called 'alliterative enjambement' by Griffith, and 'strong-linked alliteration' by Orchard (433). Orchard would probably label the alliteration of a secondary element in one a-line with the primary element of the preceding line as 'back-linked alliteration' (433), although his examples show coalliteration of the final stress of the b-line with the preceding primary alliterator.

18 I might also note that *The Ruin* shows 'cluster alliteration' as described in *Judith* in lines 3, 4, 14, 31, and 33, for a density (five lines out of forty-nine) even higher than *Judith*'s.

19 'Marvellous is this wall-stone, broken by the fates. They burst the city-place; the work of giants crumbles.'

20 In Orchard's terms, this is strong-linked alliteration accompanied by back-linked alliteration. But note also that secondary elements in verses 1a and 2a coalliterate, beginning with the 'st-' cluster, probably to be understood as a variety of 'weak-linked alliteration' (Orchard 433).

21 'Mind ... [he] braided something swift, a quick plan in rings: the one famed for thoughts bound the wall-braces wondrously together with wires.'

22 Here, where the explicit content of the lines themselves refers to the notion of braided and bound elements, we may have the clearest indicator that 'interlace' may not be an inappropriate metaphor for thinking about the poetic effect of cross alliteration. Note also that lines 17–19 stand as a trio of lines with end-linked alliteration (cf. Orchard 433), where the final stresses of consecutive lines coalliterate. The final syllables of those lines, then, add an additional dimension to the alliterative interlace effect of this passage.

Chapter 3.1: Late Old English Verse

1 One notable exception to this trend is Thomas Cable, whose book, *The English Alliterative Tradition*, does attempt the sort of evolutionary perspective I suggest is too infrequently pursued. And while Cable's analysis and my own differ in important ways, I have no wish to undervalue his numerous

insights. The analysis undertaken here in Chapters 3.1–3.3 has recently
been published (in substantially different form) in *Anglo-Saxon England*; its
argument was anticipated, in some ways, in chapter 4 of my book on the
Anglo-Saxon Chronicle, although the arguments made there were only brief
and suggestive.

2 *For the Water-Elf Disease* was written into British Library MS Royal 12 D.
xvii by scribe 3 of the Parker Chronicle and so must have been composed
near or before mid-century; the *Chronicle* poems under annals 975DE and
later (with the notable exception of *The Death of Edward*) are generally char-
acterized by late Old English verse rules; and the Sutton Brooch is usually
dated on artistic grounds to about 1000.

3 Below, I will offer more precise scansions for such verses, including there
the probability that both 'ungemete' and 'ungerydre' should probably be
scanned with two stressed positions; in both cases the relevant a-lines indi-
cate vocalic alliteration, and thus I scan primary stress on the 'un-' prefix.
Note, however, that regardless of how we scan these words, the four-posi-
tion initial foot was disallowed by classical verse, as I indicated on p. 28.

4 Note Thomas Cable's comment on the decline in types C, D, and E (all with
secondary stress): 'After the mid-tenth century, there is a significant drop in
the percentage of lines with three levels of ictus' (Cable, 'Metrical Style' 80).
To this degree, Cable's analysis and my own are in complete agreement
here, although I associate the decreased usage of 'compound-like' verse-
types with the transition to late Old English verse.

5 The signficance of this shift is played out most compellingly in the realm of
diction: classical Old English verse used (and, indeed, needed) a complex
and traditional compound-oriented poetic diction, resulting in the familiar
poetic register shared by most classical compositions. The metrical use of
poetic compounds, of course, kept otherwise archaic words and forms cur-
rent (within poetry) long past the time when they were otherwise being
used. Late Old English verse, by contrast, needed no such archaic com-
pounding techniques, resulting in its simpler diction, which is frequently
interpreted by modern commentators as comparatively prosaic. The inter-
pretive choice between 'verselike' and 'prosaic' is a false dichotomy, how-
ever, based on the position that classical verse is the only sort of verse
under consideration. As such, it is a dichotomy that has hindered the
proper identification and appreciation of late Old English verse.

6 See Russom, *Linguistic Theory*, esp. 67–82.

7 Note that this verse, which has the second element of a compound in the
'dip' of a verse corresponding to a classical B-type verse, also supports the
notion that relevant stress levels were reduced to two. The secondary ele-

ment of the compound must be scanned with either full stress or no stress, and the placement of the compound in this position thus causes no problems in late Old English verse, although it was somewhat unusual in classical verse. See Russom's account of a similar verse, *Beowulf* 501b (Russom, *Linguistic Theory*, 35). Similar verses with the second elements of compounds in the 'dip' of B-type verses are quite common in *The Metrical Psalms*.

8 Note in particular the following innovative alliteration patterns. AA-, BB-, or AABB-alliteration is seen in these lines: *PPs* 54.8 2 (BB-alliteration); *JDay II* 28 (AA); *JDay II* 152 (BB); *MCharm2* 10 (AABB); *MCharm5* 3 (AABB); *MCharm7* 11 (BB); *MCharm10* 5 (BB). Also, there are clear examples of double alliteration in the b-line linked to an alliterating syllable in the a-line. Alliterating syllables on the fourth (or final) stress are fairly common in late verse; consider the following examples: *Mald* 29, 75 and 288; *CEdg* 19; *JDay II* 169; *Pr* 18 and 41; *Seasons* 86 and *MCharm2* 34.

9 The 'frequent use of anacrusis' (Gordon, *The Battle of Maldon*, 29) is often cited as one of the late features of *Maldon*; see also Fulk's comments on the frequency and variety of this feature in *Maldon* (259), *Judgment Day II* (263), *Durham* (260), and other poems in his chapter, 'Late Developments.' The 'BA' types used by Cable (*English Alliterative Tradition*) in the analysis of works from late in the Old English period capture this feature, and their increasing prevalence is precisely the point to which Cable calls our attention.

10 The reanalysis of anacrusis seems to have also resulted in the identification of any initial x-syllables in classical s-feet as extrametrical.

11 Although the system described here may seem to be so general that virtually any potential half-line can be accommodated within it, it is worth noting that no verse described by this system may have three stressed trisyllabic words (since no single foot has two Sxx sequences). Although many verses have SxxSxx sequences, it appears that such sequences are always scanned in separate feet. In my reading of late Old English verse (and Ælfric; see chapter 3.2) I have found no verses with three trisyllables or with three metrical Sxx sequences (three such sequences, of course, would demand that two of them be scanned in the same foot).

12 In other words, we should expect that the consequences of these changes were evolutionary in nature. The verse system adapted slowly to these metrical changes, and (in general) poems early in the late period retained much more of the feel of classical poems than later, more innovative poems did.

13 It seems worthwhile to note that the existence of three-stress verses in the

late tradition accounts for the loss of hypermetric lines and clusters in late Old English verse. Classical Old English verse and its use of hypermetric verses depended upon a clear distinction between two-foot and three-foot verses, but in late verse, two-, three- and even four-stress verses could be derived from classical two-foot verses and the normal/hypermetric distinction could not be maintained. Note that four-stress verses have been identified in Layamon's *Brut* (e.g., Noble, 'The Four-Stress Hemistich in Laʒamon's *Brut*'). Connections of this sort suggest the plausibilty of the analysis undertaken in chapters 4.1 and 4.2 of the present book, where I suggest that late Old English verse (as described here) can be understood as a clear antecedent of Layamon's verse.

14 Examples from *The Battle of Maldon* are also included on the basis of this poem's date; its sporadic use of typical late verse types, however, does serve to confirm the currency of these types even in an otherwise relatively classical poem. Although it is not always easy to determine if a poem belongs to the late Old English verse system or not, I believe the following poems should be considered as late Old English verse: *The Metrical Psalms*; *Metrical Charms* 2, 4, 5, 6, 7, 9, 10, 11 and 12; the *Chronicle* poems in annals 959DE, 975DE, 975D, 979DE, 1011CDE, 1036CD, 1057D, 1067D, 1075D (1076E), 1086E, and 1104E; *The Judgment Day II*; *The Battle of Maldon*; *Instructions for Christians*; *An Exhortation to Christian Living*; *A Summons to Prayer*; *Durham*; and the Sutton Brooch inscription. Together, these poems total over 6000 lines of verse; such a corpus is surely large enough to support the metrical analysis I undertake here, especially since so much work on classical Old English metre uses a corpus of lines half this size: the poem of *Beowulf*.

15 Note that all of the cited xx/SxSx verses would be unmetrical in classical verse, since anacrusis there is limited to two syllables in the a-verse and one syllable in the b-verse. The b-verse examples might be taken as hypermetric (if hypermetric verses were, in fact, acceptable in late verse), but in the context of the other items in the table, such an interpretation seems improbable.

16 Sx/SxSx verses also appear to be indistinguishable from one variety of classical hypermetric verse, but once again, such an explanation does not seem very compelling for these verses, which do not appear in hypermetric clusters. It is probable that hypermetric verses never appear in the late Old English verse under discussion; cf. notes 13 and 15 above.

17 This verse might better be scanned as S/SxSx, but it nevertheless stands as a diagnostic late type; note also that the *Chronicle*'s 1065 poem, *The Death of Edward*, contains a verse of the SSx/Sx type (28a: 'soþfæste sawle').

18 Note that, while in classical verse, the link accomplished by verse rhyme could not stand as the primary linkage in a line (since it would link the final stress of the a-line to the final stress of the b-line, a link excluded in the classical tradition), the changes in alliterative patterns during the late Old English period did allow final stresses to be linked. Thus, changes to possible alliterative links also seem to have allowed the (formerly) secondary poetic effect of rhyme to become primary in the case of verse rhyme. Somewhat surprisingly, the analysis presented here allows us to see the origins of verse rhyme as a straightforward development of a secondary poetic effect into a primary effect occasioned by the shift in allowed alliterative patterns. Verse rhyme, which has often seemed (to modern interpreters) to appear somewhat mysteriously in late Old English or early Middle English verse, is actually a simple and obvious development.

19 Note that I scan 'Her' as part of the poem here, although metricists have traditionally excluded this word from the *Chronicle* verse (a habit extending back to Campbell's edition of *Brunanburh*). The reasons for doing so, however, seem dubious to me, as they are either based on an assumption that the poems were not written for the *Chronicle* or based in Sieversian metrics. In my work on the *Chronicle*, I have argued that even *The Battle of Brunanburh* (the *Chronicle*'s first poem) was probably explicitly composed for the *Chronicle* (*Textual Histories*, 72–3 and 99–102). The argument from Sieversian metrics, of course, is not strictly relevant for this poem, which is in the late verse tradition, and it is possible that, even in *Brunanburh* 1a, we might see a mid-tenth-century example of a late Old English verse form.

20 See S3 below for a statement on just what sorts of rhyme seem to have been functional in the late Old English tradition.

21 Line numbers from the *William the Conqueror* poem are taken from the lineation used in chapter 3.3.

22 This is the third and final line of the Sutton Brooch; see Okasha, *Hand-List*, 116–17.

Chapter 3.2: Ælfric and Late Old English Verse

1 In 1995, for example, Andy Orchard was able to suggest that the question of whether Ælfric composed verse was 'no longer seriously posed by scholars' (458, n. 96). More recently, Haruko Momma has attempted to summarize the debate: 'The debate has never come to a close, but it now seems to be agreed that Ælfric's writing is not poetry when placed within the strict regimen of traditional verse in Anglo-Saxon England' ('Rhythm and Alliteration' 255). Momma's 'traditional verse,' of course, corresponds to what I

have labelled classical Old English verse; my argument in this chapter will suggest that a comparison between Ælfric and late Old English verse yields a different conclusion.

2 Consider John C. Pope's comment, 'It [that is, the rhythmical prose] is better regarded as a mildly ornamental, rhythmically ordered prose than as a debased, pedestrian poetry' (*Supplementary Collection* 1:105), for one influential suggestion that the choice lies between good prose and bad poetry. More recently, Paul Szarmach, ('Abbot Ælfric's Rhythmical Prose') has usefully summarized the responses of textual editors and others to the problem of how to visually present Ælfric's texts in modern editions, citing a particularly telling opinion from Bruce Mitchell's *Old English Syntax*: 'To me, Ælfric's alliterative prose is good prose, not bad poetry ... I do not agree with [Pope's] decision to print this prose in verse lines' (*Old English Syntax* 2:998, quoted in Szarmach, 103, with Szarmach's ellipsis). It seems clear that the unstated assumption continues to be that, since Ælfric's works do not match up well to Sieverisan metrics, the choice in identifying their form is one between good prose and bad poetry.

3 Perhaps the most cogent articulation of 'rhythmical alliteration' as the origin of Layamon's verse form is that of S.K. Brehe's essay, 'Rhythmical Alliteration'; Brehe's detailed analysis of similarities between Ælfric and Layamon is telling, and he suggests 'if we recognize Ælfric's rhythmical form as the source of the Middle English loose metre, we will find it easier to explain the enormous differences between the loose metre and Old English classical verse' (78). Other scholars have also either noted such similarities or suggested the importance of Ælfric for understanding Layamon, notably Cable, *Alliterative Tradition*, and Angus McIntosh, 'Early Middle English Alliterative Verse.' Taking an opposing position, Douglas Moffat, in 'The Intonational Basis of Laʒamon's Verse,' uses an argument based in intonation patterns, deciding, 'I cannot agree with Norman Blake, who regards the *Brut* as a regularized, poeticized outgrowth of rhythmical prose of the Ælfrician sort' (142).

4 Friedlander, 'Early Middle English Accentual Verse,' traces Layamon's use of rhyme to a tradition extending back at least to the *Chronicle*'s poetic entry in annal 1036, but she appears to draw no clear distinction between the late Old English examples and the early Middle English texts. In chapter 4.2, I will suggest that Layamon actually knew at least some of the *Chronicle* poems, and that his use of rhyme stems either directly from them, or through traditional links to such late Old English rhyming verse.

5 See Godden, *Introduction*, 412, where he describes Ælfric's *Life of Cuthbert* as being 'written in a new and apparently experimental style.' Note the reser-

vations of Haruko Momma who notes that 'this homily seems to represent
an experimental stage of Ælfric's writing, because its style varies widely in
its degree of similarity to verse' ('Rhythm and Alliteration' 261). Momma's
caveat that not all of Ælfric's rhythmical compositions remain as rhythmi-
cal or alliterative as the most regular sections is an important reminder that
Ælfric apparently felt free to deviate from some of the expectations of late
Old English verse, although his general adherence to most of those stand-
ards in his alliterative compositions is also clear.

6 'One upright man likewise had great familiarity with the holy Cuthbert
and often enjoyed his teaching – then his wife gave birth, with much more
difficulty than necessary, to the point that she was a greatly afflicted with
madness. When the pious man came to the blessed Cuthbert (and he was at
that time situated as provost in the monastery that is called Lindisfarne),
then he might not, for shame, openly say that his pious wife lay in mad-
ness, but asked that he might send some brother who could administer the
last rites before she was led away from this world.'

7 Cf. Pope's comment: 'Ælfric allows *sc, sp,* and *st* to alliterate with one
another and with *s* followed by a vowel or any other consonant, though
with *st* especially he seems to prefer exact correspondence. The alliteration
of *sc* and *s* has been observed in the metrical psalms, and Ælfric may be
reflecting, or exaggerating, a tendency of late Old English poetry' (*Supple-
mentary Collection* 1:128–9).

8 Although Pope does not accept such continuing alliteration as a significant
feature of Ælfric's practice, he does note that '[Brandeis] demonstrated that
such concatenated alliteration is abundant, and that it appears frequently
in lines that lack internal alliteration' (*Supplementary Collection* 1:134).

9 Without making an exhaustive survey, we can note that the following lines
from the *Psalms* that apparently feature no alliterative link do share at least
one probable alliterator with the primary alliterator of the preceding line:
PPs 71.11.3; 76.10.3; and 79.10.2.

10 Cf. O'Brien O'Keeffe, *Visible Song.* Similar 'half-line' pointing occurs in
other Ælfric manuscripts, as well as examples of b-line pointing. Sherman
M. Kuhn's essay, 'Was Ælfric a Poet?' lists the following manuscripts as fea-
turing one or the other system of pointing with at least some regularity:
London, British Library, Cotton Julius E. vii (the base manuscript for
Skeat's *Ælfric's Lives of Saints*); London, British Library, Cotton Vitellius C.
v; Cambridge, Trinity College B. 15. 34, and Cambridge, Corpus Christi
College 178. The metrical effect of such pointing was recognized by Skeat: 'I
have divided the matter into lines as well as I could, usually following the
guidance of the points introduced into the MS. itself; these usually occur at

the end of what is meant to be a line, and frequently also at the pause in the middle' (*Ælfric's Lives of Saints* 2:li).

11 Of course, CUL Gg. 3. 28 is often closely associated with Ælfric or his scriptorium: the points in this manuscript may even reflect an authorial habit, rather than scribal habit, and the evidence of pointing therefore may well suggest that Ælfric himself felt that he was writing verse. Even if that is not the case, the significant issue is the similarity of this pointing practice with the pointing practices encountered in the classical Old English verse tradition.

12 It is worth pointing out that the changes were even more extensive than I have described here: virtually the whole machinery of oral-formulaic composition is no longer relevant to either Ælfric or late Old English poets in general. Formulaic themes, kennings, and poetic compounding (things which have often been seen as basic to the distinction between Old English verse and prose) turn out to be relevant to only the classical verse tradition. Late Old English verse, it appears, was formally distinguished from prose primarily through metrical or rhythmical criteria alone.

13 The manuscripts of the late Old English *Chronicle* poems from the tenth century, of course, are far removed in time from that century (manuscript D dates from the latter eleventh century, and manuscript E from 1121 or a little later), so they tell us little about how the earliest exemplars of the late *Chronicle* poems might have been pointed. But it may well be significant that while the *Metrical Psalms* and the *Chronicle* poems evidence a fairly slow, even evolutionary, development away from classical norms, the works of Ælfric seem to use relatively few classically acceptable forms virtually from the start. The development of 'metrical pointing' in Ælfrician works right as (or soon after) they were being composed may indeed be directly connected to the extent to which these works embodied innovative metrical forms.

14 In addition, the scribe writes the first line of the alliterative portion in capitals, as he does the very beginning of *The Life of Edmund* itself. The beginning of the alliterative passage, then, is visually marked almost as insistently as the beginning of the entire text. A facsimile of this page is included in Szarmach's essay 'Abbot Ælfric's Rhythmical Prose.'

15 See Bredehoft, 'Boundaries.' For an especially close analogue to the treatment of the 'prose'/'rythmical prose' boundary at this point in Julius E. vii, see the treatment of the Alfredian Boethius in London, British Library, Cotton Otho A. vi (s. x med.), where heavy punctuation, blank space, and display letters (or space left for such letters) generally mark the transitions between prose and verse portions of the text. Plate I of O'Brien O'Keeffe's

Visible Song is a photograph of folio 87v of the Otho manuscript, perhaps the best-preserved relevant page of this manuscript.

16 'Bede, the wise teacher of the English nation, wrote the life of this saint in order, with glorious praise, both in the manner of a simple narrative and in the manner of poetical singing.'

17 As Godden notes, 'The account of St Cuthbert, II.10, seems to be an early and experimental version of this [rhythmical] style, with very marked rhythms and a more extravagant use of poetic and colourful language; since one of its main sources was Bede's metrical life of the saint, and it is indeed the first and perhaps only work by Ælfric that used a poem as its main source, it seems likely that the inspiration and model for the use of this style *in extenso* was the use of Latin verse for historiographical narrative' (Godden, *Introduction* xxxvii)

18 Although Ælfric's verses frequently have three full stresses, verses with four stresses are somewhat unusual. But they are not, apparently, excluded, as the following examples from the *Life of St. Sebastian* suggest:

198a: þurh ænig þing gehælon magon.
284a: and þæt þa riht-wisan beon ge-herode.

For reference, I will use Skeat's line numbers, as here.

19 Pope's analysis of rhyme in Ælfric includes examples of possible rhymes (including rhymes of '-lic') in positions other than the last stressed positions of each verse (*Supplementary Collection* 1:132–3); however, it seems best to treat Ælfrician rhyme, at this point, as operating on the same principles as rhyme in late Old English verse.

20 Pope suggests that 'alliteration of minor syllables' is often used in Ælfric, especially when 'the main stresses were recalcitrant' or failed themselves to alliterate (*Supplementary Collection* 1:124). Brehe's summary of Pope's description of Ælfric's metre identifies these minor syllables as 'auxiliary verbs, copulas, pronouns, demonstratives, conjunctions, prepositions, and prefixes' ('Rhythmical Alliteration' 70). It does not seem to me to be necessary to hypothesize alliteration in Ælfric on 'minor syllables' other than prefixes and prepositions.

21 One of the anonymous readers of this book for the University of Toronto Press noted that three of the lines in this list (80, 127, and 468) include verbs with the 'fore-' prefix, which, as noted by Campbell, regularly takes stress on the prefix (*Old English Grammar*, 32). Such examples, therefore, may more properly belong in the lists of lines showing normal alliteration, but it is useful to include them here on the principle that they may well have

served as precedents for Ælfric's apparent willingness to employ alliteration on other prefixes.

22 In each of these cases, late Old English verses scansions would allow the relevant prefixes and prepositions to be scanned on S positions; a full examination of Ælfric's alliteration patterns would be valuable to determine if this is always the case. That is, it is at least possible that Ælfric allows occasional, nonstandard alliteration on x-positions; but if no examples can be found where a preposition or prefix seems to alliterate that cannot be scanned as S, that would seem to suggest that Ælfric continues to demand that alliteration be associated only with S-positions. As far as *St. Sebastian* goes, the evidence seems to be that Ælfric may allow prefixes and prepositions to be scanned as S, but that the rules for alliterative linking otherwise remain unchanged.

23 See above, note 8.

24 ' ... and left him as lying for dead. Then came a widow (she was a martyr's widow) on the same night to where he lay greatly wounded. She wished to bury his body, and she found him living, and led him then to her house alive.'

25 I consider here only examples where an unlinked line shares an alliterator with the primary alliterator of a neighbouring line. Cases where one stressed word alliterates with one stress in a neighbouring line are considered to be accidental. The lines in question, then, are 11, 126, 152, 153 (continuing 'c' alliteration from 151–2), 181, 282, 292, 381, 430, 431, 433, and 462.

Chapter 3.3: The Poetics of Late Old English Verse

1 O'Brien O'Keeffe describes the work as 'poor verses' (135); Julie Townsend's essay 'The Metre of the *Chronicle*-verse' ignores the 1036 poem altogether, with the disclaimer, 'My concern is with the five regularly alliterative' poems (143). The 1036 poem is one of McIntosh's specimens of 'the late "debased" Old English verse' ('Wulfstan's Prose' 112).

2 It is at least possible that the first portion of the 1036 annal is also intended as verse; Sedgefield prints it as such. I hope to address this issue in a future reconsideration of the *Chronicle*'s late Old English verse passages.

3 I have scanned this verse with stress on 'hwile' and understand alliteration between 'w-' and 'hw-'; it may be possible that 'hwile' is unstressed and that the two verses in this line are linked only by inflectional rhyme; see the discussion of alliterative patterns with 'h-' in the previous chapter as well as the discussion of 1086E below.

4 'But Godwine then hindered him and set him in captivity, and drove off his companions. Variously he slew some, some were given to people for

money, some killed roughly, some bound, and some blinded, some hamstrung, and some scalped. There was no more miserable deed done in this land since the Danes came and made peace here. It is now that we should believe in the dear God that they rejoice happily with Christ, who were, innocent, so horribly killed. The prince yet lived, each kind of wickedness promised to him, until they counselled that he be led to Ely, bound as he was. As soon as he arrived, they blinded him upon the ship, and brought him thus blind to the monks, and he dwelt there the time that he lived. Afterwards they buried him as was fitting, full honourably, as he was worthy, at the west end, right near the steeple, in the south porch; his soul is with Christ.'

5 Line 7 gives the most difficulty; it is likely that the final fricatives in 'todraf' and 'ofsloh' are intended to be similar enough to allow the line to feature verse rhyme, and I count it as a rhyming line.

6 Fulk notes that some of these rhyme-pairs may reflect true rhymes if the original poem had been composed in an Anglian dialect (282, n. 31).

7 The matching of inflectional syllables is not paralleled in the *William the Conqueror* poem from the *Chronicle*'s annal 1086E, as the following rhymes suggest: 'befeallan'/'ealle'; 'hinde'/'blendian.'

8 Recall, of course, the fact that single-stress A3 verses are allowed only in the a-line in classical verse, while b-lines generally have two stressed positions. *The Death of Alfred*'s use of single-stress a-lines (balanced with two-stress b-lines) may be inherited from this feature of the classical Old English verse system.

9 See Roberta Frank's important essay 'Some Uses of Paronomasia in Old English Scriptural Verse.'

10 The rhymes in this line and in line 7 are of particular importance for confirming the claim made in chapter 3.1 about stress levels in late Old English verse. In line 7, *William the Conqueror* rhymes 'deorfrið' and 'þær wið,' with the compound word necessarily scanned as SS. In line10, the 'headeor'/'fæder' rhyme indicates that the compound must be scanned as Sx. These rhymes, then, show that there was no intermediate stress level in late verse, and that compounds that would have been scanned Ss in classical verse were now scanned as either SS or Sx.

11 The scansion of line 18 given here reflects manuscript pointing and rhyme; it might be possible to lineate the line as:

Wala wa. þæt ænig man   sceolde modigan swa.   SxS/(x)SxS Sx/SxxS

Such a relineation would give the line alliteration as the primary linkage, rather than rhyme, and it would also prevent the a-line from having only three syllables. As noted above, the status of three-syllable verses remains uncertain in late Old English verse, although the pointing of the present line suggests the possibility that three-syllable verses were acceptable.

12 'He ordered castles to be wrought and wretched men to work greatly. The king was very harsh, and demanded of his underlings many marks of gold and more hundreds of pounds of silver that he seized by weight and with great injustice from the people of the land – and for little need. He was fallen in avarice and loved greed above all; he established a great deer park and made a law for it that whosoever should slay hart or hind would be blinded. He forbid the killing of harts and likewise boars; he loved the stags as greatly as if he were their father. And he ruled that the hares might roam freely. Powerful men complained and the poor lamented, but he was so rigid that he cared not for the enmity of them all; but they must entirely follow the king's will, if they would live, or have land, land or possessions, or even the king's favour. Alas – that any man should so proudly raise himself up and consider himself above all men. May the almighty God make mercy known to his soul and give him forgiveness of his sins.' Note that I use 'þæt' for Plummer's crossed thorn, the common manuscript abbreviation for 'þæt.'

13 Note that the roughly contemporary *Durham* does not use rhyme so extensively, and that, when Layamon uses an early Middle English descendent of the late Old English verse form, rhyme and alliteration function as complementary systems of half-line linkage (for Layamon, see chapter 4.1). The *William the Conqueror* poet's extensive use of rhyme therefore would have probably stood out as unusual even in the late eleventh century.

14 Alternatively, it may be better to treat line 20 as simply having no linkage: late Old English verse does seem to allow occasional lines with neither rhyme nor alliteration, and this line may be such an example.

15 Further, line 16 has a stressed syllable beginning with 'l,' continuing the alliteration of the preceding line; see the similar examples in *The Death of Alfred*, p. 92.

16 It may be more accurate to scan 'Aidanes sawle' as SxxxSx, if the two initial vowels are treated as separate syllables, rather than as a diphthong.

17 'Afterwards, the holy Cuthbert, when he was still a youth, saw how God's angels carried the soul of Aidan, the holy bishop, happily to heaven, to the eternal glory that he earned in this world. The holy Oswald's bones were later brought after many years to the land of the Mercians, into Gloucester, and there God often made many wonders manifest through the holy man. May there be glory to the Almighty always and ever. Amen.' This relineated passage is cited from Needham, rather than Skeat's edition, as Need-

ham indicates that a reviser has added five words in the last line. I use Skeat's line numbers for reference only, since Needham's edition uses a 'proselike' layout.

18 The count of lines with cross alliteration should probably be expanded here if we take 'h' plus vowel as alliterating with vowels (l. 286; as I noted above, I believe there seems to be clear evidence for optional h/vowel alliteration in other Ælfrician texts). In late Old English verse, ABBA-alliteration should be understood as a variety of cross alliteration, rather than transverse alliteration, because late Old English verse does not exhibit the metrical subordination which makes the distinction between the two types of secondary alliteration meaningful. For an especially clear example of how Sieversian thinking has hindered how scholars approach Ælfric's texts, consider that Haruko Momma ('Rhythm and Alliteration' 258) quotes the first four lines of the present passage as exemplifying Ælfric's tendency to use an xa/ay alliterative pattern. Using late Old English verse scansions allows us to see three of those four lines as actually employing cross alliteration, making this passage far more effective poetically than Momma credits.

19 See my essay, 'Estimating Probabilities,' (and above, chapter 2.4) for an argument that cross alliteration is sometimes used for effect in classical verse, including an example of four consecutive lines with cross alliteration.

20 See my argument about *The Order of the World* in my article, 'Estimating Probabilities' (22).

21 Further evidence that Ælfric's works should not necessarily be considered prosaic can be found in the observation made by Godden (*Introduction* xxxvii), noting that Ælfric's rhythmical works are 'accompanied at times by a sprinkling of poetic vocabulary,' including words such as 'metod,' 'rodor,' and 'folme.'

22 'God shaped his creation all in six days, and ceased on the seventh so that afterwards he shaped no other creation, but mightily renews that selfsame one among men and beasts until today. He shaped then two humans, and established all the hours, but he has never since shaped novel creations from the old arrangement that he set at first. But he shapes each day new souls and fastens them in bodies (as we learn in books) and those souls are not created anywhere before God sends them to their appointed bodies in their mothers' insides, and so they become men' (spaces added to mark the caesura).

23 For brief discussions of 'consecutive alliteration' see Bredehoft, 'Estimating Probabilities' (19–20), and Grinda, 'Pigeonholing Old English Poetry.' Orchard, 'Artful Alliteration,' also discussed this phenomenon, labelling it 'continued alliteration.'

24 Note the manuscript point in the middle of 16a. This point may appear because points had become conventional before the Tironian '7,' or it may be that this point signals a mistake on the scribe's part about the verse boundary (note that no point appears in the middle of 14a). It seems worth noting that this line is the heaviest line of the passage under consideration and thus perhaps the most likely to be mis-scanned by the scribe. Further study of mid-verse points may well offer additional insight into scribal perceptions of the structural units of late Old Engish verse.

25 'Edmund the blessed, king of the East-Angles, was wise and worthy and constantly honoured the Almighty God with noble customs. He was blessed-minded and distinguished and remained so resolute that he would not stoop to shameful vices, nor on either side did he lay down his practices, but was always mindful of true learning. If you are made a chief-man, do not lift yourself up, but be among men just as a man of them. He was generous to the poor and to widows just as a father, and with benevolence he led his folk and steered the violent always to righteousness and happily lived in true belief' (space added to mark caesura).

26 It seems unlikely that Ælfric's works served as a direct source for either *The Death of Alfred* or *William the Conqueror*, especially considering the extensive use of rhyme in both poems. It seems far more likely to suppose a continuing tradition, as opposed to direct influence.

Chapter 4.1: Layamon and Early Middle English Verse

1 The following comment from Françoise Le Saux is typical: 'Laȝamon's verse is a descendant of the Old English long line; but critics have had some problems in ascertaining its exact parentage' (*Laȝamon's Brut* 192).

2 Of course, many writers have addressed the relationship between Layamon, Ælfric, and Old English verse; besides the works of Blake and Brehe cited here, my work in this chapter has also benefitted in various ways from works by Friedlander, Cable (*Alliterative Tradition*), McIntosh ('Early Middle English'), and Minkova.

3 The Caligula text is often seen as keeping remarkably close to Layamon's own text and intentions, but there can be no question that the Caligula scribe does sometimes nod. Besides the kinds of issues to be raised below, half-lines are occasionally dropped and mispunctuation is frequent. The latter issue (mispunctuation) is especially important, since it seemingly arises from a misapprehension of metrical structure. Although the Caligula and Otho scribes share the habit of pointing a-lines with a punctus elevatus and b-lines with a medial point, mispointing by both scribes raises the pos-

sibility that their ultimate ancestor may not have shared that pointing system. A study of mispointing in these manuscripts might illuminate much about these scribes' perceptions of metrical form.

4 London, BL, Cotton Caligula A. ix. 'When he best expected to hold his land, then Hengest had it in his hand.'

5 London, BL, Cotton Otho C. xii. 'When he best expected to hold his people, then the queen held it, together with Hengest.'

6 The presence of the 'cwene' in the Otho version does not seem to be the type of innovation that the Otho scribe is normally responsible for, so we might suspect that, here at least, the Otho version is closer to Layamon's text. But any such judgment is, of course, subjective; choosing between these alternatives is not really possible with any certainty.

7 Not all five-stress verses in Caligula have shorter counterparts in Otho, as in the following examples, where both manuscripts seem to show five-stress verses: 12112a and 12275a. It is, of course, possible that some or all five-stress verses come from Layamon himself.

8 Note that for most of the examples given, the Otho version cannot be explained as resulting from the elimination of archaic or archaistic elements: these changes do not seem to be caused by the Otho reviser's concern with updating the language of the poem, so the possible metrical explanation does seem relevant.

9 Although this chapter is primarily concerned with the forms of verses used by Layamon, it appears that the description given here will also apply to poems such as the *Worcester Fragments* and the *Proverbs of Alfred*. In this sense, I am really attempting to describe early Middle English alliterative metre.

10 It often seems that we can be much more precise: in my reading of Layamon, I believe it is the case that disyllabic forms of 'all' (e.g., 'alle' and 'alre') are regularly stressed while monosyllabic ones are not ('al'). 'Æver,' 'næver,' and 'ælc' seem always to be stressed. Short (sentence-particle-like) adverbs are often unstressed before verbs, but seemingly stressed after them. Further study of Layamon's practice might go far to identify more concretely just what sorts of syllables are scanned on S positions in the *Brut*.

11 Citations from the *Brut* that do not specify the manuscript of origin will be taken from the Caligula manuscript, unless otherwise noted.

12 That is, the principle that the final word of a verse is always stressed seems to have been a constant from classical Old English poetry to early Middle English.

13 Although the issues involved go beyond the concerns of the present work, note that Cable argues very persuasively for three-stress verses in the a-line

of poems from the 'Alliterative Revival' (*Alliterative Tradition*). If my arguments here have merit, it may be possible to suggest that the Alliterative Revival did, in fact, employ metrical forms derived from those used by Layamon and his contemporaries, restricting three-stress verses to the a-line. Cable's remarkable account of 'final -e' and metre in fourteenth-century verse indicates, however, that metrical developments between the twelfth and fourteenth centuries were probably far from simple and straightforward.

14 As discussed above, it may well be the case that Layamon wrote a number of verses with five feet; cf. note 17 below.

15 In late Old English verse, such verses would have had scansions such as (xx)S/SS or (xx)SS/S; these verses would not have any direct ancestor in the classical verse tradition. In classical Old English verse, even two stresses at the end of a verse with an unstressed onset were rare; Fulk, however, notes that xx/Ss verses may have a final foot filled by two words as early as the *Meters of Beothius* (252). We should expect to see xx/SS verses at least occasionally in postclassical verse, then, but even in that tradition, structures like (xx)S/SS seem to have been rare at best.

16 This verse (and ones closely related to it) is used repeatedly by Layamon. See, for additional examples, 1858b, 3380a, and 3461b.

17 It is worth noting here that it is somewhat easier to find five-stress verses in Layamon than verses with three trisyllabic sequences, and we may need, ultimately, to conclude that Layamon allows up to five S-positions in his verse. As should be clear by this point, I treat such verses as anomalous, even if authorial, and (as such) my system explicitly concerns itself with the most basic and common forms found (the 'normal range' of verses and lines), and assumes that Layamon could (and did) write some verses and lines that did not fall within the normal range. I limit Layamon's metrical verses to four stressed positions simply because late Old English verse had only four possible S-positions per verse, and I hypothesize a direct descent from late Old English to Layamon. Further analysis is needed, I believe, to determine if MEFC1 should allow five-foot verses, but if so, the fifth such position is one not derivable from a late Old English verse model.

18 The late Old English poem *William the Conqueror* may use a three-syllable verse, and Layamon, too, seems to occasionally have only three syllables in a verse (see chapter 4.2 below). My system treats these verses as unmetrical, in the sense of lying outside the 'normal range,' despite their occasional appearance.

19 Note McIntosh's comment: 'The interest of these early Middle English examples of "imperfect" rhyme is considerable. For we must see them not

only as phenomena which have obvious antecedents in Old English, but as richly illustrating a convention that was to spread far beyond the confines of the alliterative verse of that period' ('Early Middle English' 27).

20 A number of lines (chiefly in the second half of the poem) might appear to suggest that Layamon at least sometimes allowed rhyme to function even between non-verse-final S positions. Consider the following closely grouped examples from the Caligula manuscript:

Brut 15097: Þa while þa cnihtes wise.~   þa spechen sculden rihte.
Brut 15128: and ic hine biræuien wulle .~   at his baren liue.
Brut 15137: and þa halidomes alle.~   þa wunieð inne Rome.~

In each case, reversal of the final two words in the a-line would yield a typical example of verse rhyme. These examples fall in a portion of the Brut where Otho is defective; but in a number of similar examples, the Otho text exhibits verse rhyme: Brut 2436, 12395, 12410, 13762, 13912, 14156, 14168, and 14210. It might be possible to suggest that Otho here regularizes, but I am inclined to see this as (inappropriate) innovation on the Caligula scribe's part, providing further evidence that the Caligula scribe's sense of metrical possibilities may not have always agreed with Layamon's.

21 In the following case, Brut 14432 '7 bad alle þe ȝeonglinges.~ ȝeond þa hæðene londes,' we either have rhyme linking '-linges' and 'londes' or alliteration linking the very same elements. Alliteration may be the more attractive explanation here, although '-ling' is probably best understood as a suffix, rather than the second element of a compound. Although the proper scansion of the line therefore remains somewhat uncertain, it is an interesting example in either case.

22 Note that three of the four possible inflectional rhymes in my first group were also disyllabic; it does seem possible that disyllabic inflections could rhyme for Layamon, even if monosyllabic ones could not.

23 C.V. Friedlander was able to suggest in 1979 that 'each half-line [of early Middle English alliterative verse, including the Brut] has two principle stresses. That metrical definition is unprovable, but it has the support of all those who have studied the metre of EME poems' (220). Since then, there has been growing support for scanning some verses with three or more stresses: see, for example, Glowka ('Prosodic Decorum'), Noble ('The Four-Stress Hemistich'), and Cable's scansion of the Brut (Alliterative Tradition 157). My understanding of Layamon's metre differs in important ways from these writers, but their example in abandoning the notion of two-stress verses has been valuable.

24 'He had a gracious sister in the east end [of the land]; there is no fairer woman that the bright sun shines upon. The king of France, Louis, yearns for her fully, indeed.'

25 My point, of course, is that reliance upon a two-stress scansion system has impoverished our view of lines that use both rhyme and alliteration. Minkova ('Credibility' 434) also usefully calls our attention to the taxonomic problem of counting lines as either rhyming or alliterating, when they might actually use both types of linkage.

26 Neil Wright describes the passage as 'one of the best-known passages in Laȝamon's Brut, and certainly one of the most quoted' (161).

27 'Yesterday was Baldulf best of all knights; now he stands on a hill and beholds the Avon, how steel fish lie in the stream, gored by swords: their swimming is spoiled. Their scales shine like gold-adorned shields; there their spits float, as if they were spears (?). This is a marvellous thing that has befallen in this land – such an animal on the hill, such fishes in the welling water. Yesterday was the leader keenest of all kings, now he is become a hunter, and horns follow him. He flees over the broad field; his hounds bark. He has beside Bath left off his hunting: from his prey he flees, and we shall take it and bring his bold boast to nothing, and so we shall enjoy it, rightly taken.'

28 If we scan 'swulche' in 10645 as stressed, then six consecutive lines would feature s-alliteration.

29 We might note that thirteen of the twenty stresses in these four lines alliterate on 'k,' 'h,' or 'b.' Only ten of these stresses make up primary alliterators, and it seems likely that Layamon uses secondary alliterators here to mark this passage with especially dense sound-patterning.

30 It may well be the case that Layamon intends alliteration to include the prefix on 'bi-ȝæten' in line 10652; alliteration does seem to occur sometimes on prefixes in the Brut (as, apparently, in Ælfric; see the discussion in chapter 3.2), and it may be the case that the Caligula scribe may intend to call our attention to the possibility of prefix alliteration when he spaces prefixes, as here. In this passage, however, compare the prefixes in lines 10639, 10641, and 10649.

Chapter 4.2: Layamon's Old English Poetics

1 Interestingly, certain associations among these texts may undermine this argument: the Worcester Fragments (including the Soul's Address) are, of course, from Worcester, near enough to Layamon's home, and the Proverbs of Alfred (obviously) exhibit some interest in the Anglo-Saxon past. One

reading of this evidence, then, might hypothesize a smallish group of anti-
quaries, possibly centred in Worcester as the only practitioners of this type
of early Middle English verse; in this context, Stanley's observation that
'the relevance of the 'tremulous hand' of Worcester to Laȝamon is nothing
new' ('Sentiments' 30) acknowledges the possible relations of the *Brut* and
the Worcester fragments. An opposing position, however, is offered by
McIntosh, who suggests that the range of early Middle English alliterative
verse 'was a good deal more generally familiar in early Middle English
times than is often suggested' ('Early Middle English' p. 26, n. 13).

2 Tatlock, for example, simply says that 'broðer'/'oðer' was a 'stock rime in
M. E.' (498). Note also that, in order to make the claim that Layamon's and
Maldon's rhymes belong to the same formulaic tradition, Sklar modifies the
well-known Parry-Lord definition of formula ('a group of words which is
regularly employed under the same metrical conditions to express a given
essential idea' [Sklar, 412–13], quoting Parry via Magoun) in the following
way: 'For the purposes of this discussion, then the term "formula" will
describe not a half-line, but the rhymed pair or "couplet," that is, in the case
of *Maldon* and Layamon, the entire line' (Sklar 413). But as her examples
suggest, she includes as examples of 'formulas' any lines sharing the same
rhyme words, with little clear account of the degree of similarity (or lack of
it) otherwise.

3 Other Old English verses with 'winemagas' in a similar metrical position
are *Genesis A* 2626b; *Elene* 1015a, and *Beowulf* 65b.

4 The *Brut* verses should also be compared to *Brut* 8953b: '7 gumenene
lauerd' and 9164: 'gumenene lauerd' (*Brut* 9263b actually also reads
'gumenene ældere'). These verses seem to suggest clearly formulaic usage.
The Old English tradition shows no examples of '*gumena hlaford,' but
there are a handful of examples of 'gumena drihten' (*Daniel* 612b; *Beowulf*
1824a; and *Creed* 28b). *Judith* uses both 'gumena aldor' (32b) and 'gumena
baldor' (9b) in the context of hypermetric verses. On the other hand, the
apparent misanalysis of the Old English genitive plural that affects three of
these four verses should give us little confidence in these examples as proof
of a continuing mode of traditional, formulaic expression. These examples,
I think, may well point to conscious (and in this case, somewhat mistaken)
archaizing on Layamon's part.

5 Although I could not find any 'ungemete' verses with 'wide' in the second
foot in the Old English tradition, there are nearly twenty verses with
'ungemete' followed by a disyllable such as 'swyþe,' usually in the *Metrical
Psalms*.

6 That is, in six of the seven examples of 'wide and side' I have found, Laya-

mon uses it as a b-line. In fifteen examples in the *ASPR*, all are from the b-line; only in the *Chronicle* poem from annal 959DE do we see 'wide 7 side' in the a-line in Old English.

7 The Otho version of Caligula 10018 preserves this formulaic phrase, even while rewriting two lines into one.

8 Indeed, Le Saux remains sceptical even about the possibility proposed by P.J. Frankis that Layamon knew at least some of the works of Ælfric, especially *De Falsis Diis*: 'Whilst Frankis is indisputably right in calling our attention to the possibility that Laʒamon may have been familiar with Old English homilies, it must be admitted that they have left no recognizable mark on the *Brut*, and cannot therefore be counted among Laʒamon's sources of inspiration' (Le Saux 218).

9 In this chapter, citations of *Chronicle* poems not included in the *ASPR* are cited by annal number from the edition of Plummer and cited without line references.

10 Cf. also *Brut* 8143a, 9161b, and 12121b.

11 Cf. also *Guthlac A* 536b; *Riddle 73* 22b; and *Meters of Boethius* 26 11b, and 42b. Each of these four classical examples reads 'Cuð is wide.'

12 Cf. also *Brut* 3941b, 4927b, 6450b, 7421b, and 9789b.

13 Cf. also *The Death of Alfred* 21b (annal 1036CD).

14 Cf. the classical version 'swa him gecynde wæs' (*Beowulf* 2696b; *Daniel* 3b).

15 Cf. also *Brut* 6298a.

16 Cf. also *Brut* 6166b and 8326a.

17 Cf. also 959DE: '7 God him geuðe' and 'Ac God him geunne.'

18 Verses rhyming 'miht' (or 'mihtig') and 'Drihten' are quite common in the Old English tradition, but especially in the *Metrical Psalms*, where there are at least forty-nine examples. This is the only rhyme-pair in Old English poetry more common than 'wide and side.'

19 'He commanded them all to come quickly: those that would have land, or silver, or gold, or possessions, or land.'

20 'If they would live, or have land – land or possessions, or even his friend-ship.'

21 This conclusion is both surprising and important. While almost all of the other possible parallels discussed here between the *Brut* and the *Chronicle* poems involve poems preserved in the D Chronicle (Cotton Tiberius B. iv), the *William the Conqueror* poem is known today only from the Peterborough (E) manuscript of the *Chronicle*. It is a very important conclusion then, to suggest that Layamon knew of this poem, and it may well indicate that another copy of the *Chronicle*, one extending to 1086 and beyond, may have been available in the Worcester area. Without going too far into the realm of

speculation, the possible existence of such a *Chronicle* at Worcester may explain why the so-called Worcester Chronicle, Tiberius B. iv (manuscript D), was never annotated by the tremulous hand.

22 'Nor is it in any book written that there was ever a fight in Britain where destruction was so widespread.'

23 'Just as writings that wise men write say, that was the third greatest fight that was ever fought here.'

24 'It was never said, nor read in books, that there ever before was any army so great gathered in England by any king.'

25 'Our father was called Vortigerne; bad counsels follow him. He has brought heathen peoples into this land ... And heathen laws loved too greatly, which we shall shun for the time while we live.'

26 'One misdeed he did too greatly: he loved foreign vices and brought heathen customs into this land too firmly.'

27 It may also be worthwhile to compare *Brut* 7420 '7 þa hæðene laʒen.~ luuede to swiðe' with the 959DE verse 'Godes lage lufode,' since both include alliterating collocations of 'lage' and 'lufode.'

Bibliography

Blake, N.F. 'Rhythmical Alliteration.' *Modern Philology* 67 (1969): 118–24.

Bliss, A.J. – *An Introduction to Old English Metre*. Oxford Blackwell, 1962. *The Metre of* Beowulf. 2nd ed. Oxford: Blackwell, 1962.

– 'Single Half-lines in Old English Poetry.' *Notes and Queries* n.s. 18 (1971): 442–9.

Blockley, Mary. *Aspects of Old English Poetic Syntax: Where Clauses Begin*. Urbana: U of Illinois P, 2001.

Bosworth, Joseph, and T. Northcote Toller, eds. *An Anglo-Saxon Dictionary*. Oxford: Oxford UP, 1898.

Bredehoft, Thomas A. 'Estimating Probabilities and Alliteration Frequencies in Old English Verse.' *Old English Newsletter* 34.1 (2001): 19–23.

– *Textual Histories: Readings in the* Anglo-Saxon Chronicle. Toronto: U of Toronto P, 2001.

– 'Secondary Stress in Compound Germanic Names in Old English Verse.' *Journal of English Linguistics* 31 (2003): 199–220.

– 'The Three Varieties of Old English Hypermetric Versification.' *Notes and Queries* n. s. 50 (2003): 153–6.

– 'The Boundaries between Verse and Prose in Old English Literature.' *Old English Literature in Its Manuscript Context*. Ed. Joyce Tally Lionarons. Morgantown: West Virginia UP, 2004. 139–72.

Brehe, S.K. 'Reassembling the *First Worcester Fragment*.' *Speculum* 65 (1990): 521–36.

– '"Rhythmical Alliteration": Ælfric's Prose and the Origins of Laȝamon's Metre.' *The Text and Tradition of Laȝamon's* Brut. Ed. Françoise Le Saux. Arthurian Studies 33. Cambridge: D.S. Brewer, 1994. 65–87.

Brook, G.L., and R.F. Leslie, eds. *Laȝamon:* Brut. Early English Text Society, 250, 277. London: Early English Text Society, 1963, 1978.

Cable, Thomas. 'Constraints on Anacrusis in Old English Meter.' *Modern Philology* 69 (1971): 97–104.
– 'Metrical Style as Evidence for the Date of *Beowulf.' The Dating of* Beowulf. Ed. Colin Chase. Toronto: U of Toronto P, 1981. 77–82.
– *The English Alliterative Tradition.* Philadelphia: U of Pennsylvania P, 1991.
Campbell, A., ed. *The Battle of Brunanburh.* London: Heinemann, 1938.
– *Old English Grammar.* Oxford: Clarendon, 1959.
Cubbin. G.P., ed. *MS D. Anglo-Saxon Chronicle – Collaborative Edition.* Vol. 6. Cambridge: D.S. Brewer, 1996.
Donoghue, Daniel. *Style in Old English Poetry: The Test of the Auxiliary.* New Haven: Yale UP, 1987.
Foley, John Miles. *Traditional Oral Epic.* Berkeley and Los Angeles: U of California P, 1990.
Frank, Roberta. 'Some Uses of Paronomasia in Old English Scriptural Verse.' *Speculum* 47 (1972): 207–26.
Frankis, P.J. 'Laȝamon's English Sources.' *J.R.R. Tolkien: Scholar and Storyteller,* Ed. Mary Salu and Robert T. Farrell. Ithaca, NY: Cornell UP, 1979. 64–75.
Friedlander, Carolyn VanDyke. 'Early Middle English Accentual Verse.' *Modern Philology* 76 (1979): 219–30.
Fulk, R.D. *A History of Old English Meter.* Philadelphia: U of Pennsylvania P, 1992.
Glowka, Arthur Wayne. 'Prosodic Decorum in Layamon's *Brut.' Poetica* 18 (1984): 40–53.
Godden, Malcolm, ed. *Ælfric's Catholic Homilies: The Second Series: Text.* Early English Text Society, s. s. 5. London: Early English Text Society, 1979.
– *Ælfric's Catholic Homilies: Introduction, Commentary and Glossary.* Early English Text Society, s. s. 18. London: Early English Text Society, 2000.
Gordon, E.V., ed. *The Battle of Maldon.* London: Methuen, 1937.
Gradon, P.O.E., ed. *Cynewulf's* Elene. Exeter: U of Exeter P, 1977.
Griffith, Mark, ed. *Judith.* Exeter: U of Exeter P, 1997.
Grinda, Klaus. 'Pigeonholing Old English Poetry: Some Criteria of Metrical Style.' *Anglia* 102 (1984): 305–22.
Hieatt, Constance. 'A New Theory of Triple Rhythm in the Hypermetric Lines of Old English Verse.' *Modern Philology* 67 (1969): 1–8.
Hollander, John. *Rhyme's Reason.* New, enlarged edition. New Haven: Yale UP, 1989.
Hoover, David L. *A New Theory of Old English Meter.* New York: Peter Lang, 1985.
Hutcheson, B.R. *Old English Poetic Metre.* Cambridge: D.S. Brewer, 1995.
Keddie, James. 'Simplifying Resolution in *Beowulf.' Prosody and Poetics in the*

Early Middle Ages: Essays in Honour of C.B. Hieatt. Ed. M. J. Toswell. Toronto: U of Toronto P, 1995. 80–101.

Kendall, Calvin B. *The Metrical Grammar of* Beowulf. *Cambridge Studies in Anglo-Saxon England 5*. Cambridge: Cambridge UP, 1991.

Krapp, G.P., and E.V.K. Dobbie, eds. *The Anglo-Saxon Poetic Records*. 6 vols. New York: Columbia UP, 1931–53.

Kuhn, Sherman M. 'Was Ælfric a Poet?' *Philological Quarterly* 52 (1973): 643–62.

Le Saux, Françoise. *Laȝamon's* Brut: *The Poem and Its Sources*. Arthurian Studies 19. Cambridge: D.S. Brewer, 1989.

Leyerle, John. 'The Interlace Structure of *Beowulf*.' *Interpretations of* Beowulf: *A Critical Anthology*. Ed. R.D. Fulk. Bloomington, Indiana UP, 1991. 146–67.

McIntosh, A. 'Wulfstan's Prose.' *British Academy Papers on Anglo-Saxon England*. Ed. E.G. Stanley. Oxford: Oxford University Press (for The British Academy), 1990. 111–44.

– 'Early Middle English Alliterative Verse.' *Middle English Alliterative Poetry and its Literary Background: Seven Essays*. Ed. David Lawton. Cambridge: D.S. Brewer, 1982. 20–33.

Minkova, Donka. 'The Credibility of Pseudo-Alfred: Prosodic Insights in Post-Conquest Mongrel Meter.' *Modern Philology* 94 (1997): 427–54.

Mitchell, Bruce. *Old English Syntax*. Oxford: Oxford University Press, 1985.

Mitchell, Bruce, Christopher Ball, and Angus Cameron. 'Short Titles of Old English Texts.' *Anglo-Saxon England* 4 (1975): 207–21.

– 'Short Titles of Old English Texts: Addenda and Corrigenda.' *Anglo-Saxon England* 8 (1979): 331–3.

Mitchell, Bruce, and Fred C. Robinson. *A Guide to Old English*. 6th ed. Oxford: Blackwell, 2000.

Moffatt, Douglas. 'The Intonational Basis of Laȝamon's Verse.' *Prosody and Poetics in the Early Middle Ages: Essays in Honor of C.B. Hieatt*. Ed. M.J. Toswell. Toronto: U of Toronto P, 1995. 133–46

Momma, H. 'The 'Gnomic Formula' and Some Additions to Bliss's Old English Metrical System.' *Notes and Queries*. n. s. 36 (1989): 423–6.

– *The Composition of Old English Poetry. Cambridge Studies in Anglo-Saxon England 20*. Cambridge: Cambridge UP, 1997.

– 'Rhythm and Alliteration: Styles of Ælfric's Prose up to the *Lives of Saints*.' *Anglo-Saxon Styles*. Ed. Catherine E. Karkov and George Hardin Brown. Albany: State U of New York P, 2003. 253–69.

Needham, G.I., ed. *Lives of Three English Saints*. Exeter: U of Exeter P, 1976.

Noble, James. 'The Four-Stess Hemistich in Laȝamon's *Brut*.' *Neuphilologische Mitteilungen* 87 (1986): 545–9.

O'Brien O'Keeffe, Katherine. *Visible Song: Transitional Literacy in Old English*

Poetic Texts. Cambridge Studies in Anglo-Saxon England 4. Cambridge: Cambridge UP, 1990.

Okasha, Elisabeth. *Hand-List of Anglo-Saxon Non-Runic Inscriptions.* Cambridge: Cambridge UP, 1971.

Orchard, Andy. 'Artful Alliteration in Anglo-Saxon Song and Story.' *Anglia* 113 (1995): 429–63.

Plummer, C., ed. *Two of the Saxon Chronicles Parallel.* Oxford: Clarendon, 1892–9.

Pope, John C. *The Rhythm of* Beowulf. Rev. ed. New Haven: Yale UP, 1966.

– *Homilies of Ælfric: A Supplementary Collection.* 2 vols. Early English Text Society, 259–60. London: Early English Text Society, 1967–8.

– *Seven Old English Poems.* 2nd ed. New York: W.W. Norton, 1981.

Robinson, Fred C. 'The Accentuation of *Nú* in *Cædmon's Hymn.*' *Heroic Poetry in the Anglo-Saxon Period: Studies in Honor of Jess B. Bessinger, Jr.* Ed. Helen Damico and John Leyerle. Kalamazoo, MI: Medieval Institute Publications, 1993. 115–20.

Robinson, Fred C., and E.G. Stanley, eds. *Old English Verse Texts from Many Sources. Early English Manuscripts in Facsimile* 23. Copenhagen: Rosenkilde and Bagger, 1991.

Russom, Geoffrey. *Old English Meter and Linguistic Theory.* Cambridge: Cambridge UP, 1987.

– 'Constraints on Resolution in *Beowulf.*' *Prosody and Poetics in the Early Middle Ages: Essays in Honour of C.B. Hieatt.* Ed. M.J. Toswell. Toronto: U of Tornoto P, 1995. 147–63.

– Beowulf *and Old Germanic Metre. Cambridge Studies in Anglo-Saxon England* 23. Cambridge: Cambridge UP, 1998.

Sayers, Dorothy L. *Gaudy Night.* New York: HarperPaperbacks, 1995.

Sedgefield, Walter J. *The Battle of Maldon and Short Poems from the Saxon Chronicle.* Boston: D.C. Heath, 1904.

Sievers, Eduard. *Altgermanische Metrik.* Halle: Max Niemeyer, 1893.

Skeat, W.W., ed. *Ælfric's Lives of Saints.* Early English Text Society, 76, 82, 94, and 114. London: Early English Text Society, 1881–1900.

Sklar, Elizabeth. '*The Battle of Maldon* and the Popular Tradition: Some Rhymed Formulas.' *Philological Quarterly* 54 (1975): 409–18.

Stanley, E.G. 'Laȝamon's Antiquarian Sentiments.' *Medium Ævum* 38 (1969): 23–37.

– *In the Foreground:* Beowulf. Cambridge: D.S. Brewer, 1994.

Szarmach, Paul. 'Abbot Ælfric's Rhythmical Prose and the Computer Age.' *New Approaches to Editing Old English Verse.* Ed. Sarah Larratt Keefer and Katherine O'Brien O'Keeffe. Cambridge: D.S. Brewer, 1998. 95–108.

Tatlock, J.S.P. 'Epic Formulas, Especially in Laȝamon.' *PMLA* 38 (1923): 494–529.

Townsend, Julie. 'The Metre of the *Chronicle*-verse.' *Studia Neophilologica* 68 (1996): 143–76.

Whitman, F.H. *A Comparative Study of Old English Metre*. Toronto: U of Toronto P, 1993.

Wright, Neil. 'Angles and Saxons in Laȝamon's *Brut*: A Reassessment.' *The Text and Tradition of Laȝamon's* Brut. Ed. Françoise Le Saux. Arthurian Studies 33 Cambridge: D.S. Brewer, 1994. 161–70.

Index

Toronto Old English Series